Saint Peter's University Library
Withdrawn

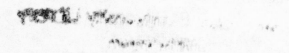

Dorothy
AND
Red

by Vincent Sheean

Dorothy
AND
Red

ILLUSTRATED WITH PHOTOGRAPHS

HOUGHTON MIFFLIN COMPANY BOSTON

The Riverside Press Cambridge

1963

Photographs used in this book have been obtained from the Dorothy Thompson Papers at Syracuse University Library, from various private sources, and from news photograph agencies. Proper credit has been given wherever possible.

Portions of this book have appeared in slightly different form in *Harper's Magazine*.

FIRST PRINTING

COPYRIGHT © 1963 BY HOUGHTON MIFFLIN COMPANY
ALL RIGHTS RESERVED INCLUDING THE RIGHT TO REPRODUCE
THIS BOOK OR PARTS THEREOF IN ANY FORM
LIBRARY OF CONGRESS CATALOG CARD NUMBER: 63-21040
PRINTED IN THE U.S.A.

To Irita Van Doren

Acknowledgments

THANKS ARE DUE TO MRS OGDEN REID, TO ARTHUR KROCK OF the New York *Times*, and to Oren Root of the New York State Banking Commission, for light on subjects of which they have particular knowledge. Dorothy's sister Peggy (Mrs Howard Wilson) recalled some very useful things, while John Gunther and Virgilia Peterson were helpful in identifying photographs of another day.

The diaries and letters used in this volume are from the Dorothy Thompson Papers at Syracuse University Library. Dean Wayne D. Yenawine, Director of the Library, should be especially thanked for his unfailing help and courtesy, along with members of his staff, James Owens and Howard Applegate, and John S. Mayfield of the Rare Book Division. Helpful also have been Alan U. Schwartz of Greenbaum, Wolff and Ernst; Melville Cane, Sinclair Lewis' executor; Martin F. Shea of the Morgan Guaranty Trust Company; Conrad Oberdorfer and Dale Warren in Boston; Alexander Sachs in New York; Lilian Mowrer (Mrs Edgar Ansel Mowrer) in Washington. Mrs Michael Lewis (Bernadette) unearthed a quantity of photographs at Twin Farms, some of which are used in this volume. Thanks to them all: the errors that remain are my own.

V. S.

Contents

Illustrations

following page 178

Dorothy and Red Lewis, photographed by Edward Steichen, in the early 1930's.

Dorothy Thompson and Sinclair Lewis in Berlin, 1927–1928, the time of their meeting and courtship.

The drawing room of Dorothy's flat at Händelstrasse 8, across from the Tiergarten in Berlin.

At the Ungarische Weinhaus, Vienna, in the fall of 1927.

Dorothy in Red Square, Moscow, in November of 1927.

Red's letter to Dorothy of May 1928, a few days before their marriage.

Mr and Mrs Sinclair Lewis just after their wedding at Savoy Chapel, London, on May 14, 1928.

The Lewises visiting with Hugh Walpole in the garden of his Lake District home during a honeymoon stopover.

On the steps of the honeymoon caravan in which they toured the English countryside during the summer of 1928.

The newlywed Lewises in London shortly after their marriage, and returning to the United States on the *Hamburg* in late August 1928.

The original old farmhouse at Twin Farms, Barnard, Vermont.

The Big House (or "Dorothy's House") at Twin Farms as it became after extensive remodeling.

Dorothy with Michael Lewis, born in June 1930.

Red Lewis revisiting Berlin in December 1930, after receiving the Nobel Prize in Stockholm.

Dorothy

AND

Red

I

The Meeting

ON THURSDAY EVENING, JULY 9TH, 1927, MISS DOROTHY
Thompson gave a dinner party at her Berlin flat, Händelstrasse 8, facing the bosky glades of the Tiergarten. Miss
Thompson was thirty-three years old on that day and felt
inclined to celebrate the event. It was the first time in at least
two or even three years that she had felt inclined to celebrate
anything: after a marriage which had caused her great turmoil,
humiliation and suffering, she was beginning, as she says,
"to live again." Her final divorce decree from the courts in
Budapest had arrived that very week and her first husband,
Josef Bard, poet and philosopher in her mind — journalist in
the minds of others — was at last beginning to recede a little
(not much but a little) from the dominant position he had long
occupied in the foreground of her universe.

Dorothy Thompson was at that moment the Berlin correspondent for the Philadelphia *Public Ledger* and the New York
Evening Post, both of which belonged to Mr Cyrus H. Curtis
of the Curtis Publishing Company and were completely different from the newspapers which later carried the same names.
Miss Thompson had in a very few years, no more than seven,
made a name for herself as a foreign correspondent in Central
Europe, and the Curtis newspapers had now appointed her the
head of their whole service for that part of the world, with
Budapest, Prague and Vienna as well as Berlin within her
bailiwick. She was beautiful, intelligent and highly (perhaps

too highly) informed, with a confident manner which was
becoming to her fresh and original personality, although in
other women it might not have been so. The fact was that in
1927 there were few women correspondents of recognized
attainment in Europe; the profession, which had been tiny
before the war of 1914–1918, was now larger than before, but
perhaps as a result of the war it consisted almost entirely of
men, chiefly (in the older ranks) of war correspondents who had
never gone home. Dorothy stood out, rather, in a world of
men: in Berlin itself only Sigrid Schultz, correspondent of the
Chicago *Tribune,* was an American woman with the same
regular status. (Irregulars, "free lances," often only tourists
with some vague newspaper connection, were not as frequent
then as now and, in the small world of the foreign correspondents, seldom counted for anything.)

Dorothy's prowess as a correspondent had given her a special
consideration, perhaps something like a special rank, both in
Berlin and Vienna. She owed her prowess not only to skill,
intelligence and luck, along with a good deal of hard work, but
also to the fact that she early learned and long retained a real
familiarity with the German language. Those who heard her
speak German in her later years can have no idea of the fluency
with which she handled it in the 1920's. She must have had a
true affinity for it, since she was never able to get beyond the
merest pidgin-talk in French or Italian. I do not say that she
could not make mistakes (she often did), but hardly any
foreigner can be exempt from them in an inflected language.
She was fluent in numerous kinds of German, could put on
(for at least some phrases) the accents of Berlin or Vienna, so
notably diverse, and had a wide familiarity with different
vocabularies from different regions of experience. She could
talk the special lingo of the theatre world, which in Berlin as
much as anywhere else (perhaps more) abounds in meanings
unknown outside it; she was thoroughly at home in the pom-

pous language of diplomacy; she could also talk straightforward upper-class German comprehensible to any university profes- sor, bishop, countess or novelist. If she could do all this with her own German speech, it may well be imagined that nothing escaped her ear. In those years I never saw Dorothy at a loss for the meaning of any German word or phrase addressed to her, and at whatever speed. She was also in perfect possession of her hearing, her actual auditory faculty, which drifted away so gradually thereafter that she did not know for many years that she was deaf.

At this point in time — Thursday, July 9th, 1927 — no shadow of ill health, no hint of affliction or sorrow or even of frustration in the great sweep of the future could have shown itself to Dorothy. The one sorrow of her life — the heartbreak of her marriage to Josef — was now in the past. As we shall see, it did not go away altogether (does any heartbreak go without a trace?), but it no longer had the power to make her miserably unhappy for months on end. She was fresh, smiling, pink-and-white, bright-eyed, an American girl very well pleased with her general situation in the world and perfectly equipped to go on with it, conscious that there were few rivals on the horizon and many rewards in view. So far as I know, Dorothy never at any time (until the end of her life, perhaps) questioned herself or her future: confidence was her keynote at all times. She had suffered greatly over Josef but it was a private suffer- ing. We learn it now from the papers she left — fully intending, as I believe, that they should be published — but we who knew her at the time could never have guessed. I did not know her well, of course (I had met her the year before, only once, with Josef), but I have consulted others who knew her better at that time, and all agreed that her suffering had no effect upon her appearance. The heartbreak didn't show.

And it has always been my opinion that, whatever happened (and there were disasters!) was in that same case: the heartbreak didn't show. It was a vitally important element in Dorothy's greatness that she could always step over the corpses and go on, steadily, resolutely, right to the end, with her head held very high indeed.

She seems to have had, if we judge by letters and diaries of a few weeks later, some fatalistic feeling that Josef's departure from her life might be the prelude to some more satisfactory relationship. At least we know that she had her own ideas of the man who must exist, somewhere on earth, with whom the perfect "creative" marriage (her favorite word) would be possible for her. Her work and her life were inextricably one: she wanted to work, and in her misery it was a form of salvation to be able to do it at all, and to do it well; but she did not think, as she says in a letter to Josef, that it was possible to "feed my soul on daily newspapers." Thus she wanted in him or in his work a completion of her own ("to bring the wheel full circle," she says), so that, in a way, we see that the "creative marriage" was possible only with a "creative artist." These ideas haunt her imagination for years, as we shall see in many documents. At the root of them is the feeling that her own work, whatever its merit, is not "creative," and that only through the artist-husband could this necessity, real or imagined, be realized.

Dorothy's thirty-third birthday dinner, which was to be momentous in her life, was small but choice, like so many of her gatherings at Händelstrasse 8. No doubt the food was choice, too: her maid Hedwig was an excellent cook. She knew her wines, both German and French, and had a skilled hand with flowers. In that charming drawing-room, with furniture more Viennese than anything else (with its deep bow to the French eighteenth century), there was conversation in two or three languages. The guest of honor was Count Karolyi, that liberal prime minister of Hungary who had been extruded from his post and his country by the opposition of the wartime allies. The Countess von Moltke and her wonderful son, Helmuth, one of the tallest and handsomest young men in Berlin or anywhere else, were present, as they often were. Helmuth it was, this same Helmuth, whose participation in the Christian-aristocratic opposition to Hitler afterwards cost him his life (July, 1944). The American guests, aside from Lilian Mowrer, are less certain, but probably H. R. Knickerbocker was there.

Lilian Mowrer, herself a correspondent for some English newspapers at that time, was (and is) the wife of Edgar Ansel Mowrer, then Berlin correspondent of the Chicago *Daily News*. The Mowrers had obtained the official papers for the rent of a very large apartment on two floors, much too big for them, and Dorothy had gone into it with them — they on the second floor, she on the third — in separate households which were (to the housing authority) one. Such permits were not easily obtained at the time, and especially in this charming house over the park. Both Mowrers had been expected at the birthday dinner but Edgar had a severe cold and could not come.

The momentous American guest was Sinclair Lewis.

Lewis was, at the age of forty-two, the most famous and by far the most successful American writer in the world. His five early books being set aside as apprentice work, little noticed or read, his career on the great scale begins with the publication of *Main Street* in October, 1920. This book made an impression which hardly anything since has equaled, because it was not only a novel but a work of social satire such as American letters had never known — a sociological document, a contribution to history. It was as such that practically all the writers of English in that period received it, writing to Lewis in terms of astonishment and admiration. Their letters are in the Lewis Collection in the Yale Library. (There is a tale to be told about them, in its right place.)

After *Main Street* the mammoth, posterlike novels had succeeded each other every two years, each with its trail of endless discussion, enormous sales and quick translation into almost every language. They were (up to now): *Babbitt* (September, 1922), *Arrowsmith* (March, 1925), and *Elmer Gantry* (March, 1927, the present year). With all their exaggerations and grotesqueries, these sprawling, exuberant compositions trembled with the vitality of a genius unlike any other and had been quite differently received from other novels. By this I do not mean that they were amongst the over-all "best sellers" of the modern time — not at all. Any religious romancer (Harold Bell Wright, later on Lloyd C. Douglas) and any writer dealing in moonlight and roses (Gene Stratton Porter) distanced them by far. Indeed, the novels of Lewis, like those of Hemingway and many others who form the literature of our time in America, never got into the category of the true best-sellers, those fabulous books which, independent of taste or criticism, go on selling for ever. (Many of these, by the way, would be unknown even by name to the public which has read Lewis, Faulkner, Hemingway and Scott Fitzgerald.)

No: the novels of Sinclair Lewis did not sell like *Ben Hur* or *In His Steps*. In common with practically all books of this century they had their season, which for Lewis meant about two years, and then dropped out of currency. His books were at least kept in print, which is more than can be said for Faulkner and some other notable novelists of our time. Most of his novels became plays and films in due course, and that process is still going on, with television now added. But during the first decade of his world-wide success Lewis was not only an extremely provocative and original novelist, read by the knowing and the noticing in all countries, but a personality of relish to the editors of newspapers everywhere. His doings and sayings were "good copy," not only because of his sudden and astonishing fame but because the man himself had a knack of commanding attention by his impetuous words and deeds, his instinctive exhibitionism, his flair for the drama of the front page.

It has been strongly suggested that a common-or-garden craze for publicity animated all of the Lewis antics during the two decades (1920–1940) when he was most before the public as a person. It is further suggested that this craze for publicity was commercial: an aid to selling books. I knew Lewis extremely well for many years and never could see any evidence of contrivance or deliberation in his oddest behavior. On the contrary: his responses were so swift and imperative as to belong in the category of the half-conscious, the instinctive and the irresistible. If you poke a lion he will roar. This, no doubt, is exhibitionism, but it is as natural as breathing to the lion. Red Lewis was a lion in his time — mangy and indeed half-broken from the start, but a lion just the same, pacing his narrow cage with irremediable fury and despair.

2

SINCLAIR LEWIS GREW UP IN MINNESOTA AND WENT TO YALE AS Harry S. Lewis. To some of his friends he was known as Hal, which, in due course, became the name under which all of his women friends (including his wives) and some of his oldest men friends knew him. To most of his acquaintance, however, he was known as Red, from his undergraduate days at Yale to his death in Rome. Red somehow suited him, not only because of his carrot-top and his general appearance, but because of something else we might call an aura: that is, he burned. In thirty years of acquaintance with him, sometimes at close quarters and for appreciable lengths of time, I never thought of him as anything but Red, and it would be false to try calling him otherwise. In this book I shall refer to him as Red (as did almost everybody else) although Dorothy herself, in her letters and diaries, constantly called him Hal. In conversation she also called him Red, merely because others did and it was understood; but to him and to herself he was Hal.

Red Lewis at forty-two was fully aware of his worldly good fortune and his many circumstantial advantages, and he did not hesitate to use them (especially after a few strong drinks). But underneath that swagger and would-be debonair manner, composed in part by the aid of London tailors and the twirl of a walking stick, Red was fundamentally insecure about his own value in life (even about his work, at times) and above all about his person. He had suffered agonies from being what is called "ugly," that is without physical attractions, and this was made even worse by the skin disease which, beginning as the ordinary acne of puberty, had grown steadily more acute and eventually marked his face like a battlefield. His childhood had been lonely; he was never strong or ordinary enough to compete with other boys; he had known no popularity or even real friendships at Yale; he had found it difficult to get into any relationship with girls although he dreamed of them constantly. All of this, as being based upon his own deficiencies of physique (the skin disease most of all, but also weak features and flabby muscles), afflicted him sorely. In his heart of hearts, he had an awful involuntary humility which came from the conviction that he was unfit for, and perhaps even unworthy of, love in its fullness. His sexual nature suffered, to the very brink of impotence, through this physical humility. Alcohol as a refuge stilled the pain but only increased the condition which was its source.

And yet he was, in the 1920's and for a long time afterwards, wondrous good company, the most inventive and salacious of wits, a true refreshment in his irreverence for the accepted persons and ideas, and, although a satirical rogue indeed in all these respects, generally kindness itself to his friends. The combination of such qualities made everybody forget, within a very few minutes, that Red was "ugly." Indeed he became positively attractive through his gaiety, charming through his wit, and so long as he could do such wonderful things with a huge vocabulary it made no difference about his features or his skin. Moreover, it is not true that he could only monologize; in the 1920's, unless he was very unhinged by alcohol, he conversed, that is with a civilized give-and-take, as well as the next one, except that his own contributions were often brilliantly funny. He was some kind of actor, or at least imitator, by his very being, and thus, beyond a doubt, enjoyed his own improvised parodies and monologues; but so long as he was sober he was not their slave. (They belonged, anyhow, to parties: those who have most often described them are persons who never knew Red alone or in the family.)

The physical humility to which I referred earlier was no doubt responsible for the alacrity with which he occupied the center of the stage at parties, always willing to improvise a speech, poem or sermon, always ready to imitate a known personage or type. It was a compensation, let us say, for more intimate delights; it reassured him, somehow, that he was not incapable of giving pleasure. And of course in the 1920's he was amazingly good at this: he did give very great pleasure, if laughter and astonishment count as pleasure.

And yet, in the midst of all the laughter, it remains true that hardly anybody could avoid feeling sorry for Red. He had, at the same time, so much and so little; his was an utterly abnormal fate; he bore the look of extreme suffering, indeed of agony, in his eyes; the world's rewards could never make up for what he had gone through and was continually going through, year after year and decade after decade. It is by now abundantly clear, as we thought even as we watched him through life, that sexual inadequacy and maladjustment tortured him beyond measure; there are documents in this respect (some of them to be printed here) which leave no room for doubt. He dreamed of a sexuality which was to him unattainable, and in the result he could never come to terms with his own nature, but lived a gruesome civil war with himself, always losing the battle and turning to alcohol for solace or (more often) oblivion.

With all this — so easy to understand now but perhaps not so evident then — he was high-spirited and charming company, as few men ever are, and his famous "ugliness" was hardly more than the most transitory impression to most people, especially men. I have known women who did not even think him ugly — who were, in fact, attracted by the sheer oddity of his peaked face and staring eyes, the eyes of a small child or a frightened animal looking through a wood-pile. Plainly Dorothy was in this case, and says so. There were others. None of them, by my guess, could ever conquer his own dreadful feeling of physical and sexual inferiority, his disgust for the body that had played him so false.

Red's first marriage, to pretty, clever and ambitious Grace Hegger, had taken place in 1914 (April 15th) after a year and a half of indefatigable proposals from him and cautious rejections or postponements from her. That marriage, which had fared ill for quite some years, was now definitely on the rocks. The two had not seen each other for a long time and Grace had already met her own future in the person of a Spanish aristocrat who was Red's opposite in every way. A divorce was inevitable, and their letters saying so (just at this period) crossed in transit; they were thus in perfect agreement except for the arrangements of time and place. This was certainly what, by now, Red wanted to the full, but it is also beyond doubt that he was made restless and uncertain by the loss of a relationship which, whatever its joys or sorrows, had been the only one in his life.

He was at this moment still relishing his tremendous fame in the world, as well as the lavish earnings it brought him. It gave him enormous pleasure to give a dinner in London, for example, to a dozen of the best writers of the time, and to be treated by them as their equal. He relished the newspaper interviews that attended his journeys everywhere in Europe and America, and quite often, through that native exhibitionistic instinct, was able to say startling things which nourished the chronicle of the day and brought him a very wide, although completely unliterary, renown among the populace. All these things gave him a kind of surface enjoyment reflected in the nervous brightness, easy laughter and incessant clatter in which he lived, moving, like an opera singer, from capital to capital, generally with a train of followers either pressed into service (like Ramon Guthrie) or merely tagging along.

Ramon, kindest and most understanding of friends, nevertheless had his own life to live and his own books to write. Red had just commandeered Ramon (who was working in the Dordogne) for a ten-day walking trip in the Black Forest, during which he drank no strong spirits, nothing but beer; it was always a way to recoup the losses to his nervous system. After such a bout of walking he was usually at the top of his form, but a week or so of Paris (in latter June) undid all the good of the Schwarzwald; he then kidnaped Ramon again (this time with his wife) and took them off to Munich with him. After a week there he said farewell to them: they were for Paris and he for Berlin.

Thus he was, by the night of July 9th, in excellent form, if one may judge by what led up to it. The Guthries were always good for Red. He drank less with them; he exercised his mind and his body; Ramon has said that on their Schwarzwald walking tour he talked a great deal about that great labor novel (the one he never wrote), not only monologizing but actually consulting, exchanging views and opinions and suggestions.

In Berlin he had gone on the day before (July 8th) to the Foreign Office in the Wilhelmstrasse to attend one of Gustav Stresemann's regular press conferences. H. R. Knickerbocker,

Dorothy's assistant and eventual successor at the *Public Ledger* bureau, took him to the conference. Stresemann was late; Red, with his usual clownishness, told the press representatives that he would be glad to take the Minister's place if questions could be held down to relations between France and Germany. At some time, before or after Stresemann's arrival, Knick seems to have introduced Red to Dorothy. It could have been hardly more than a bow and a smile, but it was enough. She had read and greatly admired his books; his interest in her was immediate. She asked him (probably through Knick) to come to her birthday dinner on the following night and he accepted. The stage, so to speak, was set, and from what I know of Red's wild impetuosity, his instinctive prescience and his inveterate habit of getting vastly ahead of himself, he probably already had a pretty accurate idea of what was going to happen.

3

THUS, AS WE SEE, SOME KIND OF WEIRD SUITABILITY HAD already linked the situations of Dorothy and Red. It was as if fate were dropping them a good strong hint. Both were at the unhappy stage of marriage broken, not really by unfettered choice; both had been, as Dorothy said of herself in so many letters, "rejected." ("You have cast me off again and again," she repeats in her letters to Josef.) Red had not been precisely rejected, but another had been preferred over him, which is much the same, and a perusal of his correspondence with Gracie, as it is to be seen in the Yale Library and in Professor Schorer's book,[1] leaves no question that both had suffered acutely from nervous exhaustion again and again before they decided to part. The woeful story of Red's restless, unhappy

[1] *Sinclair Lewis, An American Life,* by Mark Schorer. New York: McGraw-Hill, 1961.

life during these past few years with Gracie is not the material of this book, but it can be said, now that so much evidence is at hand, that it was the same, the unchanging misery which dogged him all his life, caused him to take weird compensations in exhibitionism and misbehavior, drove him into an obsessive and pathological alcoholism and left him, over and over again, with nothing but dust and ashes.

In another manner of speaking, Red's inability to make a happy marriage was within himself, at the center of his being, and his appalling subterfuges, as well as his furious assault upon the universe as he encountered it, were despairing ways out of the dilemma of sexual ambitions which, to him, were only fitfully attainable and never altogether what he thought or dreamed (God knows why) that they should be.

Dorothy's case was as different as possible. She had entered upon her marriage to Josef Bard with the highest hope and the utmost happiness. She was a very normal American girl (she says "abnormally normal") in 1921, when she and Josef married in Budapest. She was twenty-seven then, fresh and pretty with a touch of elegance and more than a touch of high-mindedness. The daughter of a Methodist parson in upstate New York, she had received a hard, spare upbringing with, at the end of her schooling, four years in Syracuse University, a Methodist institution of the "conference" (territorial unit, like a diocese) to which her father belonged. She had much to learn about life in Central Europe, as well as life in general, and Josef was her tutor, her lover and friend, as well as her husband. Her knowledge of Budapest and Vienna, not only in politics but in the theatre, music, the arts and even to some extent in philosophy, came originally through Josef and his friends. She became convinced that Josef's true work lay in poetry and philosophy rather than in the occasional journalism he had been doing (some of it for the *Daily Mail* in London) before she came along. She then evolved a system of life by which Josef would do this "creative" work (his own work, it was called) while she became the wage earner of the household by more and better journalism.

Discoveries in later years were numerous and unpleasant. "I have been faithful to you in my way, but I never could be faithful in your way," Josef says only shortly before their divorce. (One wonders what he meant, aside from the oldest and hollowest paradox.) She found that her money had been spent on others; the others included friends and acquaintances, since his pasture was her own immediate circle; she discovered that he discussed her very freely during these dalliances; she found that all Budapest and Vienna had been aware of this since the time of their marriage. The explanation given was that he could not control himself: he was Don Juan! His heavily underlined copy of *Don Juan*, which she found after his departure from the Berlin flat, was at the same time justificatory to himself and insulting to her.

This long story trails through a large number of letters preserved at the Syracuse University Library. There are special reasons why so many of these letters survive. Dorothy herself often wrote letters, then and afterwards, which she never sent; they were kept in her own files and sometimes she rewrote them or parts of them. Occasionally we have two or three versions of the same letter, without any indication if any of them had been sent. We know (because she says so) that most of the longest letters to Josef in 1927, when she was in Berlin and he was in London, were never sent.

In addition to this instinct of accumulation, if it were that, or aid to memory and reflection, if it were that, it seems that when Josef decamped he left all her letters and all her gifts through five years ("my gifts of love") in the Berlin flat where she found them and mourned over them for a year and a half. He also (perhaps in haste or carelessness, perhaps with intent) left his diaries there and his heavily underlined copy of *Don*

Juan, together providing her with a shocking revelation of his true attitude.

Her letters of January, 1926, are exceedingly bitter, as are the others in that year, leading up to the one on December 16th from Vienna (where she had taken refuge with her friend Genia Schwarzwald) asking for a divorce. In this decisive letter she says:

"I have in me the capacity to be deeply faithful to one man whom I love and who loves me; what I want is to find that person and build a life with him which shall have breadth, depth, creative quality, dignity, beauty and inner loyalty. If I do not find him I shall go it alone."

A perusal of the letters shows that Dorothy suffered most in the early part of this year, as might have been expected; she had been given too many revelations at once. And the wounds to her *amour propre* never grew less. Even so, from time to time she reverts to the language of love with him, perhaps because it was too familiar to shed all at once, perhaps because the recurrences of emotion were stronger than her own will. In her bitterness she quotes him constantly: the "woman who gave you stones instead of children," obviously, is from some letter of his which wounded her deeply and she cannot let it drop. His cynical remark (out of *Don Juan*) that when one loses a friend one goes to the coffee shop and picks up another — in these or variant words — also comes into a number of these letters.

A scattering of his own letters preserved in the Syracuse papers might tend to show that he never defended himself against any of her charges: on the other hand, there are not enough of his letters through the years 1922–1927 to justify a conclusion. His letters of 1922, when she was in Berlin and he in Budapest, begin "Darling Wife," as a rule. In the last two years of their marriage they begin "Dear Dorothy." There may have been many letters in a contrary sense, for all we know, but those preserved seem to show a rather gentle (and perhaps bored?) acceptance of everything she says, so far as facts are concerned, while contesting interpretations or meanings.

It is noteworthy indeed that in all of his letters Josef, when he wishes to praise the distinctive qualities of his remarkable wife, speaks of her energy, ambition, will power, her "will-to-life" and other elements in a character which sounds more masculine than feminine. Dorothy, in one letter to him (probably never sent), inquires how and why she loved him, and replies: for beauty, through beauty, because of beauty. Thus she seems to have loved him as a man is supposed to love a woman, and he (if it be love) loved and cherished her strength, her various powers.

Her very intense suffering, anyhow, finds no echo in him — all the feelings shown in his letters are gentle and dim, there is little resentment even of her most vigorous accusations, and on the whole he does not sound (during the last two or three years) very interested.

Her own language was bold and resolute.

From a letter of January 12, 1926: "You married me knowing that you could never be true to me."

From the same: "I was a girl and you made me a woman, and a woman and you made me into a man."

Budapest, in this and other letters, plays its part as an abode of lust and laziness, Josef being its syndrome child. Thus about Lake Balaton (in a really slashing letter of February 27th): "I feel that the weeds of the Balaton have been wrapped around my legs too long."

And again, a little later in the same letter: "I want air and am going to get it. I am going to find myself, the self I lost in the Ritz Hotel to a pathological Don Juan whose love is only fantasy and self-justification."

This reference to the Ritz in Budapest, which is repeated

elsewhere in the correspondence in many forms, refers to the afternoon when Dorothy first saw Josef. She was staying at the Ritz in Buda, having tea with Marcel Fodor (her journalistic mentor in Hungary) when she looked up and saw Josef standing in the doorway. He was, by all accounts (especially Dorothy's), phenomenally handsome. It was the thunderbolt, the *coup de foudre*, love not only at first sight but at a glance. Fodor knew Josef and introduced him. There was no turning back thereafter.

One complete letter — whether it was ever sent or not — may give the sense of Dorothy's turmoil, resentment and outrage better than any number of excerpts. This is of uncertain date, probably early 1927, and the unsteadiness of its emotional tone reveals much: we are in sentimentality verging on bathos at moments, but there are dagger thrusts and shrewd observations as well. My own guess is that this letter was never sent; it looks like one of those meditations which Dorothy liked to write out before she went to bed at night — her diaries contain quite a few of them. It has neither salutation nor signature and is written on the ordinary office paper of the Philadelphia *Public Ledger:*

Here tonight in the solitude of this quiet flat, in the lonesomeness and the emptiness which is me, I sit and try to find something to say: some little flower of word or thought to lay on a grave growing cold. I feel I owe you that flower. But none blooms: I am afraid the ground has gone sterile. So many flowers bloomed for you: such hardy ones: perennials like phlox and zinnias: hardly an orchid. Strange that flowers which bobbed up even when they were trampled on should have ceased blooming.

You asked me something — in one of those blue letters — innumerable blue letters which first brought messages like big soft crushing hammer blows: so must Mrs Angerstein have felt under Angerstein's axe, I thought when I got them: and then with nasty little stings: little knife thrusts — quick — and the knifer runs away — and then, at the last, just tiresomeness. You can be so very tiresome, Josef: so excruciatingly boring. Did anyone ever tell you that? And you are so stupid. In all my life I have never known anyone with such *ein Herzensdummheit*. But in one or another of these letters — I can't be bothered to look which — you asked me whether there needs be any barricade between us. Odd question. No. But no bridge, Josef, either. All the bridges burned. Not one left on which to walk into friendship. *Schade*. Because you and I might have been such friends, Josef, so close and loyal as brother and sister.

Memories might have been a bridge. Memories of a boy and girl who wept on a couch in a city of laziness, music and lust, and of a girl who held lilies-of-the-valley in her hands. But *muguets* were spoiled for me. They were, at the end, a kiss of betrayal. I might remember a warm night in a hotel room in Vienna — in the Grand Hotel — if I did not have to recall the curious insensibility of a man who took his other choice there. I might remember a little blue flat in a proletarian street if I did not have to remember a cruel wedding night there: I might remember rooms full of light and air, with the loveliest palace outside their windows, if I did not have to remember seductions, and confidences given to others. I cannot think of a place that belongs to just our memories. So they all fade. Left is only a feeling in me, welling up now and again like some cruel tide drowning my heart: the feel of my own finger stroking a brow, my own lips against a temple: and the sight of your clear forehead and eyes straining wistfully and darkly toward something not me. It is curious how I always knew everything about you from the beginning. When you sat in Mrs Salay's boudoir combing your hair, looking so **vain**, "He is vain," I said to her, half laughing, half appalled, and she said fiercely, "He is horribly cruelly vain . . . don't marry him." Or on the slope of a hill, when I saw you pulling lazily at grass, looking lazily at me. "I feel you will let me down," I said, and terror was in my heart. "Don't be boring," you said coldly. I felt freezing. And in September, sitting here, in this room, on that couch. "I have the feeling if you met a woman who would offer you even more freedom, more economic security — a woman who had money and didn't have to work you would leave me like a shot," I said. I wanted you to deny it. But you didn't. Nor did your expression change. Curious. I wonder, idly, what you thought then. You have a talent for treachery, Josef, don't you? They say it is a Jewish talent . . . I am afraid I am becoming anti-Semite. This simplification of the mind-form (I have been reading your article in Harper's)[1] when it carries its owner to the last simplification of pure self-interest is rather ugly, Josef. I often wonder what you thought when you got your check from Harper's for that article. Because of course you must have got it long ago. Did you perhaps not think at all? Or did you think: "Dorothy has given me so much she won't mind this last three hundred dollars. She's a born masochist and it will suit her to finance my honeymoon." I am sure it would amuse Eileen to know about that $300. She would be pleased, no doubt. And the fifty taken from Dashiell was a master touch. And the lie afterward. Oh, Josef, you need to be a much cleverer liar now, for me. Tell me — do you know when you lie or do you believe it yourself? That is the one thing not quite clear to me.

Why do you do it, Josef? Why did you run to other women and talk about me? To Phyllis, to Dorothy B— to Karlie? About my erotic failures, my unsatisfactoriness as a wife, your own erotic instability, my unpleasant nature? It isn't

[1] "Why Europe Dislikes the Jews," published in *Harper's*, March, 1927.

nice for a man to talk so of his wife. It isn't done, Josef, by English gentlemen. Dear me, no. And it only makes a good impression on women who are in love with you. Others find it rather caddish. This as a tip for the future. And all the time, Josef, you might have come to me: you had taken so much from me, my love, my life, my work and its fruits: you might have said "Here, Dorothy, are my two hands: I want to tell you about myself. I want to tell you because I love you, and, because I see our lives going on the rocks. Help me, and help me to help you." But you didn't. I wonder why. Did you, then, never care whether it went on the rocks — if you had another boat to spring in. I'm afraid so. *Schade* . . . we might have been happy. I doubt whether the chance will ever be so good again.

* * *[1]

I meant to put a flower on the cooling grave. But perhaps it is a flower: Sincerity. I was often unkind to you. I cannot say I am sorry. I told you what I thought of you. The worst things I ever said weren't a far shot from the truth, were they, Josef? And I never called you Judas. You called yourself that. Remember? Afterward you fell into a peaceful sleep.

* * *

It was all so unnecessary, Josef. Only a little courage, a little sincerity, a little power to see outside yourself, — and all this pain, this futility, this waste would have been spared. What a five years! To grow gray, and bad-tempered and ugly: sterile and overworked. Years have rolled off me since you left: years and pounds. I feel the sea blowing through me again. And better emptiness and heart-break, than a

---

[1] These asterisks are in Dorothy's letter and do not indicate any omission of text. She seems to have used them here and elsewhere in her letters and diaries to mark a change of mood or subject.

stone which should have been a child, an eternal, futile, earth-binding pregnancy.

* * *

Don't do it again, Josef. But you will. All lies, what you say, that you are not made for marriage — you write this to me, and say, "Never again." But you will marry again, the moment you need to do so to hold your newfound security. Too bad. You would be happier as an Oberkellner and a better man. Even perhaps a better writer. But you won't be one. Mama wanted you to marry a little fortune and Mama, I see quite clearly, is much in your life. You're a lot like her in lots of ways.

And by the way — Have you told your mother? I might write to her if I knew. I still have a good heart, and I am sorry for her, you her Benjamin — and you, too!

* * *

I wish it had never happened, Josef. I am afraid I wish I had never looked up to see you standing in a door in the Ritz hotel. I am afraid being hurt too much isn't good for one's soul. It kills something childlike in one.

Oh, well — all this introspection — this pawing over the remains — I don't do it often. That's why I don't write. Because I can't write casually, as you suggest, of the day's news. Why in God's name should I? You can read the newspapers. Besides you don't mean it. You don't want me to write, you don't want me to come to London. And you certainly don't want me to meet Eileen. You don't, of course, know exactly what you do want, but I fancy you think subconsciously that you may make rather a plume out of me as an ex-wife. Knowing my talent for playing-up. And that I never make public scenes. And knowing your charm.

I know it too, you see. Only that charm led me to the letter I did write before you left, led me to that farewell

St. Peter's College Library
St. Peter's Co

donation, led me to all my exaggerated and rather silly gestures. Charm and an inveterate habit of believing you. If I see you I shall no doubt burn again with the ache to hold you, with the passion to help you, with that sudden illumination of imagination which I thought was a seer's gift but which I am now convinced was hallucination. No, Josef, it is better for me to sit at home with two portraits, one representing you and your first failure of Eileen: the other you according to O.K. Both help to reconcile me.

Ah, my dear, how long will you live in shadows? How long chase such devious ways? Is it well with you, Josef, my dear one?

4

THE DINNER PARTY FOR DOROTHY'S THIRTY-THIRD BIRTHDAY was a great success and the celebrated American novelist, Mr Sinclair Lewis, was much appreciated by the Central European guests. The only person who was there that night and is here today (in Washington) is Lilian Mowrer, who says she was rather bored with Red, who sat next to her, and rather worried about her husband Edgar, who was downstairs dosing a very bad cold. Consequently Lilian departed as soon as she could decently do so and retains hardly any recollection of the evening.

Others who were there have recounted it, and certainly Dorothy told of it often enough. When dinner and coffee were over and there was some movement of the guests Red maneuvered Dorothy into a corner and asked her to marry him. She was astonished into quick laughter and could hardly believe he meant anything, least of all marriage. "I don't even know you, Mr Lewis," she said.

Just the same, it was a flattering proposal to any woman who had spent the past two years in an effort to patch up her broken heart. Red was a *parti*, the most successful writer of the time, with an importance which, although hard for his contemporaries to estimate correctly, was bound to be monumental in the long run. Dorothy was extremely susceptible to the "creative artist" or the "creative man," and her letters indicate that Red's curious, peaked face and knobbly head had some attraction for her, evidently from the start. All these things made her ready to listen as he paid his court.

It was a peculiar sort of court, just the same. The thunderbolt, the *coup de foudre*, the electrical phenomenon she had experienced when she first saw Josef, was not in this at all. (One of her best friends tells me he thinks this is what disappointed her most.) Red engaged in a long story about a house in Vermont which he had either seen or invented in a dream. He described it to her. It was not Twin Farms, where they afterwards lived (as did I, also). Red had not yet seen Twin Farms. But, as Dorothy told the story, it bore a remarkable resemblance to Twin Farms. In this idyllic spot, far from the madding crowd, Red would like to live and work and be happy, but the only girl in the world that he could be happy with, or even live there with, was Dorothy. Fate had thrown her in his path; he would never give up; he would propose marriage publicly and privately henceforth, every time they met, until at last she must consent.

No doubt this was all embellished with a rare foliage of nonsense, since Red's conversational style was like that, and yet Dorothy was left with an uneasy sense (half terror and half delight) that this madman was deeply in earnest and meant precisely what he said.

As indeed he did. Only a few days later, when he was asked to speak at a public luncheon, he got up and said: "Dorothy, will you marry me?" and sat down again without another word. I have heard stories of his proposals in the park or the streets, in other people's houses, at the theatre and elsewhere. All Berlin must have known this within a very few days. It was too good a joke to keep — and Red was too famous.

Yet, at this moment, nothing had been decided about his divorce, whether it should be obtained in Paris or Reno, by him or by Grace, and what the terms. Dorothy found to her amusement, two or three days after her impetuous swain had first proposed, that he was in fact very legally and solidly married. It was very like him (always so far ahead of himself) not to mention this little detail. But he was constantly pressing his court and Dorothy was discovering that she took delight in his company. They had a similar taste for tomfoolery, at which Red was always more inventive and funnier than anybody else. He was winning, touching, appealing as a child is appealing (women always said so) and was so tremendously taken with her that she would have had to be a superwoman not to be pleased. They were constantly together. She was "beginning to live again." He changed all his plans, cabling his publisher Harcourt and others that he would not return to America as intended; he pushed on the inquiries about his divorce; he looked for, and found, a flat of his own in Berlin (what the English call a "service flat," out at the Herkules Haus in Charlottenburg).

All experiences were not good experiences where Red was concerned. We shall see that in due course. But in July, 1927, and during the magic vacation month of August, the sun was shining for both of them. It seemed a promise of happiness.

2

The Time of Decision

DOROTHY'S ANNUAL VACATION FROM THE *Public Ledger* WAS now coming up and she decided (upon his urging) to give it to Red: that is, to go with him wherever he wanted her to go, and spend the time as he pleased.

It might seem that this in itself was a decision implying all that followed. It had been preceded by another such decision and my own guess (upon knowledge of the two personalities) is that neither one was yet final. For Red, yes: for Dorothy, no. She was enough of a woman of the world, in spite of her long fidelity to Josef, to know that a few weeks spent in travel with a man need not inevitably conclude with matrimony. Her letters and diaries show that she was not at all sure of what she should do, or when or how. She was greatly attracted to Red and immensely flattered by his headlong pursuit, but from the very beginning she had strong misgivings and was slow to pledge her word. (This had nothing to do with his "ugliness," his physique or his disastrous skin; she hardly seems to have noticed such things, or seems to have found them puckish and delightful, somehow. It was, instead, a question of character.)

She had to go to Vienna on July 18th to write about a flare-up of workers' rioting. Red heard of this at the last moment, pursued her to Tempelhof airport, and got into the plane with her, although he had never flown in his life and was nervous of the experiment. She said she would let him come with her, and begin to take him seriously, if he would write three articles for the *Public Ledger* on the Vienna riots. He agreed at once. Frances Gunther (John's first wife), who had gone to Tempelhof to see Dorothy off, was also thrust into the plane as a chaperone and all three of them took off for Austria.

Red did indeed write three cablegrams for Dorothy (appearing July 19, 20 and 21 in America), to which she afterwards referred as "not much good — all about me." They described the funeral of the dead workers (the best of the three), the native and irrepressible laughter of the town and, as a sort of résumé, an account of the abortive revolution now ended. In an oblique way it was a sort of declaration of Red's intentions — or even of his determination — since a novelist of his rank had no real business writing news dispatches for a woman correspondent who was amply equipped to do it herself. The American press, always keenly aware of Red, immediately took the Vienna episode to be a declaration of love: Red, who had often proposed marriage publicly in Berlin, was now doing so on the front pages of the press in the United States. From then on his plans for, with and about Dorothy were Punchinello's secret, so far as the newspapers were concerned. They did not persecute him — they were always pretty considerate of both Red and Dorothy — but they accumulated facts and photographs against the wedding that must, sooner or later, result.

Perhaps Dorothy, who always had more common sense than Red, saw that the Vienna episode rendered further caution unnecessary. At all events, she agreed to take her vacation with him. Since Red had talked so much about his walking trips, and she was herself at that time (as the letters to Josef show) taking off weight as rapidly as she could, she may have said something in favor of an active holiday rather than an inert one. The choice was his, and he chose a walking trip:

this time in England, in Shropshire and Cornwall, heavenly in August. They left Berlin on August 7th.

We do not know (from documents, that is) anything about this holiday. It was (in view of the uncertainties still beclouding Red's divorce) a strictly private journey. I have heard both Dorothy and Red refer to it in later years and I gather that they loved it, but I do not remember any details at all. Red was still, at this time, in the full tide of his romantic and almost amorous adoration of England: it was mirrored in *Dodsworth* (1929), his next big book, on which his imagination was already at work although he scarcely knew it. The interior monologue of Sam Dodsworth as he approached the shores of England for the first time, in that book, is very much Red's style of thinking and feeling on the subject for all those years. Noel Coward's *Cavalcade*, only a little while later, overwhelmed him; he saw it again and again, constantly dissolved in tears and trembling at the heroism and simplicity (the celebrated "understatement" of great things) which, as is perfectly true, are native to the island.

This very sincere love of England (a kind of love he experienced for hardly any other place) and his complete infatuation with Dorothy must have made the walking tour, in that radiant August, one of the high intervals of an anxious, trembling and uncertain life. In that August Red might even have felt secure — inside himself, I mean; sure of his being, blithe in the contemplation of a future.

And also — curiously enough, those who write about Red do not say this — he was not only fond of walking but he was an exceedingly good walker. He could walk hard and fast, uphill and downhill, or he could suddenly throw himself on a grassy bank at the edge of a ditch and count the cows in a field and make up some insane but very funny story about them. He could cover the ground and at his best it was not easy to keep up with him. At times, while he was walking, he was capable of silence — real silence, not sulking or hostile, but companionable and effortless, the kind of silence that goes with real walking. Or he could (without visible effect on his breath or his pace) talk a blue streak, invent a whole novel and three plays while you were getting from one village to another.

He always walked with good stout sticks, of which he had dozens upon dozens; he was much addicted to buying them. He scattered these sticks wherever he lived; we had a great many at Twin Farms and after Red had gone and I used to walk by myself I used them for years. The stick is, he said and I agree, the indispensable adjunct to any real walking. It serves as an aid and a weapon, a sustenance and a question mark. (How else can you turn over a big rock to see the nest of snakes?) Furthermore, a psychological rather than a material advantage, you can use it, Red said, to "chastise the vegetation." You cannot know how satisfactory this is until you try it (in the real country, of course, and only with weeds).

Dorothy's love of walking was nothing like Red's. She did walk at that time and for perhaps another decade, but as a rule she did so to arrive at a destination. That is, she might wish to go down to the clubhouse on the lake (in Vermont) and decide that it would be good for her to walk. She would then walk that distance, after telling somebody in the family or servants to drive down and fetch her after she had had her swim. By this I mean that she could walk perfectly well (so many women cannot!) and often she did, but it always had a plan or a contour to it: a point of arrival and a scheme of return.

With Red, never. He walked as he breathed, because he could not do otherwise. Weather meant little or nothing to him (unless he had one of those crucifying colds of his). He was walking, although perhaps not so far or so fast, the last time I saw him, a year before his death, when I stayed in his big house at Williamstown. Walking was generally part of Red's morning, which began very early; it could equally well be part of his afternoon, particularly towards sundown. If he was working on a book he did not walk in the morning, but retired in that uniform dressing gown (he had several, all alike) to his room and his typewriter. After lunch there was a nap and then, along about four, he would unlock his door and mine across the hall (his theory being that work could only be properly done behind locked doors) and declare for a walk. At that period (not long after their marriage) Dorothy seldom came with us. Red would ramble in any direction for any length of time, "chastising the vegetation" and talking of anything on earth, until (as a rule) he began to feel the need of the evening drink. At that period on Twin Farms we never had drinks in the daytime, and in fact it remained Dorothy's rule for all but very special occasions (birthdays, etc.).

This digression about walking has its importance in the story — very much so. Red was never so well, physically, as when he was walking; he never looked so well; his mind was never so blazingly active and irresistible in its ceaseless pyrotechnic; he was never gentler, kindlier or more understanding of everybody along the way. I believe that the walking tour in England, followed by a shorter one in the Rhineland (to which Mr and Mrs Guthrie were summoned as company), had precisely this importance in the life of our two friends: it made Dorothy love him, as she had not quite before, and gave her the feeling that since she did love him and he needed her desperately, and was anyhow such a joy to be with, any scruples about character or will power or future behavior were unworthy — might be classified as sheer cowardice. Her willingness to take the risk, the very great risk, of tying her own life to Red's, which must have become explicit in early September, seems to me connected with (possibly even caused by) the walking tours, which provided the very conditions under which he was at his best. It could never be (as she probably knew by now) Romeo and Juliet, but it was something

that touched and moved her very deeply even in the midst of
her fears.

                                    2

DOROTHY LEFT RED AND RAMON STILL WALKING IN THE RHINE-
land and returned to Berlin to her job. She had already gone
over her allotted holiday time, but a foreign correspondent had
many liberties in those days. (The home office was much less
in touch than it is today, when any split second may initiate a
direct conversation either by voice or on the ticker.) When
Red arrived with Ramon, a few days later, they lived at
Herkules Haus, out in Charlottenburg, and she was, of course,
in her comfortable and rather elegant flat on the Tiergarten.

The events of September are so revealing, as shown in her
diaries, that it seems best to quote them as she narrates them,
only adding a word of explanation here or there when it may
be needed. I shall begin with the entry of September 9th,
1927, because it is (for half of the way through) purely political,
and thus characteristic of a great many of Dorothy's notes and
diaries then and for years afterwards. In these private papers
she does not distinguish between the most intimate circumstances of her life and things which were the property of the
whole world. The reader knows that she was examining all
these papers in the last year and a half of her life, and at times
making penciled notes in the margins — identifications and the
like, a clear indication that she wanted them all published.
Where she saw no point in publishing the material she crossed
it out lightly with pencil — as she has done with some of the
obsolete political detail in this first entry, September 9th. I
obey her indications. Where anything is crossed out, however
lightly, I omit it. Where the papers have passed her own eye
without emendation, decades later, I have adhered literally to

her text. Nothing has been softened down. A very few deletions have been made in order to protect the susceptibilities of persons still living. Where made, these deletions are denoted by three dots within brackets. Occasionally, a name or its initial has been changed — also marked by brackets — for the same reason. Small errors and peculiarities of spelling or punctuation — and also the frequent use of dots in twos, threes, and fours — are Dorothy's own. Such erratic dots do not indicate any deletion of text. The principle adopted is that of reproduction verbatim, as with historical documents. When Dorothy misspells a word or misuses punctuation, I have given it exactly as she wrote it, using explanatory brackets or footnotes where necessary for clarification.

Many may wonder why she wanted such intimacies to be published (at first I also wondered). Friends of long ago (John Gunther, for instance) have told me that the analysts in Vienna always thought Dorothy had a very strong "sense of mission," that is, historically speaking, and thus would regard every paper as worth preserving; she also certainly believed (and I have often heard her say so) that Red was one of the most important writers in American history, sociology *and* literature, all three. And, finally, she must have known that some part of the story would be told and retold, and she preferred, even thirty-five years later, surveying it all in retrospect, to let the papers speak for themselves — tell it all and let the future decide.

September 9
[She has penciled in, decades later,
"1927"]

Lunch with F.V.,[1] who told me they are being transferred
to Paris, and will leave here at the end of next month. He is
glad. The fight between England and France over the ultimate revision of the treaty is the chief foreign political
interest of the Guardian; hence the Paris job is one of the
most interesting for a Guardian correspondent. Quite the
opposite for an American. The Paris correspondency has
degenerated into society reporting with a few juicy divorce
scandals every week, and when a really ripping "tourist"
story like that of the Legion comes along no one could write
it for an American newspaper. Williams[2] in Geneva said
"Paris has become the important center for unimportant
things."

V. told me that he had had a talk with Gessler about the
Reichswehr, recently. Gessler admitted that the inhibitions
imposed by the Versailles treaty were becoming less and less
important as military technique evolved. For instance,
Germany does not want a large army and were the restric-
tions which now reduce her forces to a hundred thousand to
be lifted she would under no circumstances raise a force of
more than 150,000. G. [Gessler] thinks the whole tendency
of modern military theory is toward smaller standing forces
more intensively trained, and more mobile. F.V. said he
thought that the English and German armies were theoretically superior to the French "only the French are better
soldiers, and for some time still numbers will count." It is
true that every German private is a potential officer, but this
is less due to canny scheming with the idea of circumventing

[1] Frederick Voigt, *Manchester Guardian.*
[2] Wythe Williams, Philadelphia *Public Ledger.*

the treaty than to the evolution of modern technique. The British have made one-man tanks which can be moved with immense rapidity anywhere — over ditches and through hedges: the private who runs such a tank has far greater responsibility than any old-fashioned rifleman. Germany is heavily handicapped by the treaty provisions prohibiting her from building tanks . . . F.V. thinks she could stand up against Poland, though, tomorrow, because she would probably capture enough tanks and machine guns right off the bat! All nonsense about her being able to stand up to any first rate power, however. But viewing the future, the situation takes on another light.

Here Dorothy herself has lightly crossed out three-quarters of a page about strategic roads, light airplanes and small cruisers. She then resumes:

H. occupies my mind continually. For the first time since I met him . . . now, since my return from England, he and he alone intervenes in my dreams at night and is the sole object of my daydreams. I read again Arrowsmith, feeling him very near, conscious of what an immense amount of himself he has put into this book: far more than in any other. His inner self, his real longings. Leora, more than any character whom I can remember in fiction, represents the sexual ideal of the truly dynamic and creative male. But I doubt if even her creator realizes how truly her life fulfills the longing of the real woman. One is willing to be swallowed up by a man, if in his brain and heart one is transmuted into something "rich and strange," something better than one could be of one's self. Josef said it magnificently in one of his illumined, and really loving moments (the day he left me). "You must go on bearing people," and Leora said it magnificently when her baby was born dead and she knew she could not have another. "You then must be my child and must do something great." This fertilizing and re-fertilizing of the others personality is the real creative end of marriage; where it occurs women do not much care whether they have children or not. Indeed, it is the only marriage individually creative, because the physical child is just as likely to be the product of grandmothers and grandfathers as of ones own seed or womb. The real woman looks for the man whom she feels to be her male self. (Hal hits this — probably unconsciously — in Joyce: "You look enough like me to be my twin."). She looks for the man to whom she can be life, rest, energy, strength, whom she can fertilize with her own spirit. The relative passivity of woman in the actual physical fusion is more than compensated by her activity in the spiritual fusion. For his race the man is the life-giver. In the individual relation the woman is.

The reason why modern women are so unhappy and why they unconsciously hate men, is because they have gotten better and men have gotten worse. They will not let men swallow them up, because the swallowers aren't good enough. I will give my body soul and spirit to a man who can use it up to make a Damascene blade, but not to someone who will hammer out of it a lead paper-weight. Women *know* that making money to buy motors and country houses, shoving around lumps of money to the most profitable places, or selling more and better tooth paste, isnt admirable, isnt worth the expenditure of whatever flame of life is in them. Besides men who do these things haven't any use for women[.] They don't need more than themselves really[.] I've never known a woman who thought adding up a column of figures was important. All male bookkeepers do, Women will give themselves to men again when men know what to do with the gift, Leora, protesting against any cheapening of Martin's passionate dream, was only refusing to reduce the price on her own complete gift.

J. never took me wholly . . . he knew he couldn't digest me. That was both wise and magnanimous. It is true that I was never married to him. It was an enchantment of the senses and a rare intellectual companionship; no inner fusion. We learned a great deal from each other, but we never, for an instant, became each other.

Yet I am not sure that this, that I have written, is not the rationlizing of a blind urge . . . I am not sure it is true. Perhaps what we need is not to find the man who completes ourselves — perhaps, indeed, that is impossible — and what we need is to create a man *in* ourselves (or a woman if we be male). Der Mensch is neither male nor female, but like a tree, carrying all the elements of life within himself . . . So perhaps Viola Meynell was right when she married the butcher . . .

Anyway I love Hal and belong to him.

—

Went to B.M.'s for tea where we discussed — in the few interesting moments — whether or not there was any religious quality in communism. B. pointed out the ikon worship of Lenin and the power of the movement to awaken incorruptible and selfless devotion; she said it had no metaphysical quality. But it has the same attributes as the religion of the Jews — in this, that they worship the word, which was in the beginning. Talmudic . . . The Logas [logos] worship. I must write about this when I go to Russia . . . or save it for the world series on the Search for God.

September 10

(The first part is a long account of Toller's *Hoppla, Wir Leben!* and other plays of the opening Berlin season. It is omitted here because it has nothing to do with our subject —

as well as giving opinions on plays everybody has forgotten.)
It continues:

Letter from J.
I held it in my hand, turning it over a few minutes before
I opened it . . always, all my life, that small, twisted,
spidery writing has filled me with excitement and apprehension. Why, in God's name! Even today. I wondered what
hde [he?] would say . . about our meeting in London . .
those few intense words we passed in my room, when we
were alone . . I mean, now that I think of it, that they were
all my words. I have never been more sincere with anyone
than with him, always. It is curious, idiotic, that to this
day, now when everything is so definitely over, and mellow-
ing into memory, that I still, seeing his writing, wait for
the "word." Well, the letter asked me to pack up his books
and send them to him, making a list of any I chose to keep
so that he could replace them (in other words: if you keep
any, you will, of course, reduce my library by that much).
In six years all the books we bought were for him because he
needed them for the work which, since I so completely tried
to share his life, was also, to me, in some not very clear
sense, my work. Now I should send him "his" library. I
will be damned if I do. Every rapprochement with Josef is a
chance for him to begin asking new favors. I will be damned
if I will be bothered to pack them up . . when we moved
into this flat he left the whole arrangement of the library to
me . . he wasnt enough interested.
    Lunched with Margit and Jenö Feiks. Jenö is of an
unfading and unfaceted brilliance, and one feels in him the
same mingling of temperament and indolence which I have
found in all cultivated Hungarians, particularly those with a
Jewish strain. They are a terribly insincere people. Sentimental and hard, effusive and treacherous. And amusing.

Get tickets for the Massary premier [premiere]. cigarettes Soap, almonds and flowers for Hal and Ramon. Dinner Monday:

Hal	Dorothy
Ramon	Lillian
Linc	Margaret
Mongelas	Durieux
Arpad	Dina . . . Pamela.

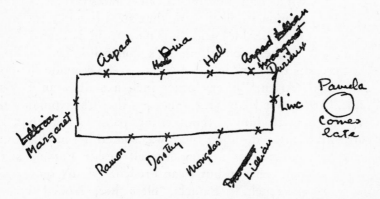

There is certainly a plethora of passable men and a dearth of even possible women in Berlin. If I were only a man and could give stag parties! This one though isn't bad. Poor Hal — I've put him between a fool and a fiend!

The next entry is quite characteristic of the turn Berlin life took for Dorothy after she was linked with Red. I give it in full.

Sept. 11

A very alcoholic party: Hal, Ramon, Tilla Durieux, Margaret, Pamela W., Linc Eyre and Lillian: afterward Diana Manners, Castleross [the name has an E on it, systematically omitted here], Arnold Bennett, Lord Beaverbrook and Kummer [the name is spelled Kommer]. Bennett, standing melancholy and bored against the big wardrobe looked at D.M. who was entertaining Beaverbrook, R. and H. with a most lewd ballad and said: "Tomorrow my friends will wonder why they made such fools of themselves." I: "Mine won't. They will only say, 'Dearie, was I *wery* lit?'" Ramon was so far gone that he encouraged H. to sing the verse about the rolling pin . . I headed him off. The catastrophe didn't occur! Bennett looks rather weasley, with his common English teeth that stick out like the mad hatter's. George Seldes said "His moustache is that droopy kind that makes you think he's concealing a harelip." Castleross is the Lord in M. Arlen's novels[1] & made the bon mot about Arlen, "Every other inch a gentleman";[2] also said, "Arlen met Lady [L.], who was the first woman who ever slept with him without being paid. After that he turned romantic, deciding there was something in this love-business." Castleross seating himself beside Pamela said, "I can't speak German but I can French. All my mistresses have been French." Pamela, bless her, looked bored. Durieux liked Hal a lot and made terrible faces at him all evening.

Hal told Arnold Bennett we were going to be married. He blessed us and said lacrymosely, "Well, one always has to choose between a good husband and a good artist," adding "I said it before & and I say it now to the man's face: Elmer[3] is a grand book." A propos Elmer: H. put his collar and vest on backwards and did a remarkable imitation of Elmer addressing their lordships from an English pulpit. He lost the drift once or twice, however, being decidedly lit.

---

[1] Not at all. He was the most unromantic of fat boys. Michael's hero was composite, but the chief element was the late Lord Alington.

[2] This ancient witticism (Oscar Wilde) dates from long before either Michael or Lord Castlerosse.

[3] *Elmer Gantry*.

I thought they would all *never* go home.

(Bennett doesn't know anything about modern German prose. Knows the French but never read Mann or Zweig or Wassermann or even Hauptmann. Jüd Süss he encountered by chance.)

The next entry is dated September 16th (merely with the numeral, as shown) but it extends, as the reader will see, through three more days:

16th

H. invited me to dinner. He moved today into the Hercules House. When I went around at 6:30 he was "asleep." R. and I pretended he was "tired" and R. promised to waken me and call me at 7. At 8 Hal himself called & I went — wore my brown frock & looked nice. But my lamb was fish-eyed! He kissed me, sat down again at his desk, positively couldn't *move*. "God, I'm lit again, darling," he said with such utter despair in his voice that I started to weep. The maid came in & lay the table for three. Ramon had gone downstairs for cigarettes and didn't come back. Hal started taking off his clothes. His coat and shoes. The maid, I thought, would *never* go. Then, he dropped on the bed. He tried to hold my hand, but he was dead to the world. I cried like a small child, sobbed, half in rage at him, half despair. But he didn't hear me. It is so awful when he just goes away like that. I tried to eat some supper but it choked me. Ramon came back finally about ten. We went to my flat, drank some wine and talked. He adores Hal but said he thought honestly he had about one chance in ten & I was that chance! I was so distressed that I couldn't sleep all night and in the morning was positively ill. Hal came for lunch, started drinking again, and wanted to go and fly on the field[.] Hagen said, "Sinclair

Lewis ist immer ein bischen blau, nicht wahr!" H. stayed at my flat — just dropped off, utterly exhausted. Sunday wasn't much better and unfortunately there was a cocktail lunch. When he saw Ramon off in the evening he was already lit, and in the bar at the Adlon (where I went to meet T.Y.[1] for dinner) said loudly "Tommy, you might as well know D. & I like each other." He wasn't aware that he was letting everyone within earshot know that we had been in England together. Oh, darling, darling, you are so different when you are you — And today (Monday, 19th) at lunch you were all you. He plans to get his book done, I mine, early in the year, take three months in England, he working on "Exile"[2] & I on my "American Protestantism"[3], and then home to a country house . . And he spun plans for new businesses, his favorite form of fiction-making. Today it was to be an automobile camp, a veritable gold-mine. We laughed and were gay and I forgot the bogey. He is altogether adorable.

Hindenburg made a damnfool speech.

To many of her old friends, as to me, this last remark about Hindenburg, on top of the intimate details of unhappiness and compensation, is so inspissatedly Dorothy that one's impulse is to laugh aloud. In a later entry (after dining at Turke's with Red) she is moved to the following reflections. The date is September 23rd.

There is something uncanny and terribly depressing about the relative stability of external things in contrast to the mutability of what has seemed at one time or another the

[1] Thomas Ybarra, New York *World*.
[2] *Dodsworth.*
[3] Never written.

most profoundly unchangeable relation in the world. That J. and I are lost to each other forever: that he no longer exists for me as he was but is really a stranger, while the waiter at Turke's is the same, while the green coat I wore in the Semmering is the same, while even the shoes I wear are, despite run-over heels, and a little shabbiness, the same or more so, than those in which I walked to him — these things which I accept intellectually outrage me innerly. Just as I accept, rationally, the incidentalness of sex, and the fallacy of the idea of union of any two individuals, yet *know* with all the peripheral intelligence of my emotions that such a break as this is a rupture in personality. (How badly said!)

This mood may have been superinduced by a night of horror on the 21st of September. The date was first written 22nd and afterwards corrected heavily to what looks like 27th. I have looked at it under the magnifying glass and am now satisfied that it is (as corrected) the 21st. It reads:

Sept. 21.
A dreadful night. We were to go to Mrs Israel's for a dance; I was invited and wangled an invitation for Hal. Hal said "We will have a fine party . . dinner somewhere grand, dress clothes . . . " I wore the little Lanvin taffeta and spent the afternoon having my hair done, and nails. So I almost missed Koennecke's flight. H. was to come at 7:45: at 8:00 I was watching for him from the window. I knew then that he wouldn't come. At 8:30 he 'phoned. His voice was thick. "I'm shot . . come here, darling." I didn't intend to go. I intended to go directly to Mrs Israel's. Yet, when I got into the taxi I gave his address to the chauffeur. At the Apartment House the porter leered at me when I asked for Mr Lewis' room. I was wearing the Lanvin frock

and my most scrumptious evening cloak. All the lights were on in H's apartment and he was on the bed in his under- clothes and a dressing gown. Dead to the world. I was beside myself. I washed his face but he only came to enough to smile at look at me with fishy, dead eyes. (Those wide aufgerissene Augen.) I cried terribly. Something in me collapsed. I shook him. I was enraged that he could lie there escaped from it all. I thought, 'I will get drunk, too," but when I went into his sitting room there was only one cognac bottle and it was empty. He is on cognac now. He said, "Take off your dress . . . You will spoil your dress — ["] I was lying on his bed — he thinks of the queerest things. I said, "No, I am going home." I knew I had to go home. I couldn't, I thought, stay all night in a man's apart- ment . . a drunken man's apartment. When I said that, he held my wrists tightly and recovered enough to say, "No, no . . Stay here . . I shall die if you go." I took off my dress, and my pretty silver shoes and the shiney rosy stockings. Suddenly he sat up, winked the sleep out of his eyes, and said "I will get you some pyjamas." He laughed when I put them on — white silk ones. I was sobbing all the time. He lifted me into his bed, clasped his arms around me, and went fast to sleep again on my breast. All the time I was sobbing. I saw how everything is going: our house in the frosty New England country, the gay wanderings about the world, the baby I want from Hal; I who never wanted J's child. I saw that everything has been a dream . . . like the dream of a child who says, "When I grow up . ." I saw that this thing will always dash the reality away — I saw all this, and thought, "I will get up and go. Somehow I will recon- struct my life. There is still work . . " And I knew that there was not even that. I saw that being a woman has got me, at last, too. I saw that if Hal goes now, I am finished. I cannot live by myself, for myself. All my heart cried out:

this is my man, the one man, and he has come too late! Nothing left for me but to become brittle or to rot. All the time Hal was making love to me. Feebly, but tenderly. I kissed his breast, and he yearned toward me. I wished I could lift him up and carry him to a high hill, where wind would be blowing. At one thirty or two he suddenly got up. "I want food," he said. Of course he could not raise anyone on the telephone. I begged him not to, but he was obstinate. If I insisted he would be quarrelsome. I said, "Take me home, Hal." And tried to put on my stockings, but he pulled them off. "You stay here," he said. I was weak as water, faint and could only beg him not to go. He stuffed his pyjama legs into trousers . . . When he went out he was swaying. "I shall bring you nice little sausage," he said, smiling and giving me a grave wave of the hand.

I was terrified after he was gone . . . in that state . . . he might be run over . . . he might fight with a policeman. They would bring him home and find me there. How unspeakably sordid it all was! My eyes burned like fires, and my heart was palpitating. He was gone over an hour. He brought back potato salad, sausages and a bottle of cognac. He had had a drink, too. He smelled dreadfully of brandy. His body like rank weeds. He tried to pull out the cork. It stuck because he had not properly cut away the tinfoil. I watched it, fascinated. It seemed as though my life hung on the tinfoil, on the tinfoil's holding. "It won't come out," he said, looking up at me, and smiling like a foiled but good tempered child. "It won't come out," he said incredulously. Then he gave up and came back, sitting on the side of the bed. I was crying again. Suddenly he looked at me. His eyes were like red moons. He started to whimper. "I cannot ruin your life . . you are wholly good . . wholly good. Get up — you mustn't stay here — I will take you home." He pulled me out of bed. "Get dressed," he said. "I must take you home . . Tomorrow I will go away . . You will never see me again. I am finished. You must never have anything to do with me again."

I was dressed now. "Hal," I said, "I will go. But don't think that you can just walk off and free me of you. Wherever you go I will be with you, in you, and you with me, in me. And if you are finished I am finished, too."

He sat down and wept a little. "Darling, darling," he said. "I am so tired — stay . . stay until morning. You have never stayed at my house."

I saw he could not take me home. Nor could I face the porter in my evening clothes, alone, at three in the morning, going out of his house like a street walker who has done her duty, gotten her pay, and been thrown out.

And so I went back to bed, and he held me close to his heart, and slept softly. I lay awake, thinking of him . . . thinking of us . . . That long figure, leaning a little to the wind, the narrow face with its wound of a mouth, its jutting nose, its furroughs like red earth disturbed by an inner volcano, its shining eyes, blue as colorless water, with their always changing pupils; the gestures of his tender, long-fingered hands, his passionate, quixotic quarrelsomeness; his ardent, mocking, obscene love of truthfulness; that sudden, swift smile, like a woman's; that way of dealing blows — with words, of mockery, of vituperation, of scorn, against himself as Babbitt, himself as Gantry. The sudden swift gusts of pity. The feeling I have with him that he knows everything and understands everything so that I become inarticulate.

In the morning, sitting up, the hand holding the eternal cigarette up before his face as though to ward something off, his thin, pale, fine hair all on end, his whole body quivering, he said — "Sweet, sweet . . I know it's giving up spirits or giving up you. And I can't give up spirits. A man takes a

drink, the drink takes another, and the drink takes the man.
And it's got me. I don't know how it began. It was my
father and Gracie. They both hated me. And you will hate
me, too. I am a rotter . . But I won't go like Verlaine —
like Oscar Wilde . . . I'll take care not to get that far.
When I get that far . . "

All my heart dissolved in me. I hid my face on his knee.
"Hal," I said, "I know it is true — If you don't give up
spirits, of course I can't marry you. Of course we must
separate. But that's no solution for me either. You're my
man. I'm thirty-three years old, and I've been married once,
and I've had lovers, but it was all a search for you. I won't
get over this." He held me so closely. So dearly. I said
"Oh, Hal, you'll get over this! It *will* be all right."

At breakfast he was quite himself. "I won't take another
drink for two weeks," he said, "or just beer. Tell me, can I
drink beer?"

I said I thought so. "Damn it, I want a whisky now," he
said, "And I don't need it at all." His hands were shaking.
All the time he talked of the future. Of our house in New
England. "I will learn to lay bricks and we will build our
own wall," he said. "If I work with my hands, that will help
me."

After breakfast he said, "Now you must go . . I must
work."

But I had the feeling he wanted me to go because then he
could take another drink.

Hedwig in the meanwhile had brought me clothes.

Such a night as this might well have induced in Dorothy
those "misgivings" and "premonitions" of which her friends
at the period have spoken. Lilian Mowrer, who was seeing
her constantly in the summer and autumn of 1927, felt that she
was, although very strongly drawn to Red, at the same time

far from sure in her own mind. The chances are, judging by the ups and downs of feeling in her own diaries, that she did not feel quite sure of herself until a more tranquil period supervened in October, when the die was in some ways cast (the arrangements for the Lewis divorce were made) and a sudden stretch of angelic behavior on Red's part veiled the essential difficulties for a while.

The diary for September continues:

I have been ordered to Russia.[1]
Sept. 28. H. has kept his word since that day. God, how I adore him for it!

"28. Von Maltzan was killed — terrible accident. It makes me sick thinking how often I had flown that stretch. He was a clever man and a good-hearted soul. I liked him lots. Only last Friday he was addressing the American Club: "Excellency, Gentlemen, and Dorothy."

Sept. 28.
Tosca with Richard Crooks — an excellent voice and a competent actor but not "hinreissend." Hal had never seen Tosca before in his life (lucky dog). "I am almost as anaesthetic to music as Josef," he said. Afterwards we had a little supper across from the opera with Bouton whom Hal liked — he talked a lot about German students, "die goldene Zeit": I couldn't help comparing him with Helmuth (who had come to supper the night before and who said "The students are the worst class in Germany.") B— is intelligent, cultivated but sentimental, one of those curiously Anglosaxon types who feel that patriotism is a vice unless practised for a country other than one's own, when it can be limitless. He pulled a good line, though, on the woman question. "The

[1] A line alone at the top of the page.

French are an intelligent nation and French feminism is on the right track . . . Bidets instead of ballots." Hal teased Bouton's little lady, a Jewess, by pretending to be a Jew. She believed him. George Seldes warned me that the German press had "rumors" of my "engagement" to Hal!

J. wrote me to send him his books, but made no reference whatever to the books he promised to send me, nor to the costs of divorce, nor — to anything involving him in any responsibility. I shall ignore him until he begins showing signs of wanting to do something for me. He makes me jolly sick.

J's poetry is *bad*. I don't know what to write him. If he will once accept his Judaism and use his good brains and stop cavorting in the sunshine so self-consciously — But how do I know!

Seeing off to America Klaus and Erika Mann . . . not without misgivings! They are naive children and Klaus's "decadence" will hardly endear him to our red-blooded males.

Charles Recht presented Ludwig Lewisohn's card and told me I was a biological monstrosity, that no mean would stick to me because I'd give them all an inferiority complex, and a lot of other very hard, nasty, and, I think, unjustified things. After all he doesn't know me at all. He's writing a book called "Whither Woman?" Doesn't the idiot see that it's "Whither the human race?" The whole "emancipation" of woman is the result of industrial civilization. In attacking the "careerist" he is barking up the wrong tree. The "new" woman is the gold-digger. The careerist is passing. There will always be genuinely distinguished women . . . there always were . . . they are as rare as genuinely distinguished men and can't be categorized.

Incidentally I am more intelligent and better educated and quite as smart as G. and I don't give H. an inferiority complex and she did. Any woman [. . .] can make any man (Napoleon or Goethe) feel inferior: it's not her wits that do it. Recht made me sick, too, with the statement that all men experienced physical revulsion after intercourse with women. Said it was biological law! As though the erotic nature of a civilized, educated and highly sensitized modern man were analyzable by jungle law. "Love" as we know it is one of the most complex of emotions. Besides — I *know* what he says isn't true.

The damned man got under my skin, though.

Lunch with Barbara, Klaus & Erica Mann & the Franks come to supper tonight: Helmuth, Alexa, tomorrow.

Sept. 30.

Lunch with H. and Coudenhove-Kalergi and his wife. She was in excellent form, high-spirited and witty and I somewhat corrected the awfully unpleasant impression I got of her two years ago in New York. I wanted to talk to Coudenhove about politics but there wasn't much chance. We agreed that the complexion of world politics is influenced almost entirely by the English-Russian situation, and that England's policy in Asia is now what her policy in Europe was after the French revolution and the Napoleonic era. Then Europe might have been an entity: she divided it and ruled. Her aim in Russia is *not* the return of a dictator (A Fascist Russia would be as unpleasant as a Bolo one) but a "liberal" régime supported by English capital and under English "influence" and conciliatory to English policy in Asia. If America stands with her, England will succeed. Coudenhove takes very seriously (more seriously than I do) England's flirtation with Italy. He believes if all else fails

England would be willing to raise a fascist army to invade Russia. I don't think even Chamberlain so stupid.[1]

G. won't go to Reno & H. has got to go to Paris for his divorce. I *feel* there is going to be a hitch somewhere. After he's gone I shall be miserable about it, perhaps — when I'm with him and he's himself I don't care about *anything*.

A propos my conversation with Recht: Ida Roland said at lunch "I felt all America was an outrage to my womanhood." She is precisely right. Never in the world was there a civilization so fundamentally hostile to women as the American. It's all tommyrot calling it a woman's country. The "rights" which have been given us are a shameless (if unconscious) price paid for robbing us of our whole life. To be sure, to a less degree, men are robbed of life, by the same civilization, but they are less jealous of it, being more abstract and romantic. (No, that's not it. But women are, somehow, closer to biological verities.)

America is a sterile country, say what you will — I think of the lush life of the Rhinelands, and the amazing hardiness of a "geist" which continues to put out green leaves on the ashpile of Vienna's ruined civilization. I am sometimes depressed, thinking of making a home there (in the U.S.). But I insist we shall have a home. I am too civilized to be wholly vagabond. I can wander forever if I've a roof waiting somewhere.

* * *

H. was too enchanting last night! He did a description of the Nov. 7 revolution celebration in Moscow (as it *will* be) after the manner of Vachel Lindsay, Swinburne, Tennyson, Browning and Wordsworth. He really is phenomenal. Of course he does a great deal with his voice, covering occasional lapses in rhythm and rhyme by inflection: nevertheless the

[1] This is Austen, of course, not Neville (1927).

stunt is *"genial"*: he gets so manificently the peculiar spirit, sentimentalities, tricks and ways of his poets. The Wordsworth parody was a masterpiece but of course today neither he nor I can remember a word! After they had gone (the guests) we sat and talked for two hours, and Hal said, "I'm going to stop doing my foolish little tricks. I bring them out, always, like a vain, spoiled child. You'll get so bored, sweet." I adore these recurrent flashes of humility.

Vincent Sheean was there, a very nice boy, with a wet lower lip, and a little too much prettiness, and he was, alas, *drunk*. It was rather poignant to see Hal's distaste — I could fairly hear his mind working drawing a moral for himself. S. kept saying "All come to Moscow . . . you must *all* come to Moscow . . . " and "Borodin — great man, Borodin." He quoted Borodin as saying of Elmer G. "I feel that this is an important book." S. made such idiotic remarks as these: "Lewis is just an artist; Borodin is mankind."

We went to sleep, coiled up together as purely as two brother-puppies. The *darling*!

It's absurd to say Elmer is an impossible character. If Floyd Gibbons had been born a Methodist, herded into a theological seminary, and had seen a good chance to get on in the pulpit, he would have been quite like Elmer. No, this isn't true. Floyd has percipience. He said, "Now that your heart is broken you can begin really to live . . . only so do women get free." Elmer could never have said that. Nor written "sunlight buttering the trees."

In this long entry, covering everything from Coudenhove-Kalergi's picture of Europe (and how quaint that seems today!) to my own lower lip, Dorothy seems more reconciled to her future than in any other extensive passage of writing during that period. Red was behaving well — that is, he drank nothing but beer, was attentive and devoted, and in his appearances before Dorothy's Central European friends he made an effort to observe the proprieties. For the fact is that he valued the proprieties, the *convenances*, the actual manners of polite society, almost as extravagantly when sober as he flouted them when drunk. He took a lot of trouble about buying the best possible clothing of all sorts and for all occasions, and so long as he cohered in other ways (which was so long as he was sober) he wore them well. I remember very well the dinner party Dorothy has just described, in which he did the fabulous parodies. He was at the very peak of his powers just then. I never heard him before or afterwards in such a vein of brilliance. Countess von Moltke and her wonderful son Helmuth were, as I remember, quite stunned by the phenomenon, as were we all.

A word about myself at my first apparition in this narrative: I had known Dorothy for about a year, Red for something less than that, but both very slightly. I had met Dorothy in Berlin, Red (and also, separately, Gracie) in London. Some of Dorothy's curious description of me (the "wet lower lip," for instance) might have been due to nervousness. I was by far the youngest member of that company, and the least distinguished. But the obsessive insistence on Moscow for the 7th of November came from another source. I had just left my friend Rayna Prohme in Moscow, was on my way to London for a few weeks, and had promised to return for the tenth anniversary of the Bolshevik Revolution on November 7th. It was this (my obsessive insistence) which set Red off on his wonderful outburst of improvisation — O you *must* come to *Mos*cow for the *Seve*nth of November — which, re-accented and as it were re-colored, served as the basis for each phase of the poetic parody.

The journey to Moscow did take place, with results felt in all of our lives for decades thereafter.

On October 3rd Dorothy writes in her diary:

Hal left Saturday night for Paris to see about his divorce. I do not know what is wrong with me. I am excessively nervous, restless, almost ill. Consumed with fears, which are indistinct — nameless. Got a beastly letter from Josef, revealing himself in his worst light, and full of resentment toward me. In all my life I only did him good and he hates me. It is this knowledge, I suppose, which is at the basis of all my fears. It is curious I do not believe, emotionally, that I am going to be happy. Something will happen. (Or is this feeling only a defense against disappointment?)

Later on the same day she writes:

Hal wires from Paris that after consulting a lawyer there he hopes to be able to persuade Grace to go to Reno. Evidently the Paris divorce game isn't so good. I shall telephone Strauss tomoro.

The next entry (or at any rate the next which has been kept) is dated October 7th:

Hal is coming back tomoro Hooray! I am a little idiot.

The period of indecision ends with Red's — Hal's — return from Paris on October 8th. He was evidently in the highest spirits, full of schemes and plans and expedients of all sorts, as delightful as they were absurd. Red could think of a dozen fascinating projects and make them all as vivid as reality while he was getting through an ordinary and not very copious breakfast. There was no standing against him — and of course, fundamentally, Dorothy did not want to stand against him. Her decision was now firm, happily and rather excitedly firm, although there was still much time to live through and a certain amount of discretion to be observed before their wedding day. The state of her mind, blissful and decided, but very pleased also in the ordinary sense of the term, is shown best in a letter to her sister Peggy (Mrs Howard Wilson) which is dated October 12th. Peggy, her only sister, was a rare and special confidante; Pam was Peggy's little girl. The letter is written on two stiff cards, letter-cards, and was evidently so sent, but at a later date Peggy left it in the files at Twin Farms, I gather, for safekeeping. It is now among the papers at Syracuse University. The letter follows:

Peggy, darling,

It was so nice to have your dear letter. I love all you tell me about Pam. She sits on my dressing table, looking at me with her wise, sweet little face while I dress — and I adore her. I knew the frocks would be too big, but I feared to get them too small. They are from Liberty's, in London. I bought them when I was in England on my vacation.

Peggy dear, I am awfully happy. I went through the most awful autumn and winter, you can imagine, and spring was even worse. I got my divorce in June. And then, when I was beginning to live a little again — it was like recovery from a long convalescence — suddenly the gods decided to be kind to me, and I met the man, who, I think, I have been looking subconsciously for all my life. *Please, honey, don't* say anything to *anybody*. He separated from his wife a year ago but he's not yet divorced. He has started to get a divorce but it may be months before he has it, and we can't (of course) be married until then. And because he's so damned famous he wants to avoid all publicity. If you tell *anyone*, that person may tell someone else, and that person someone else, and finally some newspaper person will get hold of it and there will be the devil to pay. But any how, I want you to know.

I'm going to be married again, I hope before summer, and it's Sinclair Lewis. He is the darlingest person alive. If you are *sure*[1] Howard won't tell, you *may* tell him, but *not a word.* It has all been sudden, but it's quite all right. We belong to each other. I'm not telling Willard,[2] and don't you.

I kiss you
Dorothy.

[1] Twice underlined.
[2] Their brother.

3

A Time of Waiting

DOROTHY WAS UNDER ORDERS FOR THE JOURNEY TO MOSCOW which she undertook at the end of October, but Red had cooled on the idea of following her there. He was by this time well advanced on the novel he called *Exile*, which was, eventually, to become *Dodsworth*, and in addition he had persuaded himself that the skit or spoof called *The Man Who Knew Coolidge*, originally written for Mencken and Nathan in *The Smart Set*, could be blown up into a book-length production which might reach a wide public. This was essentially no more than one of Red's monologues, and when written down at the length of 15,000 words had proved entertaining; at 60,000 words it was to be something less than that.

It was enough, just the same, to keep him from the Russian journey. It was perhaps just as well for Dorothy's journalistic purposes that he stayed in Berlin, because very little serious work of that kind could be done with Red in tow. She had a month in Russia on her own.

And then, of course, as the month of November wore on and their correspondence grew more incessant, his whim changed and he, too, wanted to see the new red world. He went to Russia on November 29th and returned to Berlin December 10th, thus affording himself at least a glimpse (his only one) of the Bolshevik experiment.

I have always thought, then and afterwards, that Red's attitude about the Russian journey, and his attitude in Russia when he got there, as well as later on, was more complex and difficult than appeared on the surface. He put his entire journey upon the head of Dorothy: he had gone to Russia "to see Dorothy," everything he did there was "because of Dorothy," etc., etc. As a novelist, a very serious and important novelist, he was more widely read in Russia than any living Russian (as he was in comparable societies); consequently the Russians expected him to say something, to observe, to comment, in some manner not merely puckish or joking. He would not. He shied off. I do not think this was merely self-consciousness about Dorothy, or the result of a desire to put her forward as the great observer. I think Red shied off the whole subject because it made him nervous and ill at ease; he did not know what to think; he distrusted his own instincts and preferred to say nothing.

He had been an avowed (a very loudly avowed) socialist for most of his adult life and still considered himself to be one. He had not surrendered, and was not to surrender for many years yet, the project for that American labor novel, of which the hero — old-time American radical merging into modern intellectual socialist — was Eugene Debs. This gave him, or should have given him, a lively curiosity about the attempt to bring socialism into existence in Russia. Perhaps he did not feel that curiosity and was ashamed of not feeling it; perhaps he thought his time was too short to do anything with it; perhaps he felt the subject was too big, unapproachable, made difficult by language and the barriers of culture. There may be truth in any of these possibilities, but what I think most likely is that Red was disquieted by stories of terror, violence and political suppression (it was the moment when Trotzky's followers were being driven off the surface of Russian life) and felt too uncertain to have an opinion. I talked to him a great deal during the next couple of years and certainly never found in him anything which could have been called a formulated opinion about events in Russia.

This, I suggest, is why he was reluctant to go, and reluctant to say anything once he had gone.

Not so Dorothy. She flourished exceedingly, worked all day every day, was fascinated by everything she saw, took copious notes and wrote at length about the whole spectacle for her newspapers in the United States. The excitement, the freshness and eagerness with which she approached everything she could see were qualities already becoming rare in journalism about the Soviet Union. At that time, when foreigners were welcome and every effort was made to make material accessible to the American or other western correspondent, it was possible to write with some insight and effectiveness about the phenomena of ordinary life under the Soviet regime, and she did so. Her letters to Red Lewis, although not organized and not journalistic — personal throughout, to a degree rare in her correspondence — give best of all the freshness of her responses, undoctored and unembellished, to the experience of an unknown society.

I saw her fairly often in Moscow after the 7th of November, as will be told. It was in Moscow that there was formed, somehow or other, the basis of that friendship which endured between us (through many vicissitudes and disagreements) until her death thirty-four years later. Dorothy and I were enough alike — and enough unlike — to make an association semi-intellectual, semi-professional, with no element of prejudged unity or fabricated accord: we were a continuous debate, as much as anything else, over the solid ground of some instinctive friendliness, as of brother and sister, which nothing could really shake. (I used to call her my "Protestant sister," whatever that means.) This relationship was well away in the future, but its groundwork came by means of events (dire events), with the instinctive actions and the unforgettable perceptions to which they lead.

The body of Dorothy's letters from Russia to Red Lewis, as

they are kept at Syracuse University, follow in order as a separate section. There may be one or two missing, but it is a reasonable guess that these are all or nearly all of them. Red evidently kept them and they wandered into the files at Twin Farms, there to remain.

2

Letters from Russia:

Moscow

NEW YORK EVENING POST
PHILADELPHIA PUBLIC LEDGER
UNTER DEN LINDEN 57
BERLIN

October 31. 1927

I've had a little bottle of redwine in the diner where everybody was chattering about Russia including a revolutionary nigger a revolutionary Syrian and dozens of revgermans rather longhaired softfaced and related to Jesus unless that story about the Roman guard is true. I thought about Russia some but mostly about you. I see always your funny darling face with the dent on one side that's sometimes a line and sometimes almost a perfectly absurd dimple or rather I feel your face, just wide enough to span with my hands when the wrists are together; your funny narrow face with its aufgerissene eyes, which I love more than anything in the world. I adore you.

Dorothy

Tues. Eve.
(nov. 1) 1927

Sweet:

We've just passed the Russian border — marked by a huge, glowing red star over the railroad track — my companions say "Now thank God we are *safe* in our own country," and all are singing the Internationale at the top of their lungs as I write this note — which I'm giving to the sleepingcar conductor to take back to you — I am distinctly conscious of coming to a different country — furrin parts.

The journey has been thoroly comfortable with plenty of company. Incidentally Dreiser's physician (the one who examined him first) is on the train & says Dreiser's condition is very serious. He thinks he has the beginning of cancer of the lungs. Of course they didn't tell Dreiser. I wish I knew whether the Doctor Berthold recommended found anything to justify this diagnosis in the Xray. Poor chap if it's so!

I have tried to learn the Russian alphabet & only found it a good sleeping draught. Govch's Germany though is first rate & kept me awake at least an hour.

Darling darling *darling*. I love you. I live in you. I kiss you.

D.

NEW YORK EVENING POST
PHILADELPHIA PUBLIC LEDGER
UNTER DEN LINDEN 57
BERLIN

Moscow
Nov. 8. 1927

I've moved into the Grand, into a very comfortable and clean room, looking over the Archway and shrine of the

Iberian Virgin into the Red Square, and I've got a nice secretary to read the papers for me, and although my trunk hasn't come, I still have hopes that the delay is only due to festivities which have held up everything, including the mail, for two days, so that I read the one letter I have had from you, over and over again.

I am getting tired of being educated by Scott,[1] being bored by Harry Dana and being facetiously nudged by old Dreiser, who has turned quite a gay dog in Moscow, constantly making rather lumbering jokes. Still, I find him sympathetic, because he has a sort of healing common sense about life. And, curiously enough, he has a genuine — if rather elephantine — sense of humor. Last night (yesterday was the great day here, one event after another) both he and I were almost in hysterics with the accumulated laughter of the day, and irritated our earnest friends highly thereby. However, one forgives even Scott his earnestness when he smiles, and he sometimes did.

Hal, I miss you so. There is more company good and bad here than one needs, and more to see than ever I did find, and more to think about and talk about than in most places — why do I have these wistful moments, when I feel like taking the next train home?

This experience is so unique for me, I wish you were sharing it, as I wish for your sharing everything which is beautiful or stimulating . . .

Oh, Hal,

D.

[1] Professor Scott Nearing.

NEW YORK EVENING POST
PHILADELPHIA PUBLIC LEDGER
UNTER DEN LINDEN 57
BERLIN

Moscow

СИНКЛЕР ЛЬЮИС   Nov. 9. 1927

That, my very dear, is Sinclair Lewis, in Russian, as I have just seen it prominently, nay, *most* prominently displayed in an Exhibition of Modern Literature arranged by the Federated Society of Writers. They've jolly well pirated everything. I saw Babbitt, Mainstreet, Arrowsmith, Wrenn, Mantrap, & The Job, and they told me they had others. You & O. Henry are, I am told, the most popular Americans at present. Upton is falling off. People are getting bored with politics. I regret to tell you that Mantrap appears rather more popular than Babbitt. And it is quite true — The Green Hat is a serious competitor, and so is "So Big" & Fannie Hurst in her lighter moments.

As far as I can see, everybody in Russia is writing something, when he isn't talking, and everything written is published: a sort of literary diarrhoea which may or may not be the beginning of a renaissance. I feel as though there were a book inflation.

x x x

A letter you wrote on the 3rd has only just arrived! It's beastly being so far from you in point of communication. Believe how near I am to you in every moment, in every breath. As for the fire sputtering — it was yours I was worrying about in that poem — not mine. And, you see, it was started without conviction and got no father than the Oxford Book of English Verse —

Condolences regarding Harris.

God!

D

I shall snatch labels off all the vodka bottles that come my way and pilfer stamps.

Vincent Sheehan has arrived but I haven't seen him. Fred Howe is also somewhere in the offing

Love to Ramon

NEW YORK EVENING POST

PHILADELPHIA PUBLIC LEDGER

UNTER DEN LINDEN 57

BERLIN

Nov.

Friday the 11th. 1927

Such days! Yesterday, for instance. In the morning foreign office, trying to get interviews — with Tchicherin, with Rykov. God knows whether. Then to The Pedagogical Seminar for a list of schools to visit and much advice about education. Then to an exhibition of the art of the Russian nationalities — a very lovely exhibition, it was, too. Then to an ancient monastery where the tomb of Tikon lies under twelve eternally burning lamps and banked with fresh flowers. Then to lunch — or whatever one may call this extraordinarily meal which one eats between four and six and which is the only meal of the day — with Junius Wood, and a very knotty and gnarled old stick he is, too but I like him for his dry kindness. Then an opera — the Love for the Three Oranges, and before that an international congress of the Friends of Russia, and at midnight to an artist's club in Moscows Greenwich village, with Restwick, the A.P. man. A typical day. Today I lunch with the wops, Erszi being back, tea with Brockdorf-Ranzau the German ambassador, and dine with Duranty.[1] Because Duranty being English,

[1] Walter Duranty, author and journalist, then Moscow correspondent of the New York *Times.*

dines. Nothing would persuade him to adapt his habits to those of this country. I work very hard, and the more I work and the more I see the more confused I seem to become. I hope to begin to see light in another week.

Your dear letters . . . and the last was from Monday. I'm desolated, truly, that you havent had any of my letters . . . it's too distressing, this delay. I suppose it was the holidays; here, for two days, no post was delivered.

The Veiller affair is too much for me. Good God didnt he know what he had on hand before he started with Elmer. What are you going to do?

I'm glad you met Vallentin, finally. She's a very clever woman with a lot of bunk about her, but nevertheless. Harris sounds filthy. But I'm glad there were some pretty girls.

Oh, sweet, I miss you like the deuce.

D.

My love to the "good baby." I gather that you have remoulded Dodsw. nearer to your heart's desire.

This being morning, and I being energetic, I give you a tiny and very fast little kiss; on the nose.

x

Moscow

Nov. 12. 1927

Two letters from you when I came in tonight from the opera: (from seeing "Esmeralda," the ballet, with the 55 yr. old pet: and I thought: How funny! There was a revolution, and what a revolution, and long before that Isadora came out of the west to tell 'em this artificial toe-stepping was the bunk, and all the "bourjuis" have been downed, and a new freedom reigns yet here's this old Queen, ex mistress of some defunct Grand Duke, twiddled her toes in the same old way to an audience of caps and smocks instead of white fronts and orders, and to a crowded one, too. Selah!) Two letters from you, and such *dear* letters. "Heinrich, Heinrich, wass hast du mir angetan," as Elizabeth moans, in Thannhauser. I am on the most interesting assignment of my life, and thrilled by it, but would I at this moment rather be here than in some "low pub" with you, drinking beers — I would *not* . . . It's a lovely idea coming here in the spring! Hal, we'll go to the desert of Karahan, and to Bokhara & Samarkand, and Astrakhan, and Mongolia, and Siberia and Karelia and really *see* the Union of Socialist Soviet Republics if you will! Do you know that this country covers $\frac{1}{4}$ of the world's surface? Well, it does, according to Baedecker! When we finish we'll only have $\frac{3}{4}$ths to see.

Sweet — this is only a goodnight kiss. I am *really* only across the street. Very near to you, dear *dearly* beloved.

Du.

A small one.

All the snow's gone away and Moscow's mud.

I'm so thankful that my letters have at last begun to come. I was desolated!

NEW YORK EVENING POST
PHILADELPHIA PUBLIC LEDGER
UNTER DEN LINDEN 57
BERLIN

Moscow
Nov. 16. 1927

You say "I can't believe you can go on liking me among surroundings so stirring. I say: Perhaps I am a little glad to have come away like this, to know, without any touch of your hands, or sound or sight of you, how you live in me, and *are* me. This comfort and this quietness.

Russia *is* stirring: I am working awfully hard, eating, thinking, breathing Russia — and more confused, more questioning, more doubtful of the verity of any impression, any sound. I find myself caring very much that this work should be good; and I'm desperately afraid it won't be. Terribly as I want to see you, too, I think two weeks' stay is much too little to be worth the journey . . . . But I will try to shorten my stay by a week.

x x x

I *need* no consolation. If Ramon does I wish him joy of Hilda Rosmach. She's a pretty thing.

And you – Hal —

I was *about* to be noble. But let me TELL *you* — if you get to casting a lascurous eye on Blondes — or for that matter brunettes.

Well —

Well – that's that.

D.

Today: Lunch German Embassy: me guest of honor; lots of good talk. I pump people like Ike Marcosson.

Afternoon — visiting factories

Eve — Dinner — Duranty; Wood; the Deuss [Ed Deuss of I. N. S.] Excellent Talk. Now. To dream of you.

Moscow
Nov. 18. 1927

Darling — I was desolated to get your telegram this evening and learn that you haven't been getting my letters. Yours have been drifting in day by day, making life so gay, so comforted, and I have thought it would be the same with you. And today is 19 whole days we've been apart — longer than ever in the long, long, *long* time we've been together. Oh, *damn* the mails.

Hal, this place is driving me crazy. Every day I change my mind about everything I'd made it up about the day before. And all the time I am excited. I don't eat much, sleep *very* little, work all the time, and feel gorgeously well. If only you were here, in the evening, so I could put my cheek against yours. But it will be so, soon. Time's moren half over.

Your waffle.

NEW YORK EVENING POST
PHILADELPHIA PUBLIC LEDGER
UNTER DEN LINDEN 57
BERLIN

Moscow
Nov. 18. 1927

Today I saw extracts from Eisenstein's great unfinished film: "October". In the afternoon — the cemetary of a nearby monastery funeral of Joffe: the only acquaintance I had in the foreign office. I knew him from Vienna. He committed suicide. Stood with a crowd in the snow; windy, gray day: Bright red coffin and black flags. Red soldiers at head & feet. And Trotsky speaking: "let out" for the day. Joffe also belonged to the disgraced opposition. Altogether — unforgettable.

No letter from you today — and I think of your four silent letterless days. Have I told you that I love you: With my whole heart, in every way a women can love a man, or one human soul another.

That happens to be true.

D

Nov. 21. 1927

Such a day! Little Rayna Prohme — you will remember
Vincent Sheehan's speaking of her; she was his friend, and a
gay red-headed girl who had balled her life up inextricably,
but was a charming thing — little Rayna Prohme died this
morning, across the street in the Hotel Metropole. Just like
that. Only a week ago we were all talking on her for wanting to join the communist party. It is dreadful, Hal: To die
alone in a beastly hotel room, in Moscow. She had one
husband (divorced) in America: You may know of him:
Raphaelson, a playwright. And she had another who loved
her, in Manila. But she though she should save the Chinese
and came to Moscow with Borodin. I liked her very much,
in the fortnight I knew her. And now all of a sudden she's
dead, from an abcess on the brain, or something. And I've
wanted all day to run home to you, because it scared me,
and I don't feel quite safe anywhere except with you, darling,
darling.

Last night: Fred Howe. We talked: he & Junius Wood,
& I, until three this morning. And

"Can you tell me S.L.'s address . . . I hear he's in Berlin,"
he said. And I could. And how is he? And I said: Jolly
well. And *he* said "Has he got a divorce?" And *I* feigned
astonishment Why, no, I don't believe so, I said. And *he*
said: Well I wish he would. And *I* said: "Have you seen the
ballet." And all the time my heart was twinkling. I *do* want
to mount the Kremlin wall, or anything else high & public
(the front balcony of the great Komintern building wouldn't
be bad, would it?) and tell the world I love and adore you.

But in Moscow there is no time nor sympathy for such a
bourgeoise thing as love.

Es lebe die Liebe, aber, doch!

x x x

I work like a fiend. I want to come home. I am home-sick. I am Hal-sick. If I go to Leningrad & I really should, I *will* come out over Stockholm: And wouldn't you like to come up and meet me. (She says very tentatively — I don't want to disturb your work . . . But they say Stockholm is adorable)

x x x

Yes, sir, I will go away with you in mid-February, if you will, to somewhere warm, and soft, and full of cafés and native costumes, west, if you like of Marseilles, or south, if you will, of Genoa, or where you will, east or west or south or north.

Because I love you.

I take your dear narrow face in my hands and kiss your temples and your eyes.

D.

NEW YORK EVENING POST
PHILADELPHIA PUBLIC LEDGER
UNTER DEN LINDEN 57
BERLIN

Nov. 22. 1927

I wonder if you know how happy your letters make me. I've just come in to my little room from the cold streets (I've been visiting an orphan asylum) and here on my table is your letter about the Baleric isles, and all the sweetness and nonsense and goodness of you. I'm trying hard to concentrate on Russia, but I'm getting so damned homesick that I'm positive I wont stick it out until the 15th. And I am getting too much material; some of it terribly interesting stuff, and as far as I know, new; the problem will be assembling it. There are such enormous gaps in it.

I think all the time — back in my mind, while I am visiting schools and talking to concessionaires all the time about us. Hal, I feel very humble. If I can ever be to you just a fraction of what I want to be, you will have a good wife. But I wish I were more beautiful, I wish I were more amusing, and more wise, I wish I were more good, and I wish I never had funny small moods . . . . and then I perversely wish that you should like me just exactly as I am even when I wish myself to be different. Which ain't logical!

It's amazing how you are with me, every moment, almost physically. I see every line under your eyes, and the almost dimple in your cheek, and the way your eyelashes turn back, and your funny knees, and the length and color of your hands; and I hear your voice, when you are suddenly your inmost self and it is very clear and singing and when you are your other self, created, for purposes, and it makes fun of what you say; and I see you as you are when you make my heart catch and a little tear come into it, and as you are when you make me laugh waffly. You see, I happen to love you.

You DArlinG.

You.

Think of how Miss M— would grace the lit'r'y salons of Europe AND America. Dont you think you'd better reconsider?

The correct answer is: You had better NOT

D

NEW YORK EVENING POST
PHILADELPHIA PUBLIC LEDGER
UNTER DEN LINDEN 57
BERLIN

Later. Thurs.
25th   1927

I am distressed about Ramon: terribly. And about you
— being alone. I want to come home. Suddenly Russia
has gone dead on me, and I feel I ought to be with you.
And yet I *can't* leave before I get certain gaps in my information filled in. And everything here goes slowly. I think
I can get away on the 2nd or 3rd or 4th — about then. I'd
like, though, not to stay in Berlin where I'm certain to be
drawn back into the office, and into telephone calls, but go
away somewhere, to the country and get my material written
up: I figure that I have stuff for twenty thousand words or
so, and I cant have it messed up by other work. Could we
go somewhere together, dear dear? Otherwise I ought to
settle down here until mid December and finish the whole
damn series on the ground. And it isn't in the least necessary
if I can get peace & quiet elsewhere. Tell me what.

Today is Thanksgiving. I'm thankful for you, for work,
and for feeling so well. I don't want anything else in the
world. I spent it (the evening) with the Hoppers, really
charming Americans & with Junius Wood, who being sixty,
crotchety, & softhearted, and living in this hotel has been my
mainstay here. After dinner, an' there was a turkey, we
went to Irma Duncan's & saw fair maidens swathed in
Scarlet dance the Internationale. All morning I spent in a
kindergarten & all afternoon at a funeral. So it was a day.

I love to work, honeyest . . only this separation is really
too long. Even though you're so vividly with me.

I bought some more linen, for the house, for our house.

I warn you, Hal, I am going to turn domestic on you. And occasionally go to Tibet.

With you.

Darling — I want to say something, in some new way, more vividly . . . and it's so late, and I'm so tired. Will it do to say "I love you"?

I kiss you goodnight.

D.

NEW YORK EVENING POST
PHILADELPHIA PUBLIC LEDGER
UNTER DEN LINDEN 57
BERLIN

Nov. 26. 1927

an' we sat in a little tiny sleigh 'bout as big sa babysled, an' we rode n rode, 'n the driver he wore a tall fur hat an' he had a sheepskin coat on, with a belt tight around his waist, an' we passed little white churches with five gold domes on a top of 'em, an' the domes were for the father God and the four best disciples. An' there were little wood houses with lights in 'em, an' the snow was thick an' soft an it kep' falling an falling, an' bymby we came to a house an' in it was a "workers club" an there was a stage and on the stage were people just like in the Chauve souris. An' I thought, funny place this; awful' funny. Looks jus' like Russia.

This is the Russianest lookin' place I ever saw.

An' I went out "investigatin'", an' I investigated a Caucasian shop and there I bought a Christmas present for a father to give to his little boy. I dont know the little boy but if he takes after his father *atall*, then he'll like to dress up an' pretend he's somebody else nhe is, and he'll like something furrin. It's a festival dress for Caucasian little boys

an' it's all white wool with a tight waist and cartridge pockets
an' in the pockets theys filigreesilver cartridge holders, an'
it has a blue satin vest an' its all trimmed with silver braid
an' it has a belt with a knife in it, an' a tall big fur hat all
white, an' the most wonderful boots. Blue, no! green, yes,
green with red tops an' all kinds other colored leather sewed
on in a design. Oh, Gee, its a nice suit.

 Now I guess I must close.

Your loving friend,
Dorothy

HOTEL SAVOY

BUREAUBINE.

MOSCOU, ROJDESTVYENCA 3.

Hotel Bolshay Moscouskaya
(Grand Hotel)
Nov. 26. 1927

I've been trying for days (I almost wrote *since* days,
and remembered in time my purist lover) to send a note to
you by hand. But the carrier pigeons didn't leave. Now
Vincent Sheehan swears he *is* leaving tonight: enviable
creature! He will see *you*. I haven't any news in the world,
for surely you are not interested in what the Lena Gold
fields representative thinks about the Gossplan. I even
doubt whether you know what the Gossplan is. "You haven't
missed much." Nor are you, probably, agog to know the
precise amount of Carborundrun exported to Russia during
the past six months.

 But are you perhaps, still, after a million repetitions
pleased to know that I — well, like you very much.

You *darling*

 Be nice to Vincent Sheehan. He's had the devil of a time

here — I've told him if he doesn't find shelter elsewhere, with a friend in the British Embassy, he should go up and use my flat. In which highly improbable case, will you tell Hedwig it's all right?

D

3

I NEVER DID USE DOROTHY'S FLAT IN BERLIN. I WAS, AT THAT moment, sick and sore and bewildered, too young by far, at least in mind and experience, for the weight of grief. Moreover, Berlin was never at any time my nest, my cocoon, my favored habitat, my second home, or whatever it was to Dorothy and other colleagues; Paris was all that to me and more. When I left Moscow I went to Paris as rapidly as possible, pausing in Berlin only a day or so to get my breath, alone in a tiny hotel room where even the street noises could not be heard. I was stricken more than Dorothy herself imagined, I think now that I read her letters. But it is necessary in this narrative to give some attention to those events in Moscow because it is from them, or through them, that I came to have such regard for Dorothy (and she sympathy for me) as could last out both our lives.

I did not know her until then except in the most superficial way. I had no notion of her indomitable courage, no concept of the grain or texture of her character, no remote idea of the heights to which she could rise, not by mind or heart alone but by some other quality containing both but containing also something else — something of a Christian configuration, something derived from her austere and powerful father in the snows of upstate New York. It was her possession of this extra quality — or, let us say more precisely, her *access* to it, since she did not always dwell on such peaks — that led me in later decades to call her my "Protestant sister," a description she could accept without a qualm because she knew exactly what it meant.

I was, as she has indicated in her letters to Red, completely preoccupied with Rayna Prohme, an American girl I had known in China in the revolutionary tempests of the year just now ending (1927). Rayna had escaped to Moscow with Madame Sun Yat-sen, widow of the founder of the Chinese Republic, when the counterrevolutionary tide — or at least the Nationalist tide — drove out the Left forces of the Kuomintang movement and took over most of the country. I had no information as to their whereabouts (such movements were secret and had to be) but it was not difficult to guess. When my work ended in Peking and Manchuria I went on to Moscow by the Trans-Siberian and saw Rayna within a few minutes of my arrival.

I had to go to Paris and London for some weeks, but it was agreed between us that I should be back for the tenth anniversary celebration of the Russian Revolution on November 7th. This rendezvous with death obsessed me; I have heard from other friends (not only from Dorothy's diary) what a bore I was on the subject. Perhaps I was most of all afraid that I might not be able to make the necessary business arrangements (whatever they were, and I have now forgotten) to get back at the time appointed, or, more significantly, to keep my promise to Rayna. There is no doubt that by this time she had become all-important to me, not only in the strictly personal sense (that was perhaps obvious) but in every convolution of thought, every pulse of being. My friends in London, Paris and Berlin could know nothing of all this and thought me more than a little strange during those weeks.

I succeeded in getting to Moscow for the 7th of November, but only just. It was the actual morning of the celebration when I arrived. I took a droshky to the address Rayna had given me and there she was, waiting. We went out into the driving snow for the parade, the tremendous show in the Red Square, the congealed and cheering masses in front of the Kremlin wall, the dignitaries (all save Trotzky) standing in their furs on top of Lenin's tomb. Trotzky was already under house arrest and was soon to be exiled; the long dictatorship of J. V. Stalin was now beginning.

The story of those weeks, except in outline, has no place here. It is fully told in my own *Personal History*, published some years later (1935). As the title of that book was intended to suggest, there are events, relationships, dramas of soul and body, which are neither public nor private but mysteriously both; there is a region where the person and the history through which he lives become so entangled that the strands cannot be separated. The year 1927 was like that, for me, from beginning to end, with a mounting tension, an almost unbearable acceleration and deepening of the whole composition (if I may so call it), whatever its author or its end.

Somehow or other Dorothy became involved in this. She was not particularly interested in either Rayna or me — certainly not in the beginning. We met her a number of times: she was full of information about the factories and schools and the countless officials she met. She became aware of the tension that there was where we were and it mystified her somewhat (as she afterwards told me). It was for this reason, as much as any other — to find out what caused the tension in the air — that she asked us to dinner one night at the Grand Hotel. Towards the end of the meal I told her the truth: that Rayna had determined to enter the Lenin School for training as an agent of the Communist International.

To me, of course, this was like suicide — the extinction of a personality. It was even worse than joining the Communist Party. Agents of the Comintern had no lives at all, and generally had to deny even the mainspring of their no-life, their belief in Communism. That this could happen to my Rayna seemed an incredible tragedy. Dorothy, although far more rational about it, saw it as I did and tried to argue the case. Before we left her that night I had pummeled poor Rayna's shoulders and told her what I have said above, what I had been thinking for days: that her decision was like suicide. "The end of Rayna Prohme," was the way I put it.

As it turned out, this was only too literally true. On the very next day, as she was talking to Kenneth Durant at the Savoy Hotel, she collapsed. He telephoned me; I got there as fast as I could; she was barely conscious, could not stand up or move, could scarcely speak. She needed far more attention than she could ever get in our quarters. I carried her through the streets to the Metropole, where Anna Louise Strong was able to get a room for her, and after hours of anxious effort I tracked down (through Walter Duranty) the doctor of the German embassy. Such difficulties would not be met today, but this was Moscow in 1927. The German doctor took a very grave view. In a few days (some days were bright with hope, but not many) Rayna was dead. The disease was encephalitis, the German doctor said, and had been going on for a long time.

Stunned as I was — stunned very nearly to insensibility — I became aware of Dorothy. She had come to the room during Rayna's illness; she was one of the first to come after its end. I do not remember what she said or did, but there was some mitigation of the numbness when she was there; I was at least aware of her.

Then came the funeral. It had been arranged by committees or delegations in Communist fashion, with a sort of parade through the streets to the crematorium. I believe the Russians who had worked in China (Comintern people) and some American labor delegations who happened to be in Moscow (non-Communist, these would mostly be) and also the students of the Sun Yat-sen University may have been responsible, between them. I hardly knew what was going on.

But the funeral itself is distinct, even now. Snow, asters, the slow tread of indifferent feet, the bells of a monastery outside the city, near the crematorium — all this, and the sound of strange voices . . . I heard one American ask another: "Who was the comrade who died, do you know?"

Dorothy walked every inch of the way, as did Madame Sun Yat-sen. Neither one was warmly enough dressed. Both had thin western shoes (no goloshes). Both, as it happened, wore navy blue capes of a kind perhaps more usual then than now, but they could not have been warm; I remember both Dorothy and Madame Sun wrapping these capes about their shivering bodies. They did not know each other and did not speak. Both could have gone in government cars in comfort. Madame Sun's Foreign Office limousine, a vast contrivance, followed her at a snail's pace all the way out to the crematorium. Dorothy's came to fetch her afterwards. I could do nothing for them if they insisted on walking — on and on and on for what seemed a space and time everlasting, while the snow fell thicker and faster and the early darkness gathered.

Still, I never have forgotten either of them on that long journey and I can see them both now. It must have meant something that they walked.

The next night I took the train to Berlin. I had been living at the Savoy Hotel since Rayna's collapse. Dorothy came there and telephoned to my room. I went down to the lobby and found her at the porter's desk. (This, too, I can see over the years.) She gave me the keys of her flat in Berlin and said that I could be warm and quiet there.

I did not use the keys, but they, too, must have been something to be so long remembered. I do not remember what I did with them (delivered them to Red? Perhaps). But I remember the keys themselves — and Dorothy in her navy blue cape with her head bent against the falling snow.

4

Callooh! Callay!

RED WAS IN BERLIN DURING MY BRIEF PASSAGE THROUGH; I remember having drinks or a meal or both with him at Herkules Haus just then, even though I cannot recall what I did with Dorothy's keys. No doubt I told him all about Dorothy in Moscow, and about Mr Theodore Dreiser, the most notable American visitor at the Russian anniversary celebration, and about anything else he wanted to hear. I am able to date this meeting with some accuracy because Ernest Hemingway, whom Red had never met, was a recent visitor to Berlin: he had in fact got out of the railway carriage (from Paris) into which I was climbing for my return to Moscow some weeks earlier. He had come and gone while I was in Moscow and Red's impression of him was very good, very friendly — a different matter altogether from the inexplicable bitterness that came three decades later. It is worth noting.

If I arrived in Berlin on November 27th, as Dorothy's letters seem to show, then I must have seen Red that day or the next, and perhaps hearing about Moscow may have determined him to go. He was often like that — particularly about journeys: he liked nothing so much as to undertake them at a moment's notice. Our one evening at Herkules Haus must have been on the 27th or 28th (the only evenings there were), and he left for Moscow on the 29th. I went on to Paris and heard nothing of the brass band and the public honors, the inconclusive interviews and unappreciated jokes, that marked Red's ten days in Moscow. I have given my own view of his weird refusal, then or afterwards, to have an opinion about anything he saw in Russia. For this record, or indeed for any account of the Thompson-Lewis marriage, it should be noted that he saw Mr Dreiser quite often and liked him better than ever. He wrote to Bill Woodward (W. E. Woodward, a successful biographer and an old friend) after the Moscow visit: "I saw Dreiser there, and didn't think he was particularly happy — impatient at the still universal inefficiency of a nation which has had to make something out of nothing. But I've never liked him so much — he was really charming."

Dorothy also liked Mr Dreiser very much and was always attentive to his health, as she had been in Berlin before. The way in which they all became embroiled a year later was one of the oddest bits of comic relief in their story. For my own part, I thought Mr Dreiser was a pompous old bore, immensely and preternaturally self-important; it was difficult for me to realize that he had actually written *Sister Carrie*. I was too inexperienced to know that eminent men, merely by the behavior of those who surround them, often become pompous old bores — it is an occupational disease and not directly their fault. Dreiser was the first of the species I had ever seen close up, except for those politicians (prime ministers and the like) whom newspaper correspondents do not really look upon as fellow creatures.

Dorothy's zest for everything she saw and heard in Moscow was not shared by Red, and by December 10th he was back in Berlin. She followed him soon. Her series of articles about Russia had been very successful in America and there already were suggestions that it be made into a book. The whole situation, both for Dorothy and for Red, was clearing up now: Mrs Lewis (Gracie) had made up her mind to go to Reno as soon as her son Wells had gone back to school after the Christmas holidays. Red would be free to remarry by, perhaps,

April. This put an end to the uncertainties which, even as late as October (just before Dorothy's departure for Moscow), had made it difficult to plan anything. Now Dorothy's main duty was to find a successor for her own job with the *Public Ledger* and, as soon as possible, to dispose of the flat on the Tiergarten. For this the Mowrers had made themselves officially responsible (they had signed the papers) and the house was much too big for them alone — it was in fact two flats, both commodious.

These difficulties were overcome during January and early February. As her successor in the *Ledger* bureau Dorothy was able to enlist H. R. Knickerbocker, who made a great reputation there during the next few years. Knick, as we called him, had come to Berlin as a student of music and philosophy, had turned into a very good Hearst reporter (I.N.S.) and now was to earn laurels as a serious analyst of the evolving giants, Germany and Russia, for the weightier part of the American press. Through Knick, in a way, Dorothy's Central European career was continued, and although he did not command as much attention as she did, he was also a part (along with John Gunther and Bill Shirer and others) of a generation in journalism which did most desperately try to awaken its employers and readers to the dangers at their feet.

Dorothy and Red decided to go to Naples for the few weeks of waiting while Gracie established her "residence" in Nevada and obtained her divorce there. There was some spurious romanticism in this, I have always thought. Dorothy did not really like Italy and never understood a word of the language; Red was still in the stage of believing that any real liking for Italy, the Italian language, Italian poetry or music, or indeed any poetry or music outside the *Oxford Book of English Verse*, was an affectation. I do not say this lightly. I *know*. I lived through many phases with both of them, and although in the end Red came to have a pathetic and indeed almost tragic regard for Italian poetry and music, which he studied faithfully as one might study Sanskrit if one were a devout Hindu, he never truly understood anything about either. Dorothy never even tried. She was content to judge Italian life and letters as a branch of the general European culture which she had remotely adumbrated from Syracuse, New York, and had brought into sharp focus, Hungarian style, with Josef Bard in Budapest and Vienna. If a play had not been produced in Vienna or Budapest it was of no interest; if a novel or poem had not appeared in German it was as if nonexistent. So far as I know of these years in Dorothy's life, the only Italian writer with whom she had any acquaintance was the ultra-fashionable Pirandello (who, poor man, never realized that he had become the spokesman of an age bewildered beyond all others).

The moon, however — ah, the moon!— is a certainty in the southern regions of Italy, and there is some sort of certificate from on high for those who spend their most blissful moments around the Bay of Naples. If you were in a dream of love, for instance, and you had anybody with whom you might share it, you would find the Bay of Naples the place for it. Red rocks, blue sea, moon on high at the moonlit hours, soft little winds (zephyrs by name) to caress the chin which is not yet quite double — these are the aids to illusion. Ever since it has been possible to travel at all, Europeans have known this. When George Sand led poor Alfred de Musset to Venice — or poor Frédéric Chopin to Majorca — she knew what play she was producing. The self-conscious literary mind, above all other kinds of mind, does this picking and choosing of the décor, this blending of the lights, so that every pulse that comes (if any come!) may be magnified by the magic of circumstance. Ordinary people fall into the ditch or the back seat of the car by sheer incidence and occurrence (that is, by the incidence of the occurrence). Occurrence is controllable for the wise old folk, over twenty-five, who have battled through incongruity. They know that you can arrange these things, not with perfect assurance of the result, but with some conducive force, some supreme suitability. Caruso sang "O Sole Mio" on the same evening when John McCormack sang "Mother Machree" at the Yankees' Stadium in New York, for the Policemen's Benefit in 1919. I have always considered this the height of suitability. I wish I had been there. Everybody must have been pleased. With a palm-leaf fan (you could get them then).

In Naples in 1928 the situation was ideal for loves unsure, for the hope for love. There were no rude reminders of ordinary life for those who had plenty (as Red had said to an interviewer just then, "I don't have a million, I have six hundred thousand"). Mussolini, Duce del Fascismo, had taken care of the currency — yes! The sea punctually washed the rocks, although not in accordance with a schedule of tides as known in more vigorous climes. Indeed it must be, and theologians should look to it, a supreme duty for the Mediterranean to operate as it does, since it is not imperatively commanded by the moon to come and go. The moon in the Mediterranean lives for love. The sea itself might (who knows?) have higher duties, if there are any.

Love alone is the duty of the moon.

Neither Dorothy nor Red was of the intellectual level to be bewitched by postcards, and yet this was very much what happened to them, in so far as they could build up the confidence to yield to the obvious. They speak of their surroundings (when they do) precisely as if they had hired their seats from a travel agency. For the first time the element of the false (of the *monté*, the preconceived entertainment) comes into their story. Up to now they have been anxious and worried indeed, trying to conceal from each other their desperate misgivings, hoping to love each other, hoping to love, hoping that love may still be possible. Now they are frankly pretending, making it up as they go along, yielding to the landscape and the brown eyes of the boatmen who are waiting for a very small tip. *Viva l'Italia!*

2

THE VILLA GALOTTI IN NAPLES, ON THE UPPER ROAD CALLED Posillipo, is one of the famous points of vantage on the incomparable bay. It is built on the side of the hill directly over the sea — that is, underneath the big motor road where the bus goes — in successive terraces which are really quite far apart, so that one climbs down or up exhaustively to get anywhere at all. There are thus sections and elements of the Villa which may be shut off or disregarded at will. During the war of 1939–1945 — called the "Second" World War, as if in series — the Villa was taken as residence and recreation quarters for the higher ranking officers of the United States Air Force. I was often there and often slept there too, since I was one of these privileged creatures at the time. Of all the pretty (though vulgar) houses up and down the Posillipo road, this is probably the prettiest, the most *cartolina postale*, the most utterly devoid of any true reason for being there. One could have imagined such wonderful things in that place! — No matter. It was the taste of the time when Posillipo became what it is, a stage setting for romanticism to claim as an aphrodisiac. George Sand, Byron, Stendhal and most of the early nineteenth century would have been happy there, at least for a while, and Dorothy and Red were, like their predecessors, enchanted. It is described in the last part of the novel *Dodsworth*, to be published a year later: a quiet, almost an idyllic time, with sun and sea and sky and moon combining with work and play.

But it had never been meant to last long. It was an interlude. We have a sonnet written by Dorothy to Red for Christmas, 1927, showing how clearly she had already discerned that the quiet life (the life he talked about, in a yet-undiscovered Vermont cottage) was unlikely to be theirs. It is a light and graceful sonnet — the sestet is skillful, anyhow — but there is a sadness in its final sting because Dorothy herself, only two or three months earlier, could not have written it. Two or three months earlier she, too, had been dreaming of the quiet cottage. She had even — in Moscow — taken advantage of some bargains that came her way in linens for the possible Vermont house. Now, with the inscription *For Hal, on Christmas, 1927,* we find this:

> *Oft have we wandered in the realms of gold,*
> *And many goodly sights and cities seen;*
> *To wander we shall never grow too old*
> *Unless pre-aged by overactive spleen,*
> *Provoked by mouthwash bottles, sure to smash*
> *Amidst the shirts and socks, and spill their gore,*
> *Or gaping kits, disgorging a sad hash*
> *Of files, and pastes, and — things which I deplore.*
>
> *I know you fondly dream to settle down*
> *With me, in some profoundly static spot,*
> *Beside a river, not too near a town;*
> *But will we stay there?   Answer: We will* not.
>
> *Old wanderlusts will all these plans unravel;*
> *Take me, and this, and be prepared to travel.*

The Berlin arrangements were completed in time for Dorothy to precede Red down to Naples, find the villa, engage servants, make all the arrangements and await him at the Villa Galotti. We find in this some remnant of the caution which so oddly and intermittently afflicted them during this period of unmarried association. It may have had something to do with Red's divorce, now under way in Reno. Gracie's arrival in Nevada had aroused the interest of the newspapers, of course, and since the engagement of Dorothy to Red was more or less an open secret for the press, it was bound to be mentioned: Red took the trouble to deny it with some vehemence, even quite late — even a short while before the wedding — because (or so I guess) he was afraid of impairing the speed or validity of his divorce.

There could be no other reason, so far as I know, for denying something everybody had known all winter and which, moreover, had never been concealed.

While Dorothy waited for him in Naples she wrote two letters which have been kept and are now in Syracuse — two out of some unspecified larger number; for we know they generally wrote to each other every day. Both are from Bertolini's Palace Hotel in Naples: one on Friday, March 9th, and the other quaintly dated March 12½. They are adult letters in their effort to understand, to analyze and perhaps to make irrefutable to both of them the strength of their emotion. The texts (again everything, even punctuation, is as she wrote it):

Friday   March 9.

It is twilight here in this little strange room, overlooking the sea. The water, and the mountains in the water, are the color of smoke, and a few little boats, far away, are hurrying home before dark. Down below in the garden the fronds of a palm tree wave softly, and it seems to me that the little evening breeze which moves them moves something in my heart.

I want to write to you a love letter. I know that a gesture or a glance tell more of love. I have seen your eyes shine when you looked at me, and you are an artist with words but cannot make them say so much. And I who can love greatly, write badly. All love-words are spoiled; we are too effusive, and use them for too many things. Simply to say "I miss you" would convey so much if one did not miss George Washington coffee and Lucky strike cigarettes, as I have heard my fellow countrymen loudly doing in this very hotel.

See, Hal, it is something like this, my feeling for you . . .

In that I feel humble toward you, who feel humble toward no other living human being. In that I must take what you give me, and be grateful for it. For I have no measuring rod for justice or generosity between you and me. So if by standard I apply to others you are unjust to me, my heart chides not you, but me, and is disappointed in myself for having failed to call more forth . . And yet I am imperious toward you, as toward no one else, and ask from you proudly what no person has the right to ask from anyone.

. . And I want to share with you everything I apperceive and cherish . . . so that I half resent this blue day because it came when you were not hear to see . . and I want to to run to you with the littlest amusing thoughts of my head and the littlest warm emotions of my heart . . . and all this I feel all the time, although I do not say so.

Yet loving you is not a simple thing, for thinking: He loves me! I am immeasurably raised in my self-esteem, yet thinking: I love him! I am enraged at myself for being so round-faced and ever so faintly — please agree faintly — sear [probably "sere"]. I am enraged, and sometimes shake a fist at myself in the glass . . that is why I would like to have a daughter for you; I feel, somehow, that I would make you a girl more worthy of being loved, for you see, in her case, I would know from the beginning that you were to love her, and in mine — I was already finished when you came along.

And this laughter . . this fact that I started to write this note in a half-melancholy mood, and now am full of amusement at myself — this is also part of loving you. .

It's quite dark now; I cannot see the palm tree or the sea, only the lights of Naples and the daggers of light which they thrust into the blackness at the shore's edge.

You are farther from me there in Berlin than you were when I was in Moscow. The south is so much farther from the north than the East is from the west . . . whatever Kipling may have thought about it.

I hope the boats got home.

D.

March 12½

You have already started to come to me in Naples — my friend, my dear, dear friend. What a strange week it has been: finding a villa, a cook, a housemaid, reading Russian books — here, in Naples, at Bertolini's, with all the blueness of the world at my feet — reading Russian books, and waiting, for my friend. In the end, Hal, it is as my friend that I think of you clearest, love you best. My comrade. Not that I belong to you or you to me but that we two together belong to something bigger than either of us, and thus, being together, serve it. Dear Hal, I wonder if you feel with me, the eternal *sense* of our having found each other. As though the gods had directed it, and were satisfied.

Dear Hal — I will marry you so gladly with the old marriage service; for better for worse in sickness in health, and forsaking all others — until death us do part. Hal — Hal!

Because in swearing this to you I swear it to something else. To a life-ideal. To the belief in loyalty, to the belief in comradeship, to the conviction that nothing comes of any relationship except through the sacrifice of the unimportant; to the belief that there is something in you greater than you — some passion for truth; some destiny to be the medium for that truth; some call to be the expression of the discontent and the aspiration of your country — Hal, my friend, my dear friend. To that I swear loyalty: not to a man who can stir me to excitement with his kisses, or comfort me to rest by his caresses; not to an active puissance — to another embodiment of what I myself deem worthy to be loved and fought for in life. Ah, my friend! I see you with your torn open eyes, your face scarred as though with flames, your long legged body leaning against the wind, the pain in you, the sweetness in you, the mad anger in you which constantly rises to defend you against becoming one of the settled and contented of the earth; the urge in you to pain, to castigation, because in you is the world, in you is your own civilization, which you will castigate until it is pure and worthy to be loved.

But I do not castigate you; salvation is by passion and by understanding. You, beloved, furnish the passion . . I shall try to understand.

Hal, you are on the train somewhere, rolling toward me — through Germany. Tomorrow you will awaken in Munich, tomorrow you will roll through the tall mountains, the pines, the wooden houses, the little crosses, the strange pagan, Christian, earthy, simple country which I love better than any in the world. Comfort it is to me to think that the Tirol is there, for refuge, when one needs refuge, for strength to begin again. Zarathustra betook him to the mountains. You are coming to me, in the body of a great, steel, fire-snorting monster, coming over mountains, to the blue sea, to me. Hal!

Hal — I do not want to touch you . . Hal, I do not want to speak . . I only want to see you . . to feel you are there . . to know you are in the world, somehow breathing into me power without divesting yourself of it, somehow receiving from me strength and thereby increasing mine. Hal! Hal!

3

THE WEEKS AT POSILLIPO WERE, IN FACT, NOT MANY — MORE for Dorothy, less for Red. He arrived on the heels of the above letter, which was certainly shown to him rather than sent, and almost at once the American press took notice. Their engagement was revealed by the New York *American* on March 15th, to be denied March 17th by Red in a telegram to the Associated Press. He remained at the Villa Galotti for a month and a week, awaiting the news from Reno. The first Mrs Lewis obtained her divorce decree on April 16th; on April 23rd Red, passing through Rome on his way to London, announced his engagement to Dorothy.

They had fixed upon England for their wedding and honeymoon because of that momentous walking trip the preceding August — the one which, I think, made up Dorothy's mind for her. This was, of course, not the sole reason. Red thought England the only "real" country in Europe; its kings, as readers of *Dodsworth* may remember, were the only "real" kings; it was the country where he could feel most at home and had most friends. To Dorothy it was ancestral: her adored father, her mother whom she had known so little, were English, and she still had relatives somewhere in the north. Both of them must have been well aware that Red's work counted for more in England than in any continental country where it was at the mercy of translation. For all these and other reasons, including the relative simplicity of legal forms, the wedding was to be in London in the midst of all those friends (Arnold Bennett, Hugh Walpole and so many more) whom Red had acquired since *Main Street* and *Babbitt*.

Dorothy stayed on in Italy, to which he duly forwarded his observations, discoveries and instructions, in nonsensical style as always. Once his own residence was proved (a short and simple matter) Dorothy was to make her first appearance at the registry office by May 10th. In the meantime he was writing invitations, making arrangements, buying the caravan in which they had elected to spend their honeymoon, and, when not otherwise engaged, finishing the first draft of *Dodsworth*. (The text of Red's letters — here and later — is also given exactly as written, including typing errors.)

SAVOY HOTEL
LONDON

Saturday Afternoon — April 28

I have just telegraphed to you, LAMB, that (poor darling innocent, so happy in your villa in Napoli, Lamb playing with Lion Feuchtwanger), you get coaxed to the slaughter on Monday, May fourteenth at Savoy Chapel. Maude Royden is in America and will remain there till fall. In any case it is doubtful if she could help. She proves not to be a non-conformist but Church of England with a position which, for all her fame, seems technically only that of lay preacher. If she *did* take part in the ceremony, it would still have to be at the Savoy Chapel, because that's the only place in the diocese of London where marriage of divorced persons is permitted (except "innocent party in case of adultery") — that and registry office. What we have to do is to be married at registrar's office, a very brief service with just two witnesses present, and then be married churchishly again, right after, at Savoy Chapel, which proves to be a charming old place, tiny and tranquil, tucked under the blatant walls of the Hotel Savoy.

I'll probably stay right at the Savoy — seems as good as any place and not much more expensive, and I don't see why you shouldn't, too. You must be here not later than Thursday, May 10, as on Friday we have to go to registrar's office. I've been there once and left your copy of divorce decree, together with mine, which arrived today. I've talked to the verger and one of the clergy at the Savoy Chapel, and Monday I'll see 'em again, and try to fix hour for marriage, then begin to invite any kings and queens who are in town. So everything goes apace, though yesterday everything looked held up, because Cape, Sidney Dark of the Church

Times, and others from who I hoped to get information, were all out of town. But today I got the right information from Cape's partner, Howard, and tout marche.

Socially, as we say, I've seen no one save your old friend Hank Wales, who is staying here, and Noel Coward. Thursday nite, when I arrived, I went to Bayard Veiller's "The Case [Trial] of Mary Duggan" — so damn' good that I was sorer than ever at the thought of his not having gone through with Gantry — and after it, sitting down here in the grill, I saw Noel Coward, whom I'd seen only once — on the stage, in The Vortex. Hm, says I, looks like a nice chap. I passed his table. He lep up, introduced himself, says Elmer is gtest bk of century, ast me to sit down — and with him was Major Seagrave, who drove a motors car in Florida at a rate which I remember as 3978 miles an hour, and whose hands and wrists are slenderer than mine, and who has a sentitive face and a bald head! Last night I went to see Coward in a play (not his own) "The Second Man," and went behind afterward. He's an awfully nice fellow; great friend of Harold Nicholson [Nicolson]. We'll see Coward's review when you come, and perhaps see him down in Kent.

The trip thru easy and uneventful. Dined with Karl Andrist and read part of his novel — not much good — and talked with Allan Updegraff and Dora Miller on phone. They had date for dinner; came over after it, but I didn't wait for them, being tired went to bed early. Enclosed is note from Dora Miller which was awaiting me at Guaranty when I arrived. Note her new telephone number. She said she'd be enchanted to take you to proper dressmakers' and I think I'd have her do it — she has expert knowledge.

Haven't done anything about car and caravan yet — I'll start on that Monday or Tuesday.

I enclose a couple of letters to you, which I thought I'd better open, case there was something to wire you, and clips from NY Herald, which you'll probably have seen, and first Holt announcement of book. Also have a second copy of divorce decree from Vombery, but that I'll hold here So. Thassa business. Now the important part of letter — on serious and solitary consideration, I consider you the darlingest person in the world. My little love!

h

Try — on whatever day you arrive — to catch a train earlier than the one I took from Paris. That left Gare de Nord at 12:05 and got here at 7:30, which made a darn short itme [time] in which to get to hotel, wash, dine, and be at theater at 8:15! I *think* there's a good 10:00 train. You old darling! Why don't you come Tuesday 8th or Wednesday 9th?

From Posillipo, Dorothy's reply:

Sunday — Posillipo.

I got your telegram this morning . . so it is to be the 14th, the 5th month, the 1st day of the week! Now I know what my lucky numbers are. Dear — dear — I am so glad. I want to be with you, always — it seems — and this is easiest, and most private . . Hal, I love you. I intended, when I sat down here, overlooking the sea, to write you a bright and witty note, and all I can find to say is Hal Hal I love you.

* * *

[A description of Pompeii then follows.]

It is absurd that I am here and you are there — it is exquisite that I feel so constantly this absurdity — it is joyous that I shall see you in *höchstens* ten days.

D

Lest my telegram should not have been clear: I stay here until Friday morning, than stay until Sunday noon in Rome, Via Ugo Bassi, I. Monteverdi. Sunday noon to Paris until Wednesday. All this unless you command me otherwise.

I began to turn the color of spinach, eggs, and orange juice, and all the weight came off my face! Also I had small moods. They miraculously disappeared with your telegrams and with a small, thin piece of veal. However, I am sticking, *generally speaking*, to the diet!

Wire me your Paris address.

SAVOY HOTEL,

LONDON,

W.C.2.

Monday

Dearest: This is about the last letter I can get through to you. And it's just to send you the enclosed letter — I fancy from your sister — & to tell you that I love you, forever, my dear!

Ferd Reyher[1] is here — just found him today. I think he'll be here

FOR

OUR

WEDDING!

I love love love you![2]

---

[1] A journalist friend.
[2] This letter is reproduced from the original in Red's exuberant handwriting among the illustrations following page 178.

AMERICAN EXPRESS CO.
SOCIETÀ ANONIMA ITALIANA
PIAZZA DEI MARTIRI

Naples. May 3rd 1928

You darling — I just have your letters — both — written Saturday & Sunday. My God what a post! It was a genuine relief — I felt you awfully far away — not hearing and there's been Sirocco with consequent effects on the temperament to say nothing of pep and spinach! I am *much* thinner but you don't notice it except when I take my clothes off.

To bring you nearer I read your novel — what there is of it here — Hal, it is *stunning* — one of the most moving love stories I've ever read. That scene with Nida! I bawled over it. You've done something which is fearfully difficult — created in Fran a perfect bitch and yet made her charming. It is perfectly easy to understand why Sam Dodsworth loves her. Everything is finished up here and I'm leaving tomorrow morning — I even have my wedding dress which is *lovely.*

I'm so glad I'm coming straight away through Paris, to you.

I kiss your eyebrows and temples & heart.

D

P.S. Lesbia will <u>not</u> be a writer. I won't <u>have</u> it!! She's going to be a lady farmer fruit-goer [grower]. Somebody <u>has</u> to be.

me before your letters came.   me afterward.

4

THE FRABJOUS DAY ARRIVED: MAY 14TH, 1928. DOROTHY HAD come to London promptly for the civil formalities, which were completed that morning by the ceremony at the registry office — St Martin's in Henrietta Street, surrounded by book publishers. Jonathan Cape and his wife were the witnesses; Jonathan was then Red's London publisher. A church ceremony (with all the vows, as both Red and Dorothy had wished) took place immediately afterwards in the Savoy Chapel in the presence of a score or more guests, friends new and old, who repaired to the Savoy Hotel for a wedding luncheon afterwards.

There is something rather touching in Red's desire to have a thoroughly conventional wedding with all the "old" vows. It made the whole thing more "real," just as being married in England made it more "real." His first marriage, at the Ethical Culture Society's Lecture Room in New York, had been nothing like this. It is not too much to suppose that by doing it in the prescribed manner he hoped (consciously or unconsciously) to make it solider, more impregnable, more certain to endure. Neither then nor at any other time did he show signs of religious feeling — indeed, his ferocious *Elmer Gantry* had been published only the year before. It was the proprieties, rather than the religious ritual, that seemed valuable to him in solemnizing the event.

And he had taken pains to dress and look the part of the eminent novelist-bridegroom. He had worn London clothes for some time now, and although there was something about him that took off the edge of their elegance, the wedding pictures (which were numerous) show him as very presentable indeed alongside his smiling bride. The press of the time abounded in these pictures, but there were also others, privately commissioned by the happy pair. Decades later (in about 1951) I found a whole drawer almost full of them in my house (Red's house) at Twin Farms, and underneath them — so careless was he! — that remarkable sheaf of letters from all the principal writers of the day saluting him on the publication of *Main Street*. Those letters (now at Yale) had lain, neglected and forgotten, ever since Red had thrown them there at some time in 1928 or 1929 when the house had just been acquired.

Neither Dorothy nor Red ever spoke to me, so far as I can remember, about their own feelings on that day, their hopes or fears: my guess would be that they were too keyed up by the excitement of the occasion to feel or think. With all the good will in the world, she must have had some misgivings, for the dangers were obvious. Red, by my guess (which is based on later knowledge, of course) was probably so elated, so proud of Dorothy, so anxious to show off the prize he had won, that he had no moment of relaxation, much less of anxiety. His highly developed sense of social temperatures (the "party" sense) would have kept him walking on air all through the day. We know that he could not resist the chance to deliver one of his monologues when it came time for the toasts after lunch at the Savoy. This time he addressed the assembly as if they were jute merchants and he were reviewing the situation in the jute trade throughout the British Empire. This one was (or so I have heard) quite funny, but many in London were wearying of Red's incessant performances: only two weeks before Arnold Bennett, after a dinner party, had written in his journal, "Sinclair did too many imitations."

The guests at the Savoy Chapel and at the luncheon afterwards included Mrs Bertrand Russell (Dora), Hugh Walpole, Mr and Mrs Pethick Lawrence, Lord Thomson, Anita Loos, Mercedes de Acosta, Gilbert Frankau and a good many others. There are guest lists among the papers at Syracuse in both Dorothy's handwriting and Red's; there are some quite surprising names on them, but we have no indication of whether the owners of these names were invited or only considered. In the main it was Red's list, since his acquaintance in London was far wider than Dorothy's at that time. He had, after all, been a lion for more than one season.

And some of the excitement of the wedding, I believe, must have come from this "lion" atmosphere, which to Dorothy, of course, was new. In a sense Red carried this atmosphere with him even on the Continent, but it is not at all the same thing: no English or American writer, even the most famous, can be quite so leonine in Germany or France as in England or America. With this marriage Dorothy was entering upon the phase known as celebrity, in its fullest sense, with the American press (and on this occasion also the English press) out in force to observe. Its advantages might be dubious — and of course in time must pall upon anybody of intelligence — but at that moment it was fresh and new, and every flashbulb must have been in some respect like a notification of things to come. To Dorothy it was quite new, indeed a transference of role, as if she had suddenly stepped up from the audience into the footlights; and if Red ever did grow weary of his public personage (which he possibly did towards the end) there was no hint of it in the zest with which he played himself in those days.

It was a golden spring, really, for America and for the West in general: prosperity was abundant to excess, the thunderous crash and the succeeding depression were well over a year off and in a month's time the Republican party would nominate Herbert Hoover for the presidency. Mr and Mrs Sinclair Lewis had every right to expect a rosy future.

5

The Honeymoon Diary

RED HAD BOUGHT THE CARAVAN — AUTOMOBILE WITH TRAILER
attached — in which they were to embark on their summer's
honeymoon in England. He had also signed a contract to write
about it for the *Herald Tribune* in New York, frugally considering that a honeymoon might as well pay for itself when bride
and groom are writers. In a short time — one week precisely —
they were ready to leave London and all its cosmopolitan delights for the open road. As we shall see, there were to be some
moments of less than bliss before it was all over, but they
started out, anyhow, with high hearts and a certain amount of
healthy contempt for those who did not understand their desire to spend a summer thus. Dorothy's diary for the summer
bears an inscription "to us," and thereupon broaches the subject in just this mood of happy pride:[1]

> Gatton Towers, Merstham,
> Surrey, May 29.

And why, people asked us, a caravan?
If you have never regretted the rutted, shadowy lanes
down which you have not passed; if you have never had an

---

[1] The Honeymoon diary is too long to reproduce here in full; much of it is simply a
digressive travel journal, concerned with observations on the English towns and
countryside and on the people they encountered — from laborers to lords. I have
retained only those entries which give the tenor of Dorothy's moods and thoughts and
seem significant for our story. Passages not included are clearly denoted.

impulse to stop, here, in the scented tent of a red hawthorne
bush, and sleep in its drowsiness; if you have never wanted
to waken on a high moor, with sunshine buttering the gorse,
the wind blowing, and clouds flying by; if it is too long ago
that you stood, half-hidden by a tree, peeking through the
rails of a fence, at gipsies camped in a field, and wondering
what would happen if you should climb through, approach
these swarthy and romantic people, and beg: "Take me with
you"; and if you never knew, or have forgotten the rest and
peace of movements springing from first necessities: the dip-
ping up of water from a brook, the frying of bacon in a pan,
the polishing of a cup with a white cloth; the drying of linen
on the grass, and the gathering of it in, it smelling sweet as
hay; if, in short, you are old and envious; if you do not like
sitting on a stoop with the work all done: if small roads do
not seem exciting and secretive; if you are convinced that
only people whom you meet in large companies in studio
flats or small and well-dressed companies in discreet houses
are interesting, then it is no use for me to answer that question. Caravans are for people who have not kept house so
long that they've forgotten how to play house. Caravans
are for those who know what beauty and change can be
packed into fifty miles of English country-side. Caravans
are for people like us.

And what can you carry in a caravan? Bacon and butter,
beer and wine, oranges and bread, cakes and beans, olives
and jam, honey and eggs, jugs and plates, cups and forks,
books and paper and pencils and ink; frocks to camp in and
frocks for dancing, shoes and boots, mackintoshes and evening wraps, ginger cookies and a tin bath; jugs for water,
jugs for milk, and a fat big jug for beer; ice and soap; blankets
and sheets, cushions and comforters, oil and alcohol, a stove
and a dish-mop, basins and pans; a fire to warm by; a lamp
to read by; beds and tables, typewriters and cigarettes. In

short everything which a civilized human being wants, if his wife knows how to cook, to make a bed, and to wash dishes without afterwards smelling of them.

And is that possible?

But of course! Out of that little top-drawer, in that little oaken chest of drawers, she takes a white pot of cream; of cold-cream, with a French mark. She rubs it thick on her hands and pulls on rubber gloves over them. That is all. And back goes the pot and shut goes the drawer. Everything is possible if you only keep ship-shape.

On the right, above the little leaded window with their orange curtains, is the larder. Little locker doors are propped up or fastened down. On the left the butler's pantry, most cunningly devised: this tiny cabinent for piles of shining plates, and that for a nest of glasses in their nickle holders, and that for jugs, and pots, and pudding basins. Up goes the top of that chest of drawers and reveals a sheet of polished tin into which a porcelain bowl has been fitted. There just above it is a little door. Push it open and you find a zinc-lined compartment, through which passes the warm pipe of the stove, drying dish-mops and towels, wet bathing suits, and toothbrushes stuck upright in glasses. In the fireplace is a little oil-stove, big enough for steaks and stews, puddings and roasts, and if you want them, souffles and crepes-suzettes. Under that upholstered seat another zinc-lined box with an outlet to the ground — for ice; for milk & butter & wine! And still there are lockers for clothes, for books, for type-writers; shelves against the wall which pull down into tables; divans which turn into comfortable beds! A house it is for a sailor, used to a sailor's tidiness; a house with more cunning cupboards than even Alice found down the rabbit-hole; a little house, with a doorway to sit in — above a stoop of maroon-painted steps to the ground; a doorway open to the garden of England; to-day to the smooth elegance of a Berkshire park; tomorrow, to a hay-scented Hampshire farmyard;

next morning, perhaps, upon the downs, where the wind flaws the grass like a green sea.

Caravans are for the unhurried, for those who wish to use a motor for hour-by-hour enjoyment, and not for merely getting somewhere. Cheap motors in America, motors for the middle classes, resulted in the motor camp, the communal wash-up; the super service-station, with parking privileges, and hot dog stands, in dusty banners announcing a trail across a continent. Massachusetts to California! Alabama to Washington! Cheap motors in England resulted in the caravan; the "my home is my castle" — on wheels; in private camping on a public common!

The motor caravan is probably not for America. It is not for our ideals of speed. Our little Chrysler can pull the 3000 pounds of our motor caravan at forty miles an hour on a good road, but with what rattling of dishes, banging of locker doors, and with what perilous swaying. Twenty miles an hour is steady and comfortable.

Long Barth-Weal-Sevenoaks-Kent

. . . We have had several kinds of days. There were the first four — Monday to Saturday — when we camped under great oaks and elms in Frilforth [Frilford], a village in Berkshire, just outside of Oxford. At the Dog House where we dined every night, the pubkeeper & his wife were city folk — a former oil salesman —"Rtired" to pubkeeping, and having a hard time to make a go of it. To be sure there's a fine golf course near tho dearth of customers, but the pub lacks sufficient bedrooms for weekend guests and the pubkeepers are tied hand & feet by the brewing association which owns the home. They told us that there are almost no "free" houses in England. This may, to an extent, account for the generally low level of English innkeeping, for there is a lack of incentive where the manager can never hope

The English
system of
licencing

to own the house. Nevertheless our friends the Chandlers were exceptions. Food was excellent, the house cosy & well-kept. But they are new at it and already Mrs. Chandler is beginning to weary of the ceaseless round. She had only two indoor servants and often was up half the night to protect chickens from foxes!

The Oxford Undergrads

Two Oxford undergrads staying at the hotel sent cards up to Hal, so we received them in the sitting room at the fire. We talked of sports and Hal dared to say that he hated all competitive sports to which one undergrad replied that he had no doubt golf developed the brain. One really did have to concentrate! Besides a fellow always had a pride in doing whatever he did *well*.

Hal: Yes, but after all life's a matter of choice; one can't do *everything* well. *Undergrad:* Well, anyhow, our ideal is certainly the all-round man. Look at Masters! His crew and Lacrosse, a crack golf player, and took a first in history. *Hal:* What do you think of Sir Ernest Sherrington?[1] *Undergrad:* Who's he? *Hal:* Well, he's one of the men at Oxford who really is influencing the future of the world . . . and probably he's no good at all at games. Now, when I was at Yale —

And then he proceeded to tell about a great chemist who was at Yale when he was there, and about whom he never heard until years later when he was writing — "Arrowsmith." But all this made no impression on the Oxford student whose outlook on life was precisely that of the American university student, who, as Hal said, even thought it a good thing to "shoot a prayer" in the Y.M.C.A. because thereby he "developed another side of his nature."

I thought of Berthold, at 27 director of a research labora-

[1] Probably Sir Charles Sherrington, English physiologist and 1932 Nobel prize winner.

tory in Edinburgh, already author of several first-rate books on biological subjects: healthy, strong, fond of long tramps & canoe trips, but who never, I wager, played a game in his life! Why *can't* there be an educational system which develops both character & brains! We were all talking together about this, later, in the Nicholsons'[1] drawing room. Vita's two boys are in a public school, of course. It's a very questionable course to send children to "experimental" schools where they likely as not grow into little snobs completely at odds with the rest of society — substituting merely one kind (and a less useful variety) of snobbery for another. After all, the public school idea of sportsmanship honor etc. is to a great extent responsible for all the amenities of English life and for its peculiar efficiency: that efficiency which depends upon the universal acceptance of a "code" and the universal enforcement of it by public opinion. (I think of the simplicity of getting a trunk, by telephone, out of the Savoy store-rooms & into our rooms in *the Mitre* in Oxford, without red-tape, receipts, tickets, or anything except the belief of everyone concerned that everybody else concerned was telling the truth, according to the code. Since most of the ease, convenience, and civilization of England depends on this, everybody is interested in its enforcement; a breach of the code is punished by universal application of "coventry.")

All attempts to build up a civilization come up, sooner or later against the necessity of a universal public *sense* of legality. I was much impressed — reading Guil. Ferrero's *Four Years of Fascism* (in the pub at Frilforth) with the emphasis which he puts upon the idea of *legitimacy* in government. Where the legal code in all its ramifications, is based on no generally accepted principal of justice and behavior (a social sense which is practically unconscious) government has neither stability nor legitimacy. The immense preva-

[1] Sir Harold Nicolson and his wife, Victoria (Vita) Sackville-West.

lence of a certain code amongst all classes in England and its especial intrenchment in the great middle class is England's greatest safeguard against bolshevism, and it is precisely the power of this code which foreigners from countries which haven't got anything similar, fail to understand.* France has to an extent — such a *mind* for legality; England has become a world empire on it; Germany lacks it completely; America lacks it.

The fact that there is in America no general sense of justice & behavior explains sporadic movements of various groups to take justice into their own hands — Ku Klux Klan etc; their legitimacy is as well-founded as any other.

* And although a great deal can be said against British education the public school is responsible for this. [Dorothy's footnote]

The next entry, undated, is headed "In a field under the Charing Hill." After describing a meeting with "two British Babbitts," Dorothy discourses on the English attitude toward America. She then writes in detail of the furnishings and gardens of the Nicolson house, Long Barn, which she particularly admired. A second entry from Charing Hill begins:

Under Charing Hill (Still)
June 8.

It's pouring today; we should have changed our pitch but we are caught here now for at least another twenty-four hours. I'm staying luxuriously in bed. With both tables down it's a fine place to work. The caravan is absolutely watertight and cosy although gales are blowing. I lie in bed writing & H is typing at the other end of the caravan.

* * *

H. said yesterday: You . . you are . . . a . . a pudding . . a bread pudding . . made of the divine host.

He was well pleased with this & after driving a bit farther said, "That's a compliment no one ever made anyone before."

* * *

Here Dorothy goes on to describe at length their excursions around the Kent countryside, visits to Canterbury and to various coast towns. At Margate, she included the following:

> There was a gipsy palmist, so I went — I cannot resist palmists. She had blue eyes, fuzzy brown hair & a pink skin. Her mouth was heavy, her nose big (rather Jewish) with thick nostrils. "I'm real English Romany . . . not like these foreigners." She said the "Romany's evidently scorn the name gipsy." She said the Gray family had their own vans, but that usually they travelled in groups or clans. I told her about our caravan. She said, "Now a real lady like you could go travelling about in a caravan, but these middle classes — they'd scorn to." I was much amused. She told me my line of marriage was broken & that there was another man of "medium color" who was "flatterin" me but " 'e was tied." My line of success wasn't much developed but I'd 'ave 'ealth, wealth & happiness un that was about all one'd want." I mahgt 'ave a cheeayld but a wouldn' guarantee as yuh'd rear hit." She had an aunt who was chief palmist in Saratoga Springs.

* * *

And of an overnight stay in the town of Sandwich:

> We loved Sandwich, with its little streets & 16th century houses. The Guild Hall in the central square is a sweet & most gracious house — We stayed overnight in the "Guild-Ford", a vast modern gray hotel sticking up bumptiously out of the flatness and greenness of Sandwich bay. The concierge inquired blandly — later in the evening — how

we'd happened to come there. (I don't think he was too glad to see us. We looked disreputable in tweeds & in a dark flannel skirt — in the dining room where only a few well-dressed gentlemen were sitting & one couple, in full evening dress whom we both swore weren't "legal") When we said "You are starred in Baedeker," he looked pained. "But I didn't know we were in Baedeker . . . we never advertise." he said. "Just a few west-end gentlemen — "

*   *   *

Apropos of nothing H. interrupted here to say: "Why ever did they call it belly-button. It should be belly button-hole." And:

> *There once was a young gent of Deval*
> *Who confused something else in the navel.*

A few moments afterward he amended:

> *There was a young lady of Reval*
> *Who said, "Dear I don't like to cavil*
> *But honestly dear,*
> *It goes better in here*
> *You've confused something else with my navel.*

The British who laugh so at our pathetic efforts to create a past & a tradition for ourselves are faking their own antiques. Next — or almost so — to the Guildford is a great & handsome 16th century half-timbered house "Built quite new," the concierge told us. "The Prince of Wales took it for six months last year."

(Probably for golf. Sandwich has a champion course) Along the sands are a row of houses exactly like those of Winnetka, Ill. "One belongs *to an American* — Lord Astor," he said. None of the houses have gardens. The sands here — the beach line — is very beautiful. We had a room on the sea.

*   *   *

This long entry concludes with the following account of an evening spent with Arnold Bennett (probably before Dorothy's marriage):

Arnold Bennett. This isn't apropos anything — but I was recalling the evening at Bennett's. When he came in I thought he was intoxicated. I didn't know then about the defect in his speech. He wore full evening dress with a soft pique shirt & H. taunted him, being himself in dinner jacket. Dinner was formal, with six or seven courses & a written menu. The house was undistinguished but comfortable. "My wife" was abroad; the only other guest was Harried Cohen, a nervous & attenuated creature who gave the impression of being excessively affected, probably by being quite appallingly natural. She is very thin, very dark, very large-eyed, & wore black velvet (with a side train) & prominent earrings. She rumpled Arnold's hair & was coy. "I've been making up titles for books," she said. "I wonder if I dare tell you Galsworthy's . . . Dare I tell them, Arnold?" Arnold though so. She giggled a little. "Puberty," she whispered. She didn't blush. "But I can't tell them Michael Arlen's. I could write it." With great effort a pencil was produced, & a match box. She wrote on it the word "Fornications." The match-box was handed around. Upstairs in the drawing room she complained that the piano had been placed with the keyboard facing the room. "It's Dorothy's room" said Arnold. She played a little, indifferently complaining that she felt ill — she'd had an injection that day. (I believe she's taking the gold cure for t.b.) Arnold said, "Play something bra — vura. Bra — vura. I like it bra — vura." But she wouldn't. Once during the eve. she said she had seen "Die Meistersinger" adding "by Wagner."

Arnold & H. talked quietly of books. I can't remember anything except that A. said something derogatory about

Hugh Walpole. At dinner H. said, "Some British people make me feel shy . . then I'm awkward . . . but you don't, Arnold." A. replied with a twinkle (I think the remark was lost on Hal, though I grinned) "I don't think I'd mind your shyness, Sinclair." Afterward H. was cutting up & I said, "Do you think he'll ever be mature." A. answered, "I hope not."

Seeing his Mss. (Old Wives Tale & Riceyman's Steps & a no. of journals) was a real experience. Beautiful things. Love of order. One of the journals described in detail the life of Maude Gonne, which interested me excessively because I always thought her a fine theme for a novel.

In any continental country he would enjoy a much greater social eminence. In England he spends his time with such people as Beaverbrook & Castleross.

| Cad |
| Bounder |

What's the difference between a cad & a bounder! I asked F.R.

"A cad — he said — "Well, Rothermere's a cad & not a bounder & Beaverbrook's a bounder but not a cad."

H.N. also agreed: A cad can be a gentleman, but a bounder can't. It was typically British that he preferred the cad!

* * *

The succeeding entry, dated "Sunday. Rye," begins with a digression on the music of Richard Strauss, goes on to a description of Kent, Sussex, and the arty "Ye Old Tearooms" of Rye. It concludes with this line:

It was a nice day. Hal didn't lose his temper with me once.

The next entry begins:

Tuesday the 13th (?)

Nothing in the world smells so sweet as a beanfield, with the breeze blowing it your way. What the English call "broad" beans. They grow a foot or eighteen inches tall, & have black & white flowers growing amongst the leaves which are gray-green, like those of olives. They have a scent — almost jasmine-sweet.

The lovely white house is "Okenbridges" & is for sale! It is a sheep farm & was used as a weaving-mill by the Romney Marsh weavers who make famous homespuns. The front is brick (part of it is stucco) plastered) and is whitewashed, and the front of the roof is thatched. The back of the roof however is tile, and so is the house — with brick. Also the white divisions bet. the panes are not there. And the rt facade of the house is clapboards, painted black. My sketch (from memory) was all wrong. It is more like this.

And *this* isn't right! If I only could develop an accurate visual memory!

I went to London for 24 hours & saw Margaret Goldsmith, Helen Augur, and dear Kokoschka.

June 14.

Yesterday a morning in an old curiosity shop where I saw a late Georgian tip-up table in a beautiful shade of oak & a most exquisite Queen Anne table, both of which I envied & desired. The antiquarian was a most gentle & charming little man who loved his wares. Prices are much higher in

England than on the continent & English wares bring higher prices than continental even in England (although many of the workmen may have been foreign) thus an English Queen Anne table, very simple in design, and a French from the same period, but with extremely beautiful marguetry of satinwood, tulip, etc. & with fine bronzes fetch the same price, although the latter is more exquisite & costly in workmanship & material . . . . but I also would rather have the English table. It is first, more comfortable, being of a better height; more homeley; ingratiating & unostentatious; between the two tables is the difference between a lady & a lovely courtesan. Oak, I found, gets that lovely silvery color by exposure to the sun.

There follows here a lengthy guided tour description of Bodiam and Battle Abbey, concluding with a lexicon of Sussex dialect. The next entry, eight days later, begins with an itinerary of their interim travels and visits:

June 22

Rye — Southwick — Brighton — Petworth — The Netherlands Farm & Mr. Wᵐ Perry — Haslemere — London — Petworth — Fittelworth & The Swan — Midhurst & Cowdray Park — Chichester — Little Hampton — Arundre — Amberley — Storrington — The Netherlands. Hampshire border — Inns — South Harting — Bertrand Russell — Winchester

In Southwick we camped in the middle of the village, on a farm belonging to a taciturn little man with shrewd eyes and a beard growing halfway around his face under his chin, like the picture of Grimes, in the Water Babies. Southwick, as far architecture goes, is an ugly little village, but the sea runs all along the end of it, and the whole village smells of fish. There's a little channel of seawater between the village and the mounds of shingle which are the real seacoast, and here fishing smacks and small yachts at rest pierce the sky with a little grove of masks. The village is built around a green, in which all day long all the children in the village and especially the little girls try to stand on their heads (and often succeed) and when I talked about it to S.P.B. Mais[1] whom we visited here, he said yes indeed, and that there was no village in England where so many children could stand on their heads as Southwick, and I could see he was full of pride. Also, he played cricket all afternoon on his green, both for pleasure and out of duty, because, he said, only by playing cricket could a foreigner (Londoner) like himself ever be really absorbed into his village; and it was clear from the way he spoke that to be counted an authentic citizen of Southwick was his greatest ambition.

He lives in a small house of the Georgian style, directly on the green, with a handkerchief of lawn in front of it behind a small iron fence. One walks off the street into a small stone-flagged room with a gatelegged table in it and some oaken chests, which are old. It is used as an eating room (the food abominable: oven-baked roasts, boiled potatoes and cabbage, and heavy sweets) and he sits there all day receiving callers. One was a youth interested in the publication of "The Adelphi") a new Brighton magazine to which young Brighton literati contribute free and impeded verse, and small essays on the universe. Hal spent an hour writing down addresses for the youth — where to send the magazine for favorable comment. H. is too absurd! He combines contemptuousness with naive good-heartedness to an incredible degree. An anaemic magazine with a most anaemic young editor: better left to perish, my own Nietzchean brutality advised. S.P.B. Mais is the John Bull type of Britisher very

[1] English writer and journalist.

like the schoolmaster in "Young Woodley" with whom he, with rare percipience, compared himself. He has actually been a public-school teacher. He must have somewhere in him tender-minded spots, because he is susceptible, as a critic, to such refined mentalities as Vita's, and I am grateful to him for giving me "The Heir" to read. And he was, he said, one of the first persons to discover Samuel Butler and Melville. He is always rude to his wife, addressing her as "idiot": "No, idiot, it's not" or "Yes, idiot, it is"; meant in fun, he would say, but not quite funny.

Brighton

Mr Harry Preston, whom we met at supper, after the theatre, in Brighton, is a most extraordinary creature. A very little man, with not much flesh, but it amorphous; eyes slightly crossed and a deformed ear. He is effusive — intolerably — and insisted on addressing us all through dinner as "Your lordship" and "Your ladyship." He greeted us by coming very close, holding our right hands (not both of us together) over his heart, and saying, in a voice, husky with emotion, "This honour . . . I had not conceived of this honour." At supper there were Preston, his wife, S.P.B. Mais, and a young man, a war invalid, who is evidently in Preston's employ, or dependent in some way upon his patronage. The ridiculous little man, Napoleon of hotel keepers, dominated all of his guests except us, and his manner toward the war invalid, while outwardly very paternal — dear boy, this & dear boy that — was, I thought, beastly. The youth — who constantly prefaced his remarks with such painful phrases as "of course I don't amount to anything . . . I'm only a poor shell-shock with one eye . . ." started to talk about his experiences, before the war, with an American motor firm which had sent him to England to study English selling methods. This greatly interested Hal, who is on the search for just such material; Harry Preston, I could see, was outraged. For all his obsequiousness he wished to dominate the company. His expression grew more & more bad-tempered. Finally, he interrupted rudely. "Let us not discuss business now, my dear boy. There is a time for everything." The one-eyed man collapsed at that, although Hal protested warmly. He said nothing more during the meal. H. Preston's eyes kept roving around the room, and often, without any change of expression in his eyes, he would lean forward and say. "My dear Mr. *Sinclair;* your lordship . . . . this honour . . . ." apropos of nothing. His wife was a vulgar, complacent-looking woman, who seemed somewhat confused by her husband without minding.

Mr. Milbank

And we looked up Mr. Milbank, taking him to luncheon at the Metropole, a very flashy place with excellent food. Mr. Milbank, a Church of England clergyman, who had spent many years in America, "in forty states" had written Hal enthusiastically about his books, and Hal, who cannot resist preachers had determined to look up this rector who had left America "upon the acquisition of a small fortune" and "because of prohibition." He lived in a small apartment, its furnishings comfortable but indicating no particular refinement of taste, and although the family portraits on the walls, and the old prints of ships which his grandfather had commanded, indicated that he was technically a gentleman, his thirty years in America had removed any *patine*. He drank a great deal of whiskey and encouraged Hal to do so. He had no honesty of opinion. As we came in, Hal remarked about the prayer book crisis, and said he was sympathetic to the Anglo-Catholics. Milbank, believing Hal to be a total agnostic, thought him to be joking; only later, when he saw that he was serious, did Milbank acknowledge that he himself was Anglo-Catholic. He talked a great deal about actors: his cousin is Charles Cherry, and he had been much in the society of actors and told us a great many anecdotes about Maxine Elliot [Elliott], whose younger sister (if I remember rightly) is Countess of Something-or-other (or was it her niece) Anyhow Maxine, not pure herself had seen to it that her younger female relatives were.[1] One could see that Milbank himself was an actor, of sorts. A poisonous combination of worldly clericality; genteel Bohemianism. He was not in the least shocked by Hal's atheism, his attitude being "Das kann man auch sagen." But I was interested in what he said about the prayer book. All the churches for miles around reserved the host, he said, and believed they would go on doing it — chiefly because it was more practical. He described the administration of the last sacrament as the Catholics would do it, with the reserved host, in an open hospital ward — a mere wafer on the tongue and no one disturbed — and as the Church of England prescribes; a ceremony involving the setting up of a communion table, candles, and a service which lasted at least twenty minues — distressing and "medically undesireable" for the whole ward. He said that the adoration of the host was a general practice. The failure of the bill was encouraging to Roman Catholics. Undoubtedly the most honest Anglo-Catholics would leave the church and go where they belong.

> The Netherlands
> Farm. & Petworth

And now, from the shore, we started into the heart of West Sussex; trailing the caravan, and trundling along at

---

[1] A great deal of misinformation in small compass. Maxine's sister was not Countess of Something, etc., but, having married the notable actor Johnston Forbes-Robertson, became Lady Forbes-Robertson when he was knighted. I later married one of their daughters. Whatever Maxine's advice to her juniors was, it came from a view of the world which was both wide and just.

fifteen miles per hour. We skirted the coast as far as New Shoreham and then penetrated inwards, so that late in the afternoon we were in Petworth, a quaint and sleepy town with one narrow circular street, ill-designed for a caravan, the whole village dominated, overpowered, indeed, by Petworth House, the estate of Lord Leconfield. The next day we returned; the house was closed, so we could not see the galleries with their fine collection, but we did walk through the park, with its magnificient oaks and beeches, its lake, wide pastures, and prolific deer, and saw the House itself, 18th century, looking like a minor Versailles or Schonbrunn, more continental than English, very dignified and handsome, but cold — without either mystery or graciousness.

It was sunset, and we had been searching for an hour for a place to park, when a wide gateway, directly upon the road, and opening into a sweep of pasture-land invited us to enter. The pasture was open and even. At the right, below a slight decline, and fronted by a neat barnyard was a group of barns, and directly in front of us, in a little hollow, so low that its roofs were below the level of our eyes, was the farmhouse, an irregular pile, of red brick, & tiles, with great chimneys, a lichened roof of gray tiles, the whole half-hidden by a mammoth oak tree.

It's front, which was turned away from us, toward the south, was plain and stuccoed, and faced a tidy but uninteresting strip of lawn & garden. But the back was irregular, mysterious and charming. The great roof, green with lichen, seemed from the slight eminence where we stood to reach to the ground; it was intercepted by a lower, one-story wing, containing the kitchen, and broken by dormers. A most lovely and ancient house. And standing under the oak tree was the farmer, William Perry, an open-faced and kindly man, whom I immediately liked. He welcomed us to his pasture, and there we camped for nearly a week.

The prospect Southward from our caravan door was idyllic: a pastoral scene relieved of sentimentality and mere prettiness by its expanse — for the vast valley stretched away to a range of low hills beyond — an occasional farm, the parti-colored fields, and the beautifully spaced groups of trees supplying satisfying detail. The comfort and seclusion of our position, sheltered by a tall tree, and cut off, by the hedge from the road, together with this lovely prospect kept us here longer than we intended.

This entry concludes with several pages of a vignette on the farmer, William Perry. The next entry, undated, follows:

Midhurst

Comment —
Such men are called "backbone" of England but they are not its brains. The trouble with England is she despises brains.

July 26.
Manesty Park

Last night was our last in the caravan! Memorable for a cloud-burst; here, in the mountains the rain falls with a beat like the hammering of drums, and all night it poured upon our roof, soaking through every crevice, running in three little streams down the glass of the mantelpiece, and making our pasture-lawn into a puddle when we awakened we were like lake-dwellers.

To celebrate the last dinner, we opened half a dozen tins; a Cross & Blackwell Hare Soup, clams, which I creamed; a bottle of Chambertin, and for sweet, an omelette with maple sirup. Both Hal and I were in mellow and exalted moods, and talked much about the books he was going to write and about the high estimate we each have of the other. But at ten we were so sleepy, that Hal suggested a nap before we tackled the dishes. He promptly fell into unconsciousness, and I, though sleeping fitfully could not rouse myself until one-thirty when I became aware that the caravan, which was practically sealed against the rain, was stinking horribly of leftover dinner. I tried to rouse Hal to help with the washing up, but it was no good. He merely grunted. I washed the grease into the dishwater . . . horrid is the smell of soup & soap in combination . . . and was tidy by three. When I lay down, in Hal's pyjamas — he was sleeping on my bed & I couldn't get at my own night clothes — and wound myself up in a down quilt, the corners of which were dripping. I opened the window & rain blew on my face but I let it blow. The reward of virtue was that Hal brought coffee which he had made himself to my bedside, at seven!

It took us some three hours, two horses, & the efforts of the entire neighborhood, to get the caravan out of the lake & onto the road this morning: yet, such is perversity — when it was finally under way toward Oxford, we both looked after it wistfully.

We are comfortable here at Manesty farm. We have a big sitting room to ourselves, overlooking the mountains, a shabby kindly room, full of the atmosphere of warm-hearted, good-tempered people.

Hugh[1] came over directly after lunch & took us for a ride & long walk thru the mountains. They are melancholy & romantic, full of rapid, tumbling streams, and with almost no habitation, even today. In these mountains I miss above everything the wayside crosses of the Austrian mountains,

[1] Sir Hugh Walpole, whose country home was Brackenburn, Manesty Park, in the lake district of Cumberland.

which, in the most remote spots remind one constantly of mankind. Those mountains are more overwhelming; but human life is more aware; they transcend man, but man is there. Hugh says that these passes were completely cut off from the world until the end of 1771, when the poet Gray rode through and recorded what he had found. Elizabeth settled Germans in here to work lead mines. But the great world has still hardly penetrated them. We walked and talked as walkers always do — idly.

The entry continues with their anecdotal conversation, then concludes with this single sentence, set off from the rest by Dorothy's three asterisks:

* * *

Just now Hal comes over, "I am put upon!" he says in a very small voice.

The last entries are given in full:

> July 28.
> Manesty Park.

Yesterday morning Feuchtwanger.
In the afternoon we went with Hugh & his sister from Edinburgh to the "hound trail" near Keswick, where Hugh was to be starter. It was a lovely day, bright sunshine with flying clouds after rain; the sports place was a green, open field, surrounded by moss-green mountains. Neither Hal nor I had ever seen a hound trail — the characteristic sport of all this country. The trail was first made by a man who carried the scent (annis) across the fields and around the mountain sides. The hound owners — mostly local farmers, in rusty-looking clothes, all of them speaking the unintelligible Cumberland dialect — lined up in a semicircle in the

field, holding their hounds in leash, between their knees. The hounds, lean and mottled, trembled with excitement, their noses pointed, sniffing the clean air. The the trail-maker came running in; there was a sudden keen, aromatic whiff of annis; Hugh's handkerchief, held up on his walking stick fell, and the hounds darted out from between their masters' knees and hands, flashing like a single white streak through the gateway. For a time they were lost to sight amongst the bracken; then one saw them again a moving white line along the hilltop, scattering sheep, as they passed. But the most thrilling moment was, of course, the return. After they had passed a certain point on the trail the masters were allowed to call to them, and from behind the line where they waited came such a hubbub as you never heard, such whistling & calling! And through the narrow gate the hounds came leaping home; prizes for the first six, & good substantial prizes, too: £12, and less. Breeding hounds for these events is a great business with the country people. Bookies were there taking bets although it was a tiny event. But the red-faced secretary told Hugh that it was "as clean a sport as there is in England" and that only very seldom was there any cheating. Some scoundrels had been known to make decoy trails (short cuts) and train their hounds to follow them.

On the green there were a few refreshment vans, selling soda-drinks, icecream, & fruit. The crowd was very small-townish: the pretty girls from the village in little suits of cheap serge, artificial silk stockings and cocky little hats, and the lads showing off at wrestling. I liked seeing them "take the weights" — the boys stripped to the waist & the sun gleaming on their smooth shoulders & supple backs, as they stood on the scales being weighed for the events — the girls looking at them rather shyly. There were no gentry there at all, I should say, except Hugh. Entirely village folk. Everyone's face looked happy. You could see they were having a good time. In comparison with our crowds they were very quiet. No merry-go-rounds or anything like that. Only an energetic little band playing old-fashioned marches. All the time the clouds were eternally changing the colour & contour of the mountains. The landscape was exquisitely beautiful.

Today (the 29th) Hugh took us to Buttermere; a beautiful, quite secluded lake, set in the mountains. We stopped somewhere or other for tea & talked idly enough: about Galsworthy mostly.

I don't understand why, when inns are so abominable in England, farmhouse food is so splendid. Or is this an exceptional farmhouse? We have chickens and ducks, beautiful salads, salmon, raspberry molds swimming in cream, and delicious bacon and coffee for breakfast. And quantities of everything.

July 30.

Today a wonderful drive, in our car, Harold[1] chauffeuring, to Allswater, very dark & romantic. Windermere, the gayest of the lakes, Grasmere, where I stopped at Dove Cottage — Rydal Water, The Manchester Reservoir, & back to Derwent Water & Manesty. The cottage I found infinitely touching, although the tourists & the old woman with her parrot-cry of "plain living & high thinking" was insufferable. The cottage has a tiny sittingroom, with a stone-flagged floor, dark oak walls; Dorothy Wordsworth's room had hardly more than place for bed & washstand. But the framed portraits on the walls — mostly engravings from paintings — showed noble & beautiful faces on almost all the members of that little circle. Wordsworth, Mary, & Dorothy lie in an idyllic spot in Grasmere church-yard, beside a little willow-hung stream (on the opposite bank of which an enterprising tea room has been started) The gravestones are of the sim-

[1] Harold Cheevers, Walpole's chauffeur and companion.

plest. The church is austere but interesting. It is really two aisles without a nave at all; There is a beamed ceiling and a double tiered series of arches run directly through the center of the church under the highest point of the roof. They are, like the whole interior, of masonry, covered with plaster.

July 31.

To Edinburgh. We passed through beautiful but melancholy hills. They looked like huge beasts in fells of sleek green. One could almost see the play of muscles under their skins. Edinburgh is imposing & depressing. Romantic; without gaity. The War Memorial on Castle Hill depressed me horribly. I though it ugly but Hal liked it.

Aug. 1.

Dinner with Berthold (at his house) and his Director Dr. Crewe, who said that the powers that be were placing the hope of the Empire in a unification of scientific activity which would make the Empire self-supporting. No longer a monopoly of trade & money they hoped (it seemed) for a monopoly of knowledge! B & Crewe argued on the future of a biological religion B. from a socialist viewpoint.

Aug 2. Durham.

Bad temper is the most destructive of human faults. It supplants trust with fear; it poisons love; it breeds aversion or indifference; it sterilizes emotion. Unless he stops taking me on or casting me off as the mood suits him I shall eventually cease to love H. Tonight because I disagreed with him in an argument he got up and left me, sitting alone in a public restaurant.

This is the final entry in Dorothy's honeymoon diary.

6

After the Honeymoon

WE COME NOW TO A CRUEL JUMP, MADE NO LESS CRUEL BY THE
fact that everything we know of our protagonists might lead
us to expect it. Dorothy's last entry in the honeymoon diary
was followed by their return to London and Paris. On August
22nd they sailed for America on the *Hamburg*, arriving in New
York on the 28th. During this period Dorothy did not write
in her diary, nor did she take up the little brown book again
during the crowded autumn months, her first in America as
"Mrs Sinclair Lewis," wife of the eminent novelist, with a very
large income at her command. We shall have a glance at those
months later on, but for the moment the jump must be made
— from the honeymoon to the first diary entry thereafter. It
epitomizes the progress of the drama better than any comment,
and it remains the only entry for a long time to come. This
was a period, indeed the whole of that autumn and winter of
1928–1929, when I saw much of them both, in the country and
in the city, at Twin Farms (their Vermont acquisition) and at
37 West Tenth Street, and the dolorous passage that comes
next may be unfair in some ways (I think it is, as all cries of the
heart must be, to somebody) but to my remembering eyes it
seems as true as the truth itself, without a word of exaggeration.
I give the passage here exactly as Dorothy wrote it, but the
printed page can give no notion of how her neat handwriting
gets larger, less regular, hastier and more sprawling, in proportion as her emotions run away with her and her grief (for I

think she was plainly weeping at the end) takes over for what she thinks she has lost. The passage follows:

February 13 — 1929.

Such a long time has elapsed — and so much has happened. We have bought the Vermont farm, after nearly a month of motoring, looking for it; then New York, the flat here with my furniture, from the Berlin flat & what we bought in Exeter; Christmas at Virginia Hot Springs (inexpressible boredom sustained only by my love for Hal) Now, tomoro, we are to go to Southern Florida. Hal Smith, damn him, is responsible for the idea. He wrote that he had discovered a semi-tropical stream, where grand people never go, and where the fishing is superb. And so we are off day after tomorrow, because Hal is "tired." I agree, because he has been drinking terribly again and only some such trip will make him stop it, but my heart is heavy & rebellious. My God — Florida mud flats, and all next summer in Vermont! Not one enjoyable dinner party the whole winter; not one evening at the opera; not one concert, not a single human relationship — (Can't bear it. I *won't* bear it. I had rather go & work in someone's kitchen than lead this sort of life, chased pursued, harassed by fear's fear

Tonight Hal invited the Perkins to dinner — he never asked me first — collapsed after it & went to bed leaving me to carry the party. He does this regularly. I told him I didn't want to go to Florida because of my lecture date on the 21st. He then got angry & sneered at me — "You with your important little lectures — "You, with your brilliant people . . . *You* want to talk about foreign politics which *I* am too ignorant to understand. When he talks so my heart freezes up. And then, in a minute he is very sweet again. Oh, my God, I really don't know whether I love or hate him — but tonight I was *bored* with him.

I say to myself "You are totally unimportant & you are married to a man of genius — if you give up your life to making him happy it is worth it."

But it isn't! It isn't! I can really do nothing for him. He is like a vampire — he absorbs all my vitality, all my energy, all my beauty — I get incredibly dull. If ever I begin to talk well he interrupts the conversation. He is not above calling me down in front of people because the dinner is bad — he did so when I had been too ill to bother about ordering the dinner, talking to me in a tone I would not use to a servant. He orders me to send flowers to Noel Coward who is ill in the hospital, but not once since our marriage has he ever sent flowers to me, nor did he do so while I was sick. He has insisted on my going to some party or other when I protested I felt ill. He is completely without consideration of me, yet he protests with the greatest tenderness that he loves me, and it is true: he does. He insults people in the house which is mine as well as his — the house where I am hostess. He invites strangers to dinner & goes away and leaves them. All social finesse, all delicacy & gaety of inter- course, all subtlety of contact — all the things I prize in the world, all beautiful civilized manners and forms, he violates. If I cross him in anything; if even I irritate him by weeping, out of sheer nerves & exhaustion, he yells at me that I am driving him crazy, that I have designs to make him feel like a scoundrel, and he never fails to tell me that I am just like Gracie. He thinks then that when he says he is sorry our relationship is the same. But it is not. It has never been the same since that night in Naples when he denounced me to Josef; it has never been the same since he sneered at Helmuth Von Neoltke, and I saw Helmuth's face go white (since then our friendship, which was so tender & gay, has been strained; we never write); it has never been the same since the night in Vermont when he told me "Your sister tomorrow can come & fetch you away."

No. No — too much has been piled upon too much; I am inexpressibly weary & sore. I want to get away, somewhere, forever.

I am distressed by economic cares. I could not remain in America, where I am so ill-adjusted to everything. I am afraid it will be very difficult to get another European correspondency. And I cannot live on Hal. Surely I am not fitted for marriage who have made such a ghastly failure out of two.

It's either give up my work or give up Hal. My work! I can't live & work in a world where I cannot plan from one day to the next. Yet if I give up work he will throw it up at me some day, as he now does at Gracie. Indeed, he has already done so, on several occasions, saying, "the trouble with you is you are lazy — you haven't done any work in a year." It is true.

And my very mind degenerates. But can't he see that no human being can do creative work in the atmosphere which he creates about him!

These notes are as chaotic as my heart & my mind.

I know so well what I want of life:

I want to understand all manner of things better. I know I have taste & a good head. My creative gifts are negligible. But I should like to contribute to a clearer and deeper understanding of the things I understand. My gifts are preeminently social.

What I need: More knowledge.

What I prize: Human relationships, of all kinds, passionate, tender, intellectual, understanding.

What I want: A home which will be a center of life & illumination for people who can really contribute to the development of the humanities.

My gifts: Interpretive; power to draw out & record others.
My interests: All humanities. Politics; literature insofar as
it is not precious but deals with living ideas; economics; all
the attributes of civilized living — cooking, house-furnishing
— manners.
My passion: Creative men.

And this leads me to this relationship where what I prize
what I want, what interests me — my gifts — all are stulti-
fied and rendered sterile.

                                 2

THE LEWISES WENT STRAIGHT TO THE OFFICES OF HIS PUB-
lishers, Harcourt, Brace and Company, when they got to New
York, and it was Harcourt ("Alf," at least for a year or so
longer) who took charge of their destinies. They stayed with
Harrison Smith, who is referred to in the preceding diary
entry as "Hal Smith, damn him"; they also certainly stayed
with Franklin P. Adams and his wife Esther at their house in
Westport, because I distinctly remember Dorothy telling me
that it was here, in the midst of the trees, that she became
aware of how much more luxuriant and abundant nature itself
is in America than in Europe. ("Nothing was silent," she said.
"Everything was moving, creeping, crawling, complaining, re-
joicing, all the insects, all the animals, even the sap in the
trees." She had been away from America for a long time, and
of course the abundance of life is a true fact, for many reasons,
on this side of the ocean.)

They acquired a car, driven by Red at great risk to all, and
with it they undertook to survey the possibilities for that
dream house in Vermont which he had made the basis of his
original proposal. Oddly enough, they found it almost at once.
They had rented a house in New York (that is, a "duplex,"

two floors which were half a house) from Mr E. F. Connett.
As I remember they had done this from London, by virtue of
an advertisement they found in some improbable publication
such as *The Nation* or *The New Republic*. At all events, it was
theirs as from November 1st, 1928. In September, when they
went exploring through New England, they possessed Mr
Connett's address, which was in Barnard, Vermont, near South
Pomfret, and counted upon seeing him, although they had no
notion of buying his house.

Mr Connett, an elderly and amiable gentleman, was glad to
see them. Within a quarter of an hour they had broken the
news to him that they wanted his house in Vermont — it was
what they had been looking for — and he became even more
amiable. He asked them to stay for dinner. Before the evening
was out they had signed the papers of agreement. Mr Connett
was more than willing. For some time he had been looking for
somebody who would relieve him of the obligation for his two
properties, the one in New York and the one in Vermont; he
had resolved to seek balmier climes for the rest of his life, and
indeed had already spent most of his recent time in Florida.

This was Twin Farms. It had been called by that name at
an earlier period (in the late eighteenth and early nineteenth
centuries) because two brothers had built two houses on the
opposite sides of the small valley, working the one farm between
them. (So Red Lewis always told me: I cannot prove it.)
Red and Dorothy restored the old name, but in 1928 the house
Mr Connett lived in was called, in the language of the neighborhood, Connett's "place," and the bigger but derelict house
across the valley was called the "Chase House." There were
over three hundred acres of mountain pasture, rock and valley
and stream, with the two houses looking at each other through
the bare boughs in winter and concealed from each other by
the thickets of spring and summer.

The house in which Mr Connett lived had a cornerstone with

the year 1796 incised upon it. This was the "farmhouse," although it had a system of electric bells and four bathrooms, two of them private (i.e., connected with one bedroom only). It was rustic — hardly anything had been changed in its architecture, the familiar and well-nigh perfect lines of the New England farmhouse with the roof sloped for snow — but at the same time it was far more comfortable than any ordinary farmhouse could be. It had everything the city dweller wants on his precarious ventures into the country, bells and baths and furnaces and all, but at the same time it did not *look* like something run up for the summer folk, the *villeggiatura*. It really did look like a Vermont farmhouse, which was, historically and architecturally and I dare say spiritually, just what it was.

This was the first property either Red or Dorothy had ever had. He bought and sold other houses afterwards, but as Professor Schorer says, "it was . . . to prove to be the only real home he would ever have had." It was the same for Dorothy, although the other house (the "Big House") absorbed her energy and money for twenty years or more. And, as a matter of fact, it was the same for me. The old farmhouse there is also the only property I ever owned (for a few years much later on) and the only home I ever had.

The papers in Syracuse do not tell much about the early finances of Twin Farms, and Professor Schorer's monumental book says nothing about that part of it. However, I distinctly remember how Red and Dorothy used to talk in the early years about how cheap it all was. In their eventual separation agreement (preceding the divorce) I think it was valued at $100,000, when he settled it on her — and perhaps that figure was $150,000. She also spent a small fortune on the "Big House," which was a picturesque wreck when they first came upon it. My own recollection, for what it is worth, is that Red bought the entire place, two houses and three hundred acres, plus the year's rent on the house in New York, for something like $12,000 or $15,000. Mr Connett, who owned the house in Vermont and the lease of the one in New York, merely wanted to get rid of both of them, so that he could sit in the sun, and he was delighted to get the modest sum they offered. (Of course they spent fortunes on Twin Farms afterwards.)

The readers of this book should understand where the houses were on Twin Farms and how the valley descended from the height where the public road passes from South Pomfret to the village of Barnard. The farmhouse, which we afterwards called "Red's House" and still later on "Jimmy's House" (i.e., mine), was on one side of the little valley. Above it, at the top of the valley, was the Big House. The view from its terrace led straight off to Mount Ascutney. At the end of her life Dorothy sold the Big House, resumed possession of the farmhouse, and spent her last year or so there. Although the houses were called various names at various times by Dorothy and Red (as will be seen in their letters), it seems simpler for this present narrative to call them the farmhouse (or the old house) and the Big House.

It was, in truth, a wonderful find. The old house resembled to a truly astonishing degree that Vermont farmhouse which Red had described to Dorothy in Berlin on the night he proposed marriage to her. It was not the same (he had never seen Twin Farms) but it could have been. To my mind the most significant fact about the property was that there were two houses — not one.

I had returned to New York just at this time from Paris and somehow or other either Dorothy or Red asked me to come up to Twin Farms to stay for a while. Mr Connett, the owner, had been only too glad to get out of his house on September 13th, the day they called upon him. In a few days he had, in fact, moved down to the house in New York, from which he soon went off to Florida. Dorothy found no difficulty arranging for a cook and somebody to clean; as for a gardener,

there was one already and he remained for many years. I believe that was the extent of the household. They were not in
the very least "servants" in the cosmopolitan sense, and neither
Dorothy nor Red wanted them to be. If it was inconvenient
for one of the women to come up to the house from the village,
she would simply say so and send a friend instead. They all
had their own motorcars and it was not in the very least like
Europe. Mr Quimby, the gardener, who slept over the garage,
was the most permanent part of the establishment, and indeed
he kept me in subjugation for the best part of thirty years.
He was a man who was proud of his flower beds and brooked
no trespass.

Well do I recall one morning (October, 1928) when a brisk
matron from the village of Barnard came into my bedroom
with a cup of coffee, drew the curtains and said that Mr Lewis
would be down to breakfast in a quarter of an hour. (Mr
Lewis used to eat breakfast at seven; later on it was six and
then five.) I found myself to have a tickle in the throat,
indicating the possibility of a cold, and in those days colds were
severe for me and terribly severe for Mr Lewis, so I said to this
friend: "Could I have some salt, please? I will put it into hot
water and make a gargle and it may keep me from getting this
cold which I feel in my throat."

The matron from Barnard went out and returned in a moment with a whole tumblerful of salt. (I had my own bath-
room — it was that room on the ground floor which was
Dorothy's before she died.) I said to her: "Sorry, Mrs X, I'll
never be able to use up all this salt!"

"You ain't obligated to use it all up in one go," she said
tartly.

This was the general tone of the household, which Red and
I adored and which, I think, at the very beginning caused
Dorothy some surprise. She also adored it later, but she had
been accustomed to that "gracious lady" treatment of Vienna,

Budapest and Berlin, and in fact she had not been in the United States for perhaps a decade, except one swift professional journey when she stayed in hotels. She did not fully seize the essence of Vermont just then, although nobody loved it more after a few years.

I cannot remember how I got there or when. Perhaps either Red or Dorothy drove me up — and if so, it must have been Red, because I doubt if Dorothy had a driving license until two or three years later. They had asked me to stay more or less forever, and I almost did. Anyhow I stayed about ten days or two weeks, which, for me in anybody's house, is the maximum: I cannot endure more and always feel that I, too, have become unendurable. Yet somehow this first stay of mine with Dorothy and Red at Twin Farms dwelt in all our minds forever after. Decades later, when Red had entered upon his penultimate phantasm at Williamstown, he wrote me a pathetic little note asking if I remembered our first weeks at Twin Farms and would I come and do it again. Dorothy also (decades later) referred to those first days in the house. And I, of course, could never forget.

In the first place not a single thing had been done to the farmhouse, not one. It had not been improved, embellished or amended in any particular. Dorothy and Red had only been in it a very short time, no more than about a week, when I arrived. The beds were four feet deep, the wallpaper was splashy blue flowers in my room (splashy red or pink or yellow flowers in other rooms) and the carpets were what used to be called Turkey. There were actual lace curtains. The foundations had not yet been straightened up by steel braces (as Dorothy managed eventually), so every floor was crooked, and so was every wall. The roof leaked and the fireplace smoked. The electricity wavered whimsically in the windy evenings and at times vanished altogether. A shutter was always banging. Obscure cracklings and bitter murmurs came from the stairs and the attic. One might have been in Ireland or Wales, really, so far as the spirits were concerned.

Ah, but the fun we had! We laughed until we cried, and cried until we laughed again. There were innumerable instigations, one of which was the presidential election, then going on, between Mr Herbert Hoover and Mr Alfred Smith, one of whom (and I believe it was Hoover) won in the following month. Smith was debarred from the presidency because he belonged to the Roman Catholic Church and it was thought that his election would install the Pope of Rome (the Great Whore of Babylon) in the White House. All three of us regarded this as an uncivilized taboo and yet we were not enamored of Smith as a candidate. Mr Hoover in some ways left us even more cold, although he had many more enumerable qualifications for the presidency than his rival. It was, indeed, an amazing election, and I do not know in the least how Dorothy and Red voted that time. (I did not vote at all.) Perhaps Red voted for his friend Norman Thomas — ? It is possible: and Dorothy, in that case, unless she also voted for Norman, must have voted for Mr Hoover I suppose.

Anyhow, every night of our lives we sat by the fire and roared with uncontrollable laughter at the speeches of Mr Hoover and Mr Smith. They spoke every night, and they were unbelievably funny. I do not think anybody since then has touched their ineffable silliness. Hoover was promising not only a chicken in every pot (which, in America, is not terribly rare) but silk stockings on every leg, and Smith was proclaiming the rights of the slum to govern (the city slum, the least qualified slum we have). They both said absurd things and so did their innumerable cohorts.

All of this was by radio.

The invention was not precisely new, but none of us had any particular familiarity with it. It had never been used, up to this time (October, 1928) on any great scale in American politics. All three of us knew how strange it was — what a revolution — that we should sit by the fire in a Vermont farmhouse and hear the statements of the opposing candidates. Obviously it was going to change the entire political life of the United States, but we did not then know quite how much. Nor did we have any remote notion that it was going to be accompanied within a relatively few years by the images of the speakers.

Red cared. At that moment I think he cared far more than either Dorothy or I did, even though he kept shouting at the radio and denying everything either candidate said. The radio itself was a small, rectangular box without much power in it. The thing was operated by a battery and bore no resemblance to the massive organs of a later time. As I remember, it altered its tone and even its pitch in accordance with its physical position, so that Red kept twisting it around all the time from north to south to east to west.

And then we had Wells.

Wells Lewis was Red's son by his first wife and was then eleven years old. Dorothy had insisted that he should be asked to Twin Farms as soon as possible. He came soon after I did and stayed a while — Professor Schorer says one weekend; I could have sworn that it was longer. Wells at this time was one of the most beautiful children I have ever seen. His hair was pale gold, like an aureole, standing out all round his head; his eyes were very blue and his skin pure. There is a portrait of him painted not much later which conveys the incredible candor and innocence of his aspect. He took to Dorothy right away, and she to him, but I thought he was afraid of his father and extremely uncertain of me. Our conversation on the whole bewildered him. This is perhaps in the nature of things. Red was forty-four. Dorothy was thirty-five. I was twenty-eight. None of us had anything much to say to a boy of eleven. And yet the odd thing is that this boy of eleven, also, never forgot

those days. Long years later when I found him (in the bluster-
ing storm and totally by accident), running an anti-aircraft
battery on the cold, wet coast above Casablanca, he recalled
them to me.

Red's rages were under very good control at that time. I
only remember two of them, actually. One was directed at
Wells, and was not really a rage or really against the boy. The
other was at some unidentified lawyer in Minneapolis or St.
Paul.

Rage Number One: Wells had been sitting amiably and
quietly listening, with the three of us, to some speech by either
Mr Hoover or Mr Smith. It terminated with a ripsnorting
political diapason which made us all laugh heartily. We fell
into talk in which — just for that once: it didn't always happen!
— we all three thought we'd rather have Smith than Hoover.
The boy spoke up and said, in the upper-class accent of his
school: "Ah, yes, but you can't imagine Mrs Smith in the White
House, can you?" Red rose to his feet and raged and raved for
about half an hour. The boy was terrified; Dorothy had to
intervene to quell the tempest.

Rage Number Two: A letter arrived from somebody in
Minneapolis or St. Paul who was in charge of some interests of
Red's in those regions. He had, perhaps on the advice of his
brother Claude, invested some money in farm mortgages. This
was good investment and good income. Red was rather a good
businessman, or so I think. But the lawyer or banker who
wrote the letter thought *he* was a better businessman. He had
foreclosed a mortgage. Red was on his hind legs for almost an
hour, declaiming against the heartless, stupid and shortsighted
fool who had foreclosed the mortgage, not only in defiance of
all Red's ideas but also of common sense.

But these two rages do not count, really, against the tranquil
pleasure of the time. I saw between Dorothy and Red a
genuine affection which, in a more tepid manner, spilled over

upon me and made me glad to be there. We understood each other. She was never sharp to him and he was never harsh to her. In view of their behavior (natural behavior, unthought, unstudied) in later years, and in view of the fact that Dorothy was already (as we know from the entry just quoted from her diary) beginning to wonder what she had done, this is good to remember. They were both kindness itself to me, but the best thing they did for me or ever could do for me was to be kind to each other.

As I said, Wells also felt this in some obscure manner and long years afterwards, under quite different conditions in the middle of a most uncomfortable war, he told me so.

3

THE PROPERTY THE LEWISES BOUGHT, TRADITIONALLY CALLED "Twin Farms" and soon to be given that name again, was a mountain, a hill and a valley, with the great sweep of view towards Mount Ascutney from the highest point. There stood the Big House called, in the first year or so of their ownership, the "Chase House." Somebody named Chase had evidently owned it at one time and left the name behind. It was a wreck. The framework was good enough but nobody had taken any care of it for many decades and the roofs and floors all needed a good deal of attention. Alongside it, to the left as one looked down and up towards Ascutney, there was a vast barn, also derelict and falling apart. Shattered though it was, this shell of a house had obviously once (since it dominated the view) been the chief house on the property and in the neighborhood. It had a slightly manorial look even in its desolation. From the moment they saw Twin Farms both Dorothy and Red realized that this house, the wreck, the derelict, ought to be put into condition so as to become the true domicile of the family and so as to take advantage of that wonderful view. It was a question of how and when and why and in what manner it should be restored to life. Red's idea — immediate and in-flexible — was that the barn should be made into one great room in which, as he said, various persons might do various things without interfering with one another. That is, at one end there might be a poker game and at the other end a seminar, without a clash of interest, without even an annoy-ance. It was to be high and wide and to look (by means of a huge window — the Americans later invented the word "picture window" to describe this kind of thing) out across half the state of Vermont to the dreamy peak afar off.

All this was done, during the next two or three years, just as Red wanted. The "Big Room" was created out of the barn. It adhered to the house in a somewhat awkward manner: that is, to get into the Big Room the only way, without going out to the lawn, was through the kitchen and pantry. The barn was at right angles to the house and was originally not con-nected with it at all. Dorothy solved this problem with her usual imperiousness by building a loggia, slightly Italian and obscurely wrong, on the outside of the kitchen and pantry, so that one could actually go from the dining room to the Big Room without traipsing through the working quarters; and yet for the next thirty years and more none of us ever dreamed of using the loggia to get to the Big Room. As Red had predicted right from the beginning, we all plowed through the kitchen and pantries (there were two) and since there were so many of us I often wonder how the cook and maids got their work done. We must have been a nuisance, but there was no other way to manage the traffic under those conditions. Dorothy's elegant loggia remained, to the very end, a decoration rather than a thoroughfare.

So far as the rest of the house was concerned Dorothy had a completely free hand. Red never interested himself much in kitchens, dining rooms and the like: he wanted bathrooms to be convenient and bookshelves to be more or less everywhere, on the stairs and the landings and in the bedrooms and halls, but aside from this he did not concern himself with domestic architecture. Dorothy went on and on and on, year after year, building things and changing things and adding things on to other things, so that the original shape of that house was really quite lost, and although it was to all of us a beautiful and wonderful house, I doubt if anybody concerned in the matter (including all the clever secretaries who lived there, and all the eminent guests who came and went) could have made a correct drawing of it.

There came a time, not really long after they had bought Twin Farms (and I think it may have been only four or five years after) when Red told me he liked the old farmhouse better than the new one. My recollection is not perfectly clear, but I have a notion that he said the old house was really his and this new one, with all its additions and multiplications, was really Dorothy's. It was something along those lines, because throughout the next decades I always thought of the Big House as Dorothy's and the smaller, older farmhouse as Red's. It was Red's house where I lived for years and of which I was for some time the owner; that is why Dorothy in the last fifteen years of her life usually referred to it as "Jimmy's house." These names may be a trifle confusing but they do refer to something a little more significant than mere ownership or habitation. In point of fact Red never lived in Red's house again after Dorothy's house was restored and opened; Red's house was called "the guest house" for about ten years or more; the later "guest house" (often rented) was not built until after the second world war; the big studio built on the hill dates from about 1950, long after Red's day, and what is now a farmer-caretaker's house was not in existence for the first few years of this story. That, with the garage and the apartment for servants on top of it, eventually brought the total of the houses on Twin Farms up to six. Of these the only ones which need concern any reader of this record would be Dorothy's and Red's, with the understanding that Red's was also (later on) mine, although long after their marriage had terminated.

The houses, gardens, pastures, farm and all the associated enterprises were of passionate interest to Dorothy as time went on and as her desire to be useful, to be productive, took steadily more concrete forms. She must have known from the earliest days that true farming, for profit that is, could scarcely come into being under the conditions of Twin Farms, with owners not only absent for half the year but deeply engaged in activities of a purely urban nature. Neither Dorothy nor Red could ever have been described as a farmer, even of the most theoretical kind. They would thus always be at the mercy of somebody else, and the whole history of Twin Farms from first to last was a history of these constantly changing farmers, who, whether good or bad, were not primarily concerned with the desires or interests of their employers. There were all sorts of arrangements. For example, in the calving there was some principle by which every other birth belonged to the owner, alternating with the farmer; and yet it always seemed that the bulls fell to the owner's lot. As a cow in childbirth seeks privacy, or at least solitude, and Dorothy could scarcely roam the mountains all night long to discover their hiding places, it was quite easy to arrange this. There were other possibilities with hens, eggs, fresh vegetables and other products of the land.

I observed very early, and never ceased to observe, that the difference between a farmer and a gardener was immense. I do not know why this should be, but it is. I took no part in any of these things, and at the end of thirty-five years Dorothy had still never been able to persuade me to pull up a single weed. And yet I could tell most distinctly that the gardener's interest was concerned with pride and the farmer's interest was concerned with profit. During all the dramas of Twin Farms, which were innumerable, this distinction was obscured in Dorothy's mind by her hopes, her principles, her high-minded desires and the delusions to which they led. For a great many years she was convinced that Twin Farms was productive, that it was useful to the United States and contributed to the food supply; she even thought for some years, thanks to clever book-keepers and other legerdemain artists, that it made money; she thought her herd of Guernseys and Jerseys were paying for the artesian well and the furnace and the long distance telephones; she believed the henhouse sustained the Cadillac and paid at least half the liquor bill. With the most steadfast cynicism I rejected these hypotheses for many decades, and in the end she came to agree — at least to the extent of selling off all these excrescences and living, at last, like somebody from the city who just happens to be in the country. This is precisely what she had never wanted to be or do in the beginning, and Red Lewis had known, right from the start, that her effort to avoid it was vain.

They were at odds, fundamentally, on everything about Twin Farms. That is, of course, a rockbottom philosophical concept and it did not come up in talk too often — it was not a daily subject of dispute. And yet it was always there, ever since I can remember. Red always saw with the utmost clarity that he was not a farmer and never could be a farmer and did not want to be a farmer. He had bought a farm to live on it when he was not otherwise engaged. Well indeed do I remember the first time I saw a herd on the mountain and Red told the visitors (whoever they were) that he had hired them for the effect. Actually they were all foreign cows of some sort, nothing to do with Twin Farms: the farmer of that day used to rent out the pastures. Red would never have dreamed of buying a cow. Dorothy, once she got started on this career of extravagance, was always buying cows or sheep or hens or something that might contribute to the productive justification which she felt necessary for possessing land. Worse than that: she was forever trying to bring some God-forsaken patch of rock and sorrow back into cultivation. It was her proudest boast, twenty-five years later, that she had brought back something like two hundred acres of barren land. She never stopped to consider that she was spending, like the State of Israel, a million dollars for each blade of grass. All she wanted was to restore uncultivated land to cultivation. In all these endeavors she got nothing but ribald laughter from Red Lewis and, after he had taken his jeers elsewhere, from me too.

Dorothy's noble ambitions had not germinated just yet when (1928) we were all new to Twin Farms. It can be seen from her diaries that she did not even like the simple life too much. (Strange: strange indeed: but this place which afterwards became the center of her existence seems at first to have bored her.) She was writing her Russian impressions during that first visit of mine — a book appeared, as we shall see, and Mr Theodore Dreiser also appeared in connection with it — and Red was writing his first sketches, I believe, for *Ann Vickers*. I can no longer remember what I was writing, but I know that whatever it was, Red was very stern about my doing it. In this first visit I lived on the ground floor, in the room which afterwards became my study during the years when I owned the farmhouse. Red never locked me into that room, as I recall. (He only started to lock me in about a year later when I lived on the upper floor in the room with bunches of red cherries on the wallpaper, when I had begun to write short stories.)

He had already started to call me by his own name, that is, Harry Lewis. Plainly enough, I was he, although I never knew why, and he was his own father, known as "Doc Lewis." He had one of those blue flannel dressing gowns which clothed his lanky form for the great part of his life and they were not always innocent of cigarette burns or scraps of egg. This is what he wore to breakfast, which was a full-fledged meal in the dining room at half past seven in the morning. Dorothy was not by nature or habit altogether happy with so much food so early, but she put up with it, as did I. She wrapped herself in anything warm enough, but I usually got fully dressed before breakfast. The mail came at about half past four in the afternoon at Twin Farms, but since Red thought this a barbarous hour for the reception of mail, it was always put aside to be seen the next morning at breakfast. And in it would come, more or less by the bushel basket, along with those innumerable eggs, bacons and toasts which the Master consumed at that hour. (It was his chief meal and always so remained.)

The breakfasts were incredibly funny, partly because Red was at his brightest in these matutinal times, but also because his mail itself was wildly funny. He got letters from all over the earth saying all kinds of things. Many persons thought that whatever they wished to buy — from a diamond tiara to an island in the Aegean — would be theirs if they could make Red pay for it. And evidently he had given the impression, somehow or other, either by his novels or by his public utterances, that he was quite ready to give away his princely earnings to anybody who could make out a good case. So we had countless, really countless, letters asking him to squander his money. Since he was by no means a reckless giver, and in some ways might have been reckoned a nonpareil of stinginess, these letters convulsed us daily. And we were almost equally enraptured by letters of a quite different tenor, asking him to make great efforts and sacrifices for the sake of the Eskimo orphans or the spinsters of Bulgaria or other worthy sufferers to whom he had never given a thought. Red's mail was all like that — crediting him, really, with a generosity of spirit and an insouciance of the bank account which never had been his. A more self-centered person never lived (be it said in the tenderest recollection) and the thought of our dear Red yielding to all these entreaties, or even to the tiniest part of them, was richly comic in itself.

But nobody got the joke more completely than he did. And he clowned it, too, as he did everything else. One thing may convey the idea best of all: the index. At each breakfast there were books on the table. During those years everybody who published a book in England or the United States sent a copy to Red, unless it was on some subject (such as theology) beyond his interest. He used to rip off the covers with the table knives at breakfast, since we had not yet (in the first year or two) reached the stage of the secretaries. And the very first thing he would do, as soon as the discalced book fell under his eye, was to jump for the index. "L for Lewis," he would say with fiendish delight, and read out to us whatever the author had said about Lewis. Page 23, he can't write; page 67, he can't think; page 85, why don't the Americans shoot him; page 103, we have had quite enough of this sinister mountebank; page 164, who is Lewis anyhow? This happened every single morning, since there was always some unfortunate and forgotten scrivener, English or American, who wanted to vent his spleen on Red. And how Red did enjoy it! I have never known a man who took more pleasure in the literary insults that came his way.

(So long as they were not from writers he really respected, that is — he could suffer days and weeks if anybody he revered spoke badly of him.)

Our breakfasts in this vein lasted only for three or four years, but I shall never forget them. Later Dorothy gave up the effort to eat a big meal at dawn and so did I. Red consumed his triple rations by himself, and his hours got earlier and earlier. (At Williamstown, at the end of his life, I think he was eating breakfast at half past five but I never got up to find out.)

To the very end he wanted the mail along with the eggs and viands, no matter when the mail had been delivered. I think letters went with coffee in his mind, or perhaps with his father.

"Doc Lewis" — the father — must have had a very high, sharp, scolding sort of voice, because that is what Red sounded like when he became his father and I (willy-nilly) became Harry Lewis. This was invariably at the end of breakfast, but also at other times of the day, depending upon the mood. And although the enactment was perfectly clear, serious and distinct, with the father and son as sharply outlined as if performed by professional actors on a stage, there still was a line of differentiation between real life and make-believe. That is, if I ever made any attempt to do what my "father" told me to do I would be hauled back abruptly and with some disgust, and the whole game fell to the ground. I soon learned this and never tried to break the spell.

"Harry Lewis! Harry Lewis! Get your lazy bones out of that chair and see to the wood! You know your mother's got too much to do! Are you going to let that fire go out? You lazy, good-for-nothing young 'un, get in that wood and sweep the snow off the back porch and wipe your shoes before you come back in! How many times do I have to tell you? And it's past eight o'clock, Harry Lewis, do you hear me?"

When I first became Harry Lewis I really did not know whether I was or not. Red had the most paralyzing conviction in these games. It actually was the wood that taught me the secret of the frontier between game and reality. He was nagging me about getting in the wood, and doing so in that voice which (I am sure) must have been precisely the voice of "Doc Lewis." We burned wood in the furnace at Twin Farms, and continued to do so in that house (the old one) for decades thereafter. I was so hypnotized by "Doc Lewis" that I started down the stairs to the cellar to feed some wood into the furnace. At this point Red, still haranguing me at the top of his most nasal voice, followed me down the steps in his blue flannel dressing gown. But when he saw me actually start to pick up wood from the cellar floor to put into the furnace he said in his own voice, in tones of disgust: "Oh, for Christ's sake, Jimmy, leave the wood alone! I'll take care of my own furnace."

He then proceeded to stoke the furnace, as he always did. He never would have permitted me to do so — or anybody else, either, so long as he was there to do it. I was Harry Lewis, all right, just up to the point of actually doing anything. At that point the game ceased.

But it did go on for at least two or three years, and I got sufficiently accustomed to it so that I could be Harry Lewis without overstepping the bounds of the game, without, that is, actually trying to *be* Harry Lewis.

Obviously the psychiatrists could say all sorts of things about this play; all I am trying to do is to tell what happened. There are one or two observations, first of all being that it only happened at Twin Farms (never in New York), and second that it came to an end by the time I was thirty. How it began or ended I was not to know. All I can say is that when it got started and Red was in full swing (never for more than about ten minutes) he had me hypnotized into thinking, at least with one part of my mind, that I actually was Harry Lewis and that he was my angry father, "Doc." He certainly became a different personality, and so did I.

Dorothy did not care much for this game.

4

EVERYTHING WAS DIFFERENT IN NEW YORK. THAT WINTER I was living in Fourth Street, where my friend Martin Sommers (afterwards for decades the foreign editor of the *Saturday Evening Post*) had preceded me from Paris and could give me shelter. Fourth Street, in some eighteenth-century crossing of the sheep trails, not only comes close to Tenth Street but at one point actually intersects it. I lived on that side, not far; the Lewises were in Mr Connett's house at 37 West Tenth Street, between Fifth and Sixth Avenues.

I was much in their house. Red's hospitality was incorrigible. He always asked everybody to come and never wanted anybody to go. If he felt the need of solitude, or even of sleep, he would abandon the company and retire for an hour, almost always with the solemn injunction that nobody was to go away. (Awkward: you never knew what to do.) Dorothy was also extremely hospitable but she did have the habits of civilization; she could tell lunch from dinner; if she asked you for cocktails she did not expect you to stay all night; and furthermore she always recognized that other people had other things to do, which Red treated as a chimerical notion.

Thus it happened during that winter (1928–1929) that I had numerous opportunities to observe the process which Dorothy describes in the diary entry which begins this chapter — that is, the disillusionment and incipient boredom, the fears and even dreads to which her apprehension of a future with Red had brought her. It is perfectly true that Red never wanted to go anywhere, had little interest even in the theatre just then, and had not yet developed what became (much later) a desire to hear music. No concerts, no operas and even no plays — which, considering how stage-struck he became years later, seems strange. I should have been inclined to say he liked staying at home better than anything else, except that he did not seem to like home either, and was always overcrowding it with spur-of-the-moment guests who often were trying everything short of mayhem to escape. Very possibly he, too, had some misgivings about their marriage during that first winter. If so, he never showed them in any way identifiable to me, although he did occasionally have a sharp tiff with Dorothy.

The truth is, I think, that he drank a good deal more alcohol in New York than he ever did in the country, and his way of drinking was hard on the nerves, the equilibrium of the household and even the hours of meals, work, etc., etc. Red had no particular time for drinking. If he wanted a drink he would take it at any hour — starting, that is, when he got up in the morning. If he felt he needed a rest at any time (even in the middle of dinner) he would simply go to bed. He, who was so fantastically punctual about meals when he was not drinking, now adhered to his principles only for breakfast; lunch in New York was often askew; dinner, as often as not, was delayed for hours. Red also (when he was drinking) disliked making engagements in advance, which made it difficult to have any social life of the kind Dorothy might have enjoyed; there were not many houses where he liked to be a guest; and yet he would ask almost any number of guests into his own house without regard to the food supplies or the convenience of the servants. Dorothy had brought her own German couple, man and wife, from her flat in Berlin (along with most of her furniture). They had a strange initiation into the customs of New York.

Also, I suppose, Dorothy expected something far more brilliant, more of-the-great-world, than she got. She had been making her own life for quite a few years in a highly civilized society, and had grown accustomed to its standards. She certainly must have expected (as readers of the diary in this chapter know) that life with the most famous of American writers, in the largest of American cities, on an income which even for the United States was really large, would have some elements of variety, glitter, change and excitement. Not at all. Red wanted to see only the same people every night of his life (that is, until he switched to others!) and preferably in his own house; he felt strange and ill at ease in grand New York parties, even after all his experiences in Europe; all those elegant London clothes he bought for their marriage went to waste, since he really preferred to wear the same suit for a week or so at a time. And then, as the diary shows, he was always at the mercy of a whim which might send him, on the barest possible notice, to Florida or California, Minnesota or Washington, if anybody had the skill to push his fancy in that direction.

These were all characteristics exaggerated by alcohol. Red would have denied them because he never knew (then or at any time) how fantastic these exaggerations were. Actually he wrote a letter to the New York *Times* which appeared in that paper February 17th, two days after he had dragged Dorothy off to Florida (as shown in the diary at the head of this chapter); in the *Times* letter he complained of the inconvenience of going to the theatre in New York — exactly as if he had made the effort several times a week all winter. "I am sick and tired of wearing myself out getting to and from a Broadway theatre," he said, "irritated at having to pay prices out of all proportion," and so on. The fact was, of course, that he had seldom made any such effort. Sometimes even when he had (at Dorothy's request) taken the trouble to get theatre seats he would refuse to go at the last moment, and often his condition was such that his wife and friends readily concurred in his decision.

It was not a good winter for Red. And yet it began rather well; they came down from Twin Farms in high spirits and very soon found themselves in an argument which, minor though it was in essence, made Red feel very cheerful and combative. (He loved getting angry, especially in a righteous cause.)

Dorothy's articles from Russia, from the preceding year, had been published as a book in October under the name of *The New Russia*. In November Mr Theodore Dreiser published a book called *Dreiser Looks at Russia* covering much the same ground. That was not surprising: they had both been there at the same moment, using the same interpreters, official sources, newspapers, etc., etc. A resemblance might have been expected. But Dreiser's book contained whole sentences and even paragraphs which were word for word the same as those written by Dorothy. One that I remember most distinctly — it was the one which most enraged Red Lewis — was this: Dorothy said the churches of Moscow glittered in the drab city "like jewels in a mud-puddle." One month later Mr Dreiser's book made the same comparison. How to explain it?

I have since thought it most likely that Mr Dreiser's newspaper articles were not sufficient to make up a whole book and that the young man hired by his publisher to pad them out to book length merely reached in all directions for anything he could find on the subject, taking, as a matter of course, Dorothy's articles in the *Evening Post* of the preceding year. (His publisher may not have known.) Writers of books, plays and the like do this constantly to newspaper writing; I have been plagiarized in this manner for over thirty years and know there is no recourse; but the young man who prepared Dreiser's book went too far. He put down whole phrases which had nothing whatsoever to do with factual material.

In so doing he enraged Red Lewis beyond measure. To Red it seemed deliberate plagiarism, an insult to Dorothy and therefore an insult to himself, etc., etc. (He should have known better.) He stormed the house down and threatened Dreiser with a law suit; meeting the older writer at a dinner in the Metropolitan Club, he upbraided Mr Dreiser and got his face slapped; the newspapers were full of it for a while. Dorothy, who had a far more accurate view of the probabilities, never did think Dreiser had deliberately stolen her descriptive sentences. She merely thought, as we all did, that he ought to have been more careful — and that he ought to have read his book, at least, before signing his name to it. Her good sense persuaded Red to keep still after a while and the whole thing blew over.

And yet it is obvious that the first winter in New York was a disappointment to them, somehow. I shall have to say that the following winter was worse. There arose, however, one possibility of escape for both of them from the raw nerves and harsh exchanges brought on by alcohol: Dorothy's career in journalism and as a lecturer was beginning to give some indication of that astonishing development which, later on, for almost a decade, made her unique in the field. In this very winter she made some trips to Canada to investigate the effects of American prohibition on life and economics in the neighboring Dominion. Red was ready and anxious to encourage her work, of which he was, as a matter of fact, overweeningly proud. He was not always on his best behavior during her absences, and it was during one of these (in the first winter) that there occurred a dinner party which has been variously described by all the men present. I shall give my version in due course, although it differs from the others. (Mine, at least, can be proved by the medical records!) But the point about this incipient journalism, and one or two lectures as well, is that an avenue was opening up whereby Dorothy could have some separate life and work of her own, something by which she could defend her own being against the obsessive intensity of Red's agonies and his anodynes. How were they to know — how could anybody know — that this work was to blaze up into such a conflagration, in just a few years, that instead of saving their marriage it provided the coup de grâce?

Those first articles of Dorothy's in American journalism (that is, written in America, not from Europe) appeared in June, 1929, in the Curtis newspapers, as a series "by Mrs Sinclair Lewis." She did not long continue to sign her work in that manner.

7

Love by Letter

NOBODY COULD ESCAPE THE OBSERVATION THAT DOROTHY'S diaries and letters reflect points of view which often differ. Even in the Berlin days, at the very beginning of her relationship to Red Lewis, she confided to her diary things which have no representation at all in her letters. The tendency increases from the time of these first years (1928–1930) the Lewises spent in the United States. And although Red Lewis kept no diaries, his own letters are notably more ardent than he seems to have been, on all the evidence, in life.

There is no need to call this divergence by any of the rude names — hypocrisy, pretense, make-believe, deception — which might come to mind. It is natural, perhaps even inevitable, that men and women should state themselves in letters somewhat more tensely, somewhat on a higher plane, than they do in ordinary existence. If this is so, as I think, then how much greater must be the temptation of literary folk — born writers, as both Red and Dorothy were — to yield to the magic of words, to express themselves fully, and even, at times, to express more than they truly mean! It is doubtful if either of them noticed any discrepancy, still less any contradiction, between their letters and their lives.

And yet this discrepancy, which is there from the beginning of their story, grows steadily more visible, year after year, during the decade of the 1930's. We find their protestations of love, later on, to be rather astonishing, considering how little of the time they spent together. We wonder why they both dwell upon their need for each other, their painful sense of "missing" each other, when all they had to do was to buy a ticket (either one or both) to assuage this suffering. We have not yet come to that stage, but it is adumbrated even in these early years when their separations were more infrequent and their harmony much more complete.

During the very winter when she wrote the bitter and angry entry in her diary (February 13, 1929), as quoted in the last chapter, Dorothy spent some time in Canada. These absences produced a number of letters from Dorothy to Red which are very much what she calls them so often, "love letters." One may be quoted to give the tone of them all. It is from the Château Frontenac in Quebec, dated April 16th.

"I love you because you are the renewer of my life," she says. (This seems to be a return to the mood of Berlin two years earlier.) "Sometimes, for a little while, I forget it. Sometimes, as when I woke up this morning, I remember it suddenly, overwhelmingly. Perhaps because this place is strange and I alone. I awakened to this strangeness and loneliness and remembered the time before you came when the most familiar things looked strange, and I seemed never to have seen before the most familiar faces. A dreadful time when all reality was dissolved.

"Darling, you are my reality: you are my home. Be good to yourself — preserve yourself for me."

Red's letters are sometimes quite matter-of-fact by comparison, at the same period: "You must spend at least a day out in a village," he tells her, "to see how gov liq control works there in contrast to the cities. Talk to the priest and the Ch of Eng vicar."

More often his declarations of love are breezy and slapdash, without the reflective quality which characterizes her own at the same period. For example, when she left him in Florida this same winter (after the February entry in her diary, and before her trip to Quebec) he writes a note dated merely "Monday evening" — it was sometime in March, 1929.

It's too absurd — you've been gone only four days, and yet I'm so lonely for you that I could howl. Owwwwwwww! I'm coming back in just a few days.

I haven't finished the story — I've felt rather indolent and let-down, and it started itself badly. Now I've rewritten all the first part and it's going much better. I haven't had any real parties, though I did go and lose twenty dollars on roulette one evening just on your behalf, and there's a wonderful pool for swimming over on North Beach — just warm enough. And — and I want to see the Chase house . . . . and you, I ADORE you!

H

(The short story was one of a series Red wrote for *Cosmopolitan* Magazine.)

At just about this same period, when Red was in St. Augustine and Dorothy was on a brief visit to her sister Peggy (Mrs Howard Wilson) in Pittsburgh, he sent a characteristic telegram: "During heckling after lecture please ask experts present if possible have place for flivver in studio of Chase house would say I adore you expect word adore too banal. Anatole."

After Red had returned to New York and Dorothy was in Canada (April, 1929) the following two letters (dated from the postmarks on their envelopes) give a fair idea of Red's semi-burlesque epistolary style. In the first of these, Paul and Tommy are Paul de Kruif (Red's medical collaborator on *Arrowsmith*) and Tommy Ybarra of the New York *Times*, Rhea and Lida their wives. Mary Dahlberg was an old friend

from Minnesota; Ferd is Ferdinand Reyher, journalist, and
Freeman is Red's nephew, his brother's son, then an undergraduate at Harvard. Floyd, in the second letter, is obviously
Floyd Gibbons, a war correspondent who had become at that
time a kind of idol or "star" in the newest medium, the radio.

[postmarked 4/18/29]
Thursday

An awfully nice party with Paul, Rhea, Tommy and Lida
last evening — something awfully pleasant and friendly as
well as eager in the atmosphere. They love you, all of
them! — and Rhea and Lida quite as much as Tommy and
Paul. Nor was it just compliments — it was the manner in
which they expressed their affection, and great admiration,
for you . . . Much of the talk was about Raymond Pearl's
cancer-tuberculin stuff. Paul, fond and admiring of Pearl
tho he is, feels violently that Pearl is springing the stuff
prematurely.

Mary Dahlberg for tea yesterday. She sails for France on
the Ile on Friday and she has a marvelous story of rowing
with Bror and at six in the morning from their suite getting
Paris on the long distance phone to talk to her gennulman
friend in his hotel and Bror snatching the receiver from her.
Wottawoil!

I've started the burlesque story. It's going to be hard to
do — to keep it from being as dull as the original would be.
But an interesting effort maybe.

Watkins, Ledger syndicate mgr in Philadelphia, whose
telegram I wired you yesterday, writes you here about
biographical material for boosting the series. I opened his
letter, and I'll try to supply.

Ferd goes home tomorrow morning. Freeman is arriving
from Boston and as he stays only till the next Monday, I'll

put him up here. But I wish it were something else, some one with rabbit paws, I were putting up. I do love you so!

[postmarked 4/22/29]
Sunday evening

Well, I dunno. Maybe it was great for him, and maybe it was fatal. Anyway, Freeman was here for two and a half days from Harvard, and yesterday I gave him a party. Floyd and Jimmy Sheehan came for lunch and stayed for tea and stayed for dinner and stayed for the evening — though all by request — and drank enough to loosten their tongues — no, drank more'n than not large amount — and unrolled the panorama of the seven seas and the seventy lands for the boy, who seemed to enjoy it vastly. And of COURSE a few score other people happened in from time to time, Mary Vorse, not very lit, her Mary Ellen, summoned in for Freeman to play with and exciting far less zest in his young Norse bosom than in that of Mr. Sheehan, and Ferdinand Reyher, putting in an occasional softly whispered story about Leland Powers or George Seldes when Floyd paused for breath.

AND Freeman went through the House of Harcourt, guided by Don, and liked it a lot. And this morning when Freeman and I sat talking, in casually dropped Frank Adams and Anthony Adams the Chocolate Drop, and then Grace Brown from Berlin — hern Dave have been here some time and she wants to consider renting our apartment for next summer — I rather like the idea; Dave is a careful fellow and I don't believe they'd have many wild parties.

And all the time you are gone and even when your darling voice comes in clearly from Quebec or Ottawa, it is so far away!

h

During June of 1929 Dorothy's series on Canada and prohibition appeared throughout the country and requests for her
services as a journalist and lecturer became more frequent.
Thomas Costain, then an editor at the *Saturday Evening Post*,
told Red his very important periodical would be interested in
some work from her; it was the beginning of an association
which, later on — and especially from 1932 to 1936 — was the
foundation of her work in Europe during a critical period.
Just in this year, however, she and Red were together at Twin
Farms almost the entire summer. I was there also for a week
or ten days in the autumn: it was the visit on which Red used
to lock me in my bedroom to finish a short story I was writing.

"Get to work, you good-for-nothing Harry Lewis," he would
say. "Let me hear that typewriter clacking!"

He was himself working on *Ann Vickers* at this time, at least
on its earlier sketches, although his perennial "labor novel"
(never to be written) was much to the fore. He spoke of it a
great deal and did some preliminary work on it later in the
year — along with other interests — in Pittsburgh and some
southern factory towns. We were an industrious household,
as Dorothy was also engaged on something (I think for the
Post). I remember my own visit to Twin Farms as a happy
one — Red was not drinking much alcohol, and his nerves
always benefited by a diet of beer or water. We walked quite
a lot and he seemed in high spirits. *Dodsworth*, which had been
published in March, was going great guns both in America and
England, some extremely lucrative short stories of Red's were
appearing in *Cosmopolitan*, and the general outlook appeared
rosy. At this time the work was going forward on the other,
the "big house," it would be ready for occupancy in another
summer, although it was not then as large as it afterwards
became when Dorothy added another wing. It seems to me
that Clarence Darrow, Ben Stolberg and others of note were
guests at the farm, although not at the same time I was: there

was not so much room in those days. Carl Van Doren, of course, one of Red's most valued friends, paid a visit, as he continued to do for some years. I do not believe that any observer would have said, after a visit to Vermont, that Dorothy and Red could not make a permanent marriage; I doubt if any premonition afflicted their friends, even though the preceding winter in New York had not been all it might have been. The agitations of New York seemed far away in the leafy, lovely summer on Twin Farms — as we all felt for many years thereafter. Peggy Wilson, Dorothy's sister, who spent some part of almost every summer on Twin Farms, has told me only recently that she can remember hardly anything but gaiety and good will from all those years. She feels, in retrospect, that only an excess of alcohol ever made Red misbehave, be rude to Dorothy or quarrel with others. This is perhaps not the larger and deeper truth, since Red's own misery (that which drove him to drink) was unconquerable, but it is the happy memory of a very great friend who was more often at Twin Farms than anybody else.

"I've always wanted a sister," Red used to say to Peggy, "and I'm grateful to Dorothy for giving me one."

At this moment Red, always a great man for cats, had a quantity of them in his stables, including, I believe, that big white Angora which was the ancestor of so many generations of white cats in the neighborhood. To this very day white kittens with long hair, bearing the unmistakable Angora resemblance, are sometimes born in that countryside. Red had brought the original from Europe; I think Ramon Guthrie had given him another. Ramon, too, was a visitor that summer, and is mentioned in a letter to Dorothy which must have been written during a brief absence (it is dated only "Friday"). The Cunninghams and Annie are servants; Fräulein, Bongo, Monkey, and Nuisance are all cats; Donald was the farmer of the moment. The cats, in other letters as well as this one, are not distinguished from the people in Red's way of writing.

[1929]
Friday

It was SEVENTEEN eggs, in all, that our handsome hens had produced by dinnertime last evening — less than twenty-four hours. With six adults in the house, you and me, the Cunninghams, Annie, and the cook — that would be three apiece. If we don't have too many guests, maybe we'll sell some . . . Unless the foxes, the weasels, Fraulein, Bongo, Monkey, Nuisance, the pip, and other Acts of God all get busy.

A grand clear cool day after a general raininess yesterday. Donald is plowing up a small field — in a good location, along the road between the two houses — for corn for the chicks. Ramon is sagely writing. So, as this proves, am I. And Fraulein sleeps in the sun between spasms of beating up her cheerful son.

Lookit. Read the enclosed Apartment House story and keep it for me — to remember names. I met Guy McCanles in Kansas City. He is not at all the saintly, ministerial gent that he looks in his picture. He is a real Wild Westerner, fond of booze and bad language, shrewd as the devil, fond of quoting Longfellow and gents far less elegant than Longfellow. Different though he is from Judge Bartlett, he belongs equally to the vanishing Pioneer American. Well. He is coming to New York soon, and I want to see him. If he calls up before I arrive, welcome him and give him some good Scotch . . . I have a low plan of getting him to send Kenneth Birkhead to Harvard . . . Possibility.

Dolly!
Smitty

The "Carl" of the next two letters is Carl Haessler of the Federated Press, with whom Red hoped to get to work on the

long-projected labor novel. Dorothy had gone to New York
to open the house in Tenth Street and then to go west for some
lectures.

TWIN FARMS   [1929]
BARNARD, VERMONT

Thur. Oct. 31

Good morning!
Carl got here last evening!
To work!
This is just to say that this is an important anniversary of
missing you — missing you last year, when you were in NY
and I here closing the house, missing you two years ago when
you had gone to Russia. You see to it that next year, Oct. 31,
you are with me!

h

HOTEL STATLER   BOSTON   [1929]
PARK SQUARE AT ARLINGTON STREET

Tues. morning
Nov. 12th

No, I don't think the kitties looked a bit wishful when I
left; Monkey dangled her white mittens with elegant Episcopalian elegance, & looked the superior look of a small cat
(i.e. pet) who has just caught a mouse in the kitchen. But I
was wistful enough as I took a last sulky tramp three writing-
rooms, pink room, our room, livingroom & the happy rest.
And the morning was horrible — the road as far as the
mail-box like a wriggle of wet smoke-tracks, rain steady from
a depressing sky . . . & Jo & Fred on the edge of a Light.
So I was really glad to get going. And here we are! Last
evening Carl & I spent with an old woman who remembers

pre-Civil-War days & the Underground R.R. Today we see
Sherman, great employer of Labor Spies . . . Friday I see
Dotty!
Have you seen good notice of "Pep" in Nov. Vanity Fair?

October, 1929, was the month of the great crash on Wall
Street which in turn led into the great depression. It may be
worth recording that Red Lewis had quite accurately predicted
the crash, in a newspaper interview on his arrival with Dorothy
the year before (August, 1928). I have never thought this was
very remarkable; I did the same myself, and surely it was not
beyond the capacity of any adult to see that a speculative orgy
of the kind that had been flourishing must so end. However,
hardly anybody of my acquaintance foresaw how terrible the
results were to be for the working people of the country — the
hunger and despair which were to invade the richest of all
countries. It was too soon, in 1929, to see the picture in all its
somber gloom. Red had some instinct, just the same: he was
more and more intent upon writing his labor novel, if he could,
and in those months before Christmas, 1929, he made some
journeys (to Marion, North Carolina, and to Pittsburgh)
which were partly for contemporary journalism and partly as
reconnaissance for the novel.

Dorothy at this same time had undertaken a lecture tour —
the first of many — and would be away from New York for
some weeks. Red went to Toronto in mid-October for the
convention of the American Federation of Labor, met a labor
journalist there named Carl Haessler, and asked him to come
along and help (for $150 a week and expenses) on this prelim-
inary work. Haessler went back with him to Twin Farms and
from there on the other journeys of that autumn.

Red, of course, could hardly get into an atmosphere of labor
agitation, journalism and (roughly speaking) public affairs
without taking some part himself. It was beyond his capacity
to remain a spectator in the midst of such excitements. Thus,

when he got to Pittsburgh, he took a most active interest in the trial of a miner named Salvatore Accorsi, accused of murdering a state trooper at a meeting of protest on the Sacco-Vanzetti case two years before; the evidence was fabricated and Red was indignant; perhaps his interest had something to do with the outcome, for Accorsi was acquitted. Similarly he attacked General Smedley Butler for Marine excesses in Nicaragua. He wrote from this trip:

FORT PITT HOTEL

PITTSBURGH

[postmarked 12/6/29]

Dr. 6th

The enclosed is the only dirt I have been able to stir up today, & writing it up for the Nation kept me busy till afternoon. But we've begun to Establish Contacts & I expect to spend tomorrow prowling thru steel mills & their villages. Monday begins the trial of Accarsi [Accorsi] whom the State Police are trying to frame on a murder trial — re the killing of a State Trooper after the troopers had violently broken up a Sacco-Vanzetti meeting 2 years ago. We've met the defense attorney safternoon, & we'll be at the trial.

No I haven't — haven't had one drink since the day after Thanksgiving, not even in these furrin' parts.

Has the check from Ray Long come? If not, will you please phone his secretary & ask where it was sent? I'll be here @ Fort Pitt hotel maybe a week. And — I adore you.

Col. S.P.B. Mais

Sunday

I am so horribly sorry to hear about the teeth that must come out. My littlest one — my littlest one! Yesterday we spent in exploring Rankin, edge of Braddock & one of the dirtiest, most smoky steel surburbs here. I felt depressed after it; I would have given so much to be able to fly back & sit with you by the fire . . . . just now I'm off to an I.L.D. protest meeting @ Ambridge; then meet some Liberal professors. Lookit; I'm paying the Edison Co. bill, but note that we're still charged for the basement. Will you phone & have this corrected, & praps get rebate? And on Brentano (1 W. 47) bill (also paid today): have you received the Survey of Internat. Affairs? If not, please phone. They were intended as a surprise for you — a pre-X-mas present

Sunday evening

Pore ole General Butler! He's got himself in so Dutch — with my kind help — see enclosed. The N.Y. Herald-Trib of today also carried good story, on front page of 1st news-section . . . AND I enclose a couple of Russian clips, one about Litvinoff; AND a picture of Amolbe[?]. WHY didn't we go to Amolbe?

All day today, seeing mines & mine villages (horrible) & miners, with a Univ prof who knows em. Good night, my littlest one!

H

[postmarked 12/10/29]
Monday 11 PM

Gee I'm tired — I'm going right away now to bed yet . . . As there is much mention of Accarsi in my letters now, I enclose this reprint of 2 years ago. For the murder of the cop — see pencil-marked part of report — an Italian named Accarsi has been arrested — 2 years after the event. It seems clearly a frame-up on the part of the State cops so that they may continue their bluff that they "always get their man. Apparently Accarsi was no where near the meeting or the killing . . . Yesterday, we went to an Italian Accarsi protest out in the American Bridge Co. town of Ambridge. Only about 90 protesters in the bare little Croatian Hall — with maybe 20 cops in plain clothes scattered thru & consequent feeling of strain, as everybody expected the speakers to be clubbed & arrested. Today the trial began; all day they were choosing jurors, but it was darn interesting. I chose about half the jurors — No, honest, I did! It's too long a story to write; I'll tell it to you when I come home (horray!) if you remind me. Citizen Buttunsky, b' God. Sevening, we dined with our three pals, the defense lawyers for Accarsi — old friends — one of them we'd met once before today, & the other two we met long, long ago — quite early this morning.

And so virtuously, to bed, to dream of

Mrs. Ket!

Dear Mrs. Ket!

FORT PITT HOTEL

PITTSBURGH

Fri — Dec. 13   1929

Who says Friday the 13th is unlucky? Accarsi was acquitted today! — the first serious blow to the State Police. The jury went out @ close of session yesterday; this morning we were at the court at 9:30 sharp, very sharp, even heroically sacrificing a second cup of coffee to get there. But the jury was not ready to report & tho' I'd believed in acquittal, I was awfully worried. They did not report till 10:30. The courtroom was tense as a stage scene. "Jury look upon the prisoner — prisoner look upon the jury." Accarsi (small, slim, resolute) was evidently a bundle of jangling nerves but he stood up, shoulders back, soldierly. Then the verdict, "Not guilty!" & I almost cried — so did Jake Margolis, defense attorney! . . . But as the jury came in I *knew* it'd be an acquittal, because I saw the eyes of Mrs. Schneider, the one woman on the jury, & they were shining . . . And the ass't district attorney benevolently shook hands with Accarsi whom yesterday he was trying to railroad, knowing damn well he was innocent . . . one shouldn't hold a little thing like that against him!

And then, me, I catches me a taxicab & goes out to the U of Pittsburgh to speak lovingly to mebbe 2500 students about their ignorance. (Heh? Me. I'm not ignorant — I was brought up in a Ketolic College.)

And since then I have Rested, and this evening — having refused about 4 dinner dates along of being SO Busy — I'm either going to a movie or going to read a detective story. I'll see you in a week now — you *darling!*

To Washington, D.C., Monday nite; home probably Thur. PM next.

> Phurgh
> (don't laugh)
> Saturday

Lil presents enclosed. AND I slept till ten this morning, & loaf till six — sevening we meet some liberal lawyers, then Ben's friend Professor Tyson of U. of Pitt . . . Tomorrow & Monday, inspect mines, & Westinghouse. Then to Washington.

> I adore you!

A pup
(or a ket)
(or a moos)

PS

Oh, *hon*-ey, will you please buy & send to Fred & Jo Rothermell a handsome Xmas basket, with luxuries they can't get in Vt but that won't freeze @ mail box — send parcel post — it'll be too late when I get back NY . . . AP story just came Secy Adams of Navy will investigate Genl Butler.

In haste

The Rothermells, Fred and his wife Jo, were friends whom Red had induced to keep the farmhouse open in Vermont during the winter of 1929–1930 so that, if he took the notion to do so, he could go up there and work. He never did so, and indeed the temperatures, the roads, the furnace, the deep snows and all the other conditions of life in a Vermont winter made the idea rather fantastic. It could be done far more easily today, when the roads are better and snow plows more common, but in 1929–1930 Twin Farms was really isolated from November to March or April. Years afterwards I spent a winter on Twin Farms and it was one long struggle from beginning to end. I find it difficult to imagine Red putting up with it for more than a few days.

2

DOROTHY WAS DOING WELL ON HER LECTURE TOUR, GETTING used to the audiences and learning how to formulate in spoken words what (at first) came so much easier in writing. She was just as keenly aware of the import of Red's labor novel as he was, since it had been so thoroughly discussed that summer. She tended — like an European intellectual, perhaps under the influence of Ben Stolberg — to take Eugene Debs lightly, even though he had been essentially the hero of Red's projected work and was (later on) to resume that position in Red's mind. Of course Lewis was a creator rather than an intellectual, and it was *character* he needed as a point of departure. I doubt if he had ever really read Karl Marx beyond the usual college-boy skimming of the first volume of *Das Kapital*. Dorothy's letters from Terre Haute on October 27th, 1929 — two of them on the same day — not only give a taste of how she thought and wrote on such subjects, but show most vividly how different her mind was from Red's. His letters, most of them hasty scrawls, are full of a kind of extemporaneous assurance of love, along with the merest hit-or-miss account of what he was doing; hers are long, thoughtful, and at times rather elaborate, as if there were some thought (conscious or unconscious) that eyes other than his might some day see them.

HOTEL DEMING,
TERRE HAUTE, INDIANA.

Oct. 27, 1929.
Sunday.

To
Sinclair Lewis.[1]

Mrs Eugene Debs came to my meeting and afterward we had a long talk at my hotel. (Theodore was not in town). She looks only middle-aged, fresh-cheeked and wistful. She wore a pretty lilac silk frock, and looked incredibly middle class. We found it difficult to talk because she is rather deaf, and all of her life is lived in the past before Eugene's death. I found that she follows the radical news as from a vast distance. "I never hear of socialism any more," she said. "None of Eugene's old friends and followers ever write to

---

[1] This superscription, so odd in a letter from wife to husband, appears only in this one letter.

me. As long as he was alive he seemed able to keep the movement going somewhat but since then — I guess it's all over
now." She enjoys a certain uneasy respect from the middle
class lady members of the "Women's Department Club"
(1100 members: interests: "intellectual progress") and has
settled down into their society. She herself is material for a
novel.

God, it's a lonesome business, this speaking. I'm stuck
here for twenty-four hours. I've been reading Artur
Bodansky's [Bodanzky] in the Satevepost and wondering
how I might establish some contact with that truly cosmopolitan group at the opera in N.Y. Hal, darling, I *ache* for
a society in which I feel at home. The evening at Von
Tippelskirch's was like a draught of champagne to me. But
what shall I do this winter in N.Y., with you not there &
Gertrude always there, and no contacts at all! Neither
personal nor professional. You see, I'm in a depressed mood.
Oh, well —

I feel very strange, neither sick nor well, & troubled with
the most awful dreams — dreams which would give Freud
to think. Last night, for instance, I sweated in terror,
because I had poisoned a servant with arsenic & the police
were on my trail. Then I dreamed I had become implicated
in helping Fanchon Arthur (friend of my adolescence) escape
from a convent![1] These dreams are all the worse because I
seem to desire nothing but sleep. I am not ill, but every
day I develop a new symptom. All yesterday I had headache:
today I throb from my hips down. But I haven't had that
beastly indigestion at all.

You seem, darling, so far away. In fact all of my life seems
far away.

[1] Exactly this did happen many years later — one of the most curious examples of a
dream coming true, literally true, in my knowledge. Fanchon Arthur visited Twin
Farms twenty-five years later.

I want to write you a love letter, but I can't. I don't know why I can't. But it would be like writing to someone imaginary. Do you exist, and are you you, and what *is* you? I have known so many yous. And if I wrote you a love letter would it reach the you to which it was written, or another, a stranger?

But I'd like to write you a love letter. Yes I would.

Whether it's a girl or a boy I *won't* have him or her brought up in this country. I *won't*.

She said with a flash of the old spirit.

D.

3

DOROTHY'S SECOND LETTER FROM TERRE HAUTE, WRITTEN ON the same day, shows the critical edginess with which she was making acquaintance, as if for the first time, with her own country.

October 27th(again) 1929.

I've just come from a long walk through Terre Haute — and you may tell the world that Zenith and Main Street haven't changed unless possibly for the worse. What impresses one especially is the cheapness of all standards, the shoddiness of all values. I walked through the whole shopping section very carefully. It seemed to me that nearly half of all the stores belonged to chain systems which handle especially cheap goods. Five ten and twenty-five cent stores are innumerable. You can furnish a house and almost clothe yourself from them. Not only Woolworth's and Kresge's but lots of others the names of which I had never heard — the "Grand",

McCrory's, etc. Then there was Marshall Fields', Piggly
Wiggly, chain drug stores, etc.

Clothing as displayed in the windows of all stores — chain
and otherwise — is cheap and shoddy: there was a store
specializing in women's dresses at $2.99; the average price
for shoes seemed about $5.50; coats trimmed with poor
quality fur in vast quantities cost from $25 to $39, which
seems to be about a top price. This means, of course, that
people are fashionably but shoddily clothed. Almost all the
stores, including clothing shops, offered their goods on credit,
and instalment paying.

Of course there is no theater or any other center for any
kind of art life. All the theaters are talkies or movies. But
more than that — there is as far as I can see not a single
public place in town where you can meet anyone for a quiet
talk , . This hotel is comfortable, rooms convenient, food
fair. But there is no public lounge where you can hear
yourself think. The radio is on at full blast from 9 a.m. to
midnight. I tried to talk with Mrs Debs and I had a Pilgrim's
Chorus and a "humorous" lecture to contend with. You
can't get a cup of afternoon tea in this hotel: dining room
closed between lunch and dinner. The drug stores are the
only other meeting places and they are noisy with traffic and
radio.

The houses are atrocious. The town still burns lots of soft
coal, evidently, and most of the houses are painted a dingy
gray turned almost black with smoke. They usually have
small front lawns, ragged and smoke-blackened. All of them
have their narrow verandahs on the front, in full view of the
public. There is no standardization of architecture whatsoever. The streets are a hodge podge of ugly frame houses,
also flimsily built and cheap. In fact cheapness is the main
thing.

And yet everyone seems contented. After my lecture

yesterday a lot of women came up to speak to me and almost all of them said, "Well, aren't we lucky to be living in America."

I know I am not telling you anything — but I want to put my own impressions down.

Darling — I am so lonely. This is a lonely country. It is so Goddamed *empty*. I am turning mystic. Surely there is something different in the very air of a city where civilized people have lived, worked, dreamed, loved and enjoyed civilized pleasures for hundreds of years. Living must produce some sort of radio-activity which lingers in the atmosphere. I begin to believe in ghosts. Gentle ghosts which keep one company in ancient towns. Here there are none.

It is significant that Debs came from Terre Haute. He could not be otherwise than sentimental and ineffective. —

D.

Where shall I write you next?

8

Love in Absence

FOR A WOMAN WHO HAD NEVER HAD A BABY "OR ANYTHING" (Dorothy's own phrase, as well I remember) thirty-six was thought to be rather old for child-bearing. As it turned out, she had not the slightest trouble either during the pregnancy or at the birth of her son, but all that winter of 1929–1930 it worried her. Some doctor — not our friend Traeger but some gynecologist — had planted this fear in her usually fearless brain. Consequently she had not the faintest desire to go traveling: she wanted to stay quietly in Tenth Street, hibernating comfortably with her own doctors at hand and the Woman's Hospital not too far away.

Quiet hibernation was impossible for Red's tortured and restless nature. Even if they had stayed in Tenth Street it would not have been even remotely tranquil. Except on Twin Farms (and sometimes even there) Red's very presence provoked cyclonic disturbances. Now, for no reason anybody knew, he took it into his head to go to California, to the haunts of his youth (Carmel and Monterey), and find a house for the winter. He did have one excuse — he had to appear in court at Reno, to get his alimony to Gracie reduced — but he could easily have gone to Nevada and back without disturbing Dorothy. Not he: as always, his will prevailed, and they departed, bag and baggage, for a sojourn which Dorothy mistrusted in advance and greatly disliked before it was over. Professor Schorer's valuable biography of Red says that she returned to

New York believing that her marriage had failed and that she must try to build a life of her own. (As we have seen, she was headed in that direction even the winter before.) I have no doubt that Dorothy herself told Professor Schorer this, but if I have correctly understood the documents — many of them reproduced in this book — as well as my own memory, she had more hope than conviction from the very start. During that winter, on return from four or five months in Jerusalem, I found a flat of my own and furnished it, so as to remain in New York, writing short stories, until (I think) late 1932. The flat was in Twenty-eighth Street, not too far from Dorothy and Red, and I saw a great deal of them together during December, January, April and May of 1929–1930. I was not to see them together often again, although through the decades I was in fairly constant association with them separately. It is remarkable how many reasons they could find (even before their avowed separation) to be apart. There were a few more summers at Twin Farms (and even these much interrupted) but the concept of a life in common, a life together, seems to have faded rapidly after the birth of their child. That event (June 20th, 1930), which is supposed to reconcile parents in an embrace loving if not indissoluble, performed no such miracle for Dorothy and Red. It is very doubtful if Red ever should have married; it is quite certain that he should not have had a child. Dorothy, perhaps? — but we must return to the winter of 1930.

They found a house in California with a luxuriant garden and Red continued to talk about his labor novel, although even then I suspect that it was dawning on him how impossible it would be to write. There were too many acquaintances on the California coast, and Red was (as always when not deep in work) drinking too much. It can be said of most writers, as of most composers and painters, that work is their one salvation, but never have I seen anybody of whom it was more true than it was of poor Red. He could work like a regiment of engineers,

cold sober, implacable in his resolution; but when he did not
have work to do (which, in his mind, meant a very big novel,
nothing less) he lost his power altogether and became a weak,
tremulous thing for whom one could feel only pity.

They returned to New York in April and — after a brief
journey to Twin Farms to see that the house was cleaned and
opened properly — Dorothy returned to Tenth Street to await,
through May and June, the birth of her child. They were not
quiet weeks and as a matter of fact quarrels between Dorothy
and Red became frequent and, as it seemed to me, utterly unreasonable. She was nervous over her pregnancy and he was
drinking: that was enough. Any tiny thing would be enough
to cause a quarrel under those conditions.

They had not agreed, of course, about the winter in California, either before, during or after. To Dorothy it was disagreeable because Red's condition was not good and he was
constantly being interviewed by hordes of newspaper reporters
and, according to her ideas, making a fool of himself; most of
the people they knew on that coast were rich and fashionable,
and she knew in her bones that they were making fun of Red
even when they invited him to their houses; she could have
dealt with them all, by herself, but she was self-conscious over
a pregnancy for which, she was convinced, she was too old.
Dorothy had a great deal of pride, along with other things, and
the winter in California had offended her pride.

One thing I remember about it (she told me often enough)
was a dinner party at a very grand household somewhere out
there when Colonel Charles Augustus Lindbergh played one of
his practical jokes by putting Listerine in the priceless Burgundy which had been decanted on a sideboard. Colonel Lindbergh had been much addicted to practical jokes when he was
an ordinary pilot (before his flight to Paris in 1927); I had
heard much of these from other pilots. And, of course, in 1930
Lindbergh was still very young. No doubt he never drank wine

(I think this is so) and it would not have occurred to him that to some people, in an era of prohibition, very good Burgundy was a rare and precious thing. However it may be, he did play that joke and to Dorothy, who had a real respect for good wine, it was an atrocious one. She never forgot it; it formed, or helped to form, her impression of him; and ten years later, when he spoke for the isolationists (the America First Committee) and she was one of the leading interventionists in the early stages of World War II, she made two tremendous attacks upon him which, to all intents and purposes, removed him from public life. I do not believe that Dorothy could have been so thunderous on this subject if she had not retained a vivid personal distaste based upon the experience of that practical joke. To a pregnant woman at a dinner party with total strangers a glass of Burgundy with Listerine in it must have been a horrid infliction.

Furthermore, the winter in California — far more than anything that ever happened in New York — was disagreeable in that everybody, from the newspaper reporters to the rich and fashionable hostesses, treated Dorothy as the little woman. Red was the most famous American writer and one of the most famous living Americans; Dorothy was his pregnant wife. She had never been treated like this before. Indeed, on their arrival in New York from Europe — as on other occasions in London and Berlin — she had given tongue very freely on the subjects that interested her, and she had been quoted in the press just as much, or almost as much, as her all-too-famous husband. In California she was not only second fiddle but she did not, in fact, exist except as an appendage to Red. This was to her a barbaric and unpleasant novelty. It played a part (I know full well) in her resolution to create a career of her own as soon as she could do so.

Red stayed in Los Angeles a few days after she left, ostensibly to sell a car he had bought, and instead of selling it he hired a chauffeur to drive him back to Monterey in it. (He was too far gone in alcohol to trust his own driving.) His letter about these vicissitudes is characteristic and, I think, amusing. Red's little jokes may have been childish but they were his own (not repeated from a smoking room) and I always thought them funny. The letter:

> Monterey
> Friday Apr 11
>   1930

Dearest Mrs. Small:

It proved hard to get a decent price for the Buick in L.A. — town full of used cars for sale, so Wednesday I comes up here. I took a driver & we made the whole 380 miles in one day, eleven hours straight driving. I hope I never do *that* again. I was exhausted when I got in, & all I remember of the drive is a strip of hills. Yesterday I started the diplomatic negociations necessary for the sale of the car. I hope to complete them today & be off to San Francisco tonight or tomorrow morning. Leastways I *spose* I have to go to S.F. to get to Kansas City — I'm going straight through. I spect you'll see me in N.Y. in about ten days. Oh lamb, I do miss you so!

It's been sweet to see the Morrises & Fishes & (somewhat less so) the Darmodys again. How they all love you! How they inquire after you & express such sincere unhappiness that you are not here with me. And — what you would most have enjoyed — when I arrived here, at 8 P.M., I walked in on a dinner party given by the Morrises to Dr. & Mrs. Becking & the Macks. Becking sends you his love in terms so fervid that I refuse to transmit them. The Morrises are craftily on the trail to get more money raised for his lab — that's why they had him with the Macks. for dinner. His (Becking's) wife is nice but non-committal.

Our only party yesterday — last evening we sat around,
just the family, reading aloud a joyous super-Saki book that
you must get at once, "Vile Flesh" by Evelyn Waugh — was
tea at the house of a Big Game Hunter named Boomhower
(try it on your saxophone) on the Peninsula. If, with your
fictional mind, you pictured the house of a Big Game Hunter,
what would you expect? Lions' heads on the wall & rhi-
noceroses & wapite & bilbaos & woof-woofs, with rugs of
retired lionesses with menacing mugs? Well, b' God, that's
just what he has! And he tells you that this particularly
demised head is that eg the Lion that Almost Got Him.
Yet a nice chap. Life is too much for me. I'm going to
retire from novelling & become a — a — a Big Game Hunter.
But not till I see you.

Kermit Roosevelt

Why Red says *Vile Flesh* when he means *Vile Bodies* I cannot explain, since he was (like most writers) fanatical about
getting titles straight. It does not look like one of his jokes.
The handwriting is hasty and sprawly and I can only conjec-
ture that he may have been a wee bit drunk. As for the persons
named, I assume that "the Morrises" must be Mr and Mrs
Gouverneur Morris, who lived out there, but I know nothing
of the others.

2

RED TOOK A ROOM AT THE OLD HOTEL LAFAYETTE FOR WORKING
purposes when he got back to New York in April. This was in
accordance with a fixed habit of his: he always thought he
could concentrate better in a place where there were no inter-
ruptions, no telephone calls and no household cares. It is, in
fact, a good system for somebody who is really working, but

if a man is merely marking time, as Red was that spring, it is
a delusion and a snare. What happened was that Red was in
constant communication with his bootlegger. He had his own
telephone put in, with a secret number, and he had the hotel's
telephone cut off. Thus he could call whom he pleased but
could not be called by anybody except Dorothy, and even she
was under the strictest orders not to call except in an emergency. The household was delighted to have him removed from
Tenth Street (he was always dreadful and in fact incomprehensible to any household). Dorothy could rest peacefully,
reading and writing, all day long, unless Red took it into his
head to telephone to her, which he did at unpredictable
intervals.

There occurred one of those mishaps which Red was constantly provoking or creating, and I tell it because his sense
of humor, too, like Colonel Lindbergh's, was sometimes too
much for Dorothy.

He had, as his contemporaries all knew, an inveterate passion for imitations. He imitated person, place or thing; he
imitated word or accent, phrase or idea; he imitated sermon
or sales talk. He could do this best on the telephone, of course,
where that unique face of his did not interfere with the impression. And he was particularly fond of his German imitations,
which were, as a matter of fact, rather like Mark Twain's
written German (in *The Innocents Abroad*) in structure and
feeling, although pronounced with a rich, beery accent which
I am sure Mark Twain could never manage. His Swedish,
Yugoslav, Polish and Russian imitations came next in line.
(His English imitations were frequent but very bad — he never
could manage to sound in the least English or Irish or Scottish.)

It suited Red, one afternoon as he nursed his bottle of whisky
at the Lafayette Hotel, to telephone Dorothy in a German accent. He was extremely convincing. He was Professor Doktor
Schatzheimer of the faculty of literature in the University of

Leipzig and he wanted to talk to Mr Le-vis or, in default of Mr Le-vis, to Mrs Le-vis, about some points of importance which had been found difficult of comprehension in the honored and respected works of Mr Le-vis. Dorothy talked to him at great length, both in German and in English, until he finally broke down and told her to desist. Two or three days later he did the same thing to her in a Swedish accent, varying the details of the impersonation, and again she believed him (such calls were not infrequent anyhow).

On the very next day a truly most eminent professor from Berlin called her and started the same sort of prolegomenon. Dorothy, who had been trying to write a short story, lost her temper and cut him short. "Come off it, you son of a bitch," she said. "I know you. You can't fool me again." So far as I know this imbroglio never did get straightened out; it was too embarrassing for everybody; the eminent professor must have carried back to Berlin a peculiar idea of the home life of the American writer.

And then, just at this time, Red elected to get angry with Alfred Harcourt about something — or, as I should prefer to put it, about nothing. He had never really forgiven Alfred for refusing to give him a collected and uniform edition. (Scribner's had given one to Henry James twenty-some years before and I think this is what stuck in Red's craw.) As a matter of fact Alfred was wrong: he not only owed Red some such token of esteem for the millions that had been earned by the Lewis novels from *Main Street* to *Dodsworth*, but he could have cashed in on the project. For one thing, Red himself would have bought thousands and thousands and thousands of dollars' worth of the thing in order to send them to those writers he so tremendously admired, Mr Wells, Mr Shaw and Mr Galsworthy, as well as to his beloved Mrs Wharton and a dozen others. (And half the population of Minnesota.)

Anyhow, Red was angry with Alfred and overnight was

ready to change publishers. (A letter which he chose to think
impertinent, written by a junior in the Harcourt firm, was the
immediate cause of the outbreak: it had been brewing for some
time, just the same.) Along with the pregnancy, the alcoholism,
the endless parties and the quarrels about nothing, Dorothy
now had to face the neurotic tension which surrounds a very
great "literary property" when it is about to change hands.
Every publisher in New York knew instantly, by telepathy I
suppose, that Red was going to leave Harcourt. Every publisher in New York wanted him — and why not? Nothing so
lucrative had been seen in years! I can remember evenings in
Tenth Street when rival publishers, pretending the suavity of
Versailles, looked at each other as if their hearts cried out for
murder.

For the gatherings in Tenth Street never ceased. It was
Red's custom to encourage callers. Wherever he lived, in whatever country or under whatever conditions, he liked to have
people streaming in and out of his quarters, and rather in than
out. It was as much as your life was worth to go home when
he was in certain moods. You *had* to sit there. He even expected to find you there when he returned from one of those
hour-long naps he was forever taking. And although this (the
assembly of the callers) was as a rule between five and seven
in the evening, it could be prolonged indefinitely and in any
case was continued, after dinner, from nine until all hours. In
addition to this daily charivari there were some occasions when
Dorothy, fighting for her life, would deliberately give a party
and invite the guests and hope that they, and *only* they, would
come.

Such an evening was that of June 19th, 1930. The two rooms
in Tenth Street which were used for parties, a sitting room at
the front and a dining room behind it, were crowded. H. R.
Knickerbocker, our old friend, who had succeeded Dorothy as
correspondent for the Curtis newspapers in Berlin, was on a

Dorothy and Red Lewis, photographed by Edward Steichen,
in the early 1930's.

Dorothy Thompson and Sinclair Lewis in Berlin, 1927–1928, the time of their meeting and courtship.

The drawing room of Dorothy's flat at Händelstrasse 8, across from the Tiergarten in Berlin. It was here (at her thirty-third birthday dinner party on July 9, 1927) that Red met Dorothy and immediately asked her to marry him.

At the Ungarische Weinhaus, Vienna, in the fall of 1927. Left to right: John Gunther, Marcel Fodor, Martha Fodor, Frances Gunther, Dorothy and Red.

Dorothy in Red Square, Moscow, in November of 1927, while covering the tenth anniversary of the Bolshevik Revolution.

1928

wire me your
Paris ad-
dress.

SAVOY HOTEL,
LONDON,
W.C.2.

monday

Dearest: This is about the last letter I can get through to you. And it's just to send you the enclosed letter — I fancy from your sister — + to tell you that I love you, forever, my dear!

And Reyher is here — just found him today, I think he will be here

FOR
OUR
WEDDING!

I love love love you!

Red's letter to Dorothy of May 1928, a few days before their marriage. *Courtesy of Syracuse University Library.*

Mr and Mrs Sinclair Lewis just after their wedding at Savoy Chapel, London, on May 14, 1928. *Courtesy of Syracuse University Library.*

Visiting with Hugh Walpole in the garden of his Lake District home during a honeymoon stopover. *Courtesy of Syracuse University Library.*

On the steps of the honeymoon caravan in which they toured the English countryside during the summer of 1928. Red worked on *Dodsworth* and reported the trip for the *Herald Tribune;* Dorothy kept a diary (Chapter V). *Courtesy of Wide World Photos.*

The newlywed Lewises, left, in London shortly after their marriage and, above, returning to the United States on the *Hamburg* in late August 1928. (Long after, Dorothy referred to the polo coat photograph in a 1937 letter to Red. See p. 293.) *Photo above courtesy of Culver Pictures, Inc.*

The original old farmhouse at Twin Farms, Barnard, Vermont, later called "Red's House" and still later "Jimmy's House," when it was occupied by Vincent Sheean.

The Big House (or "Dorothy's House") at Twin Farms as it became after extensive remodeling. The large window at right is that of the "Big Room" created by Red from the original barn. *Courtesy of John L. Warner.*

Dorothy with Michael Lewis, born in June 1930. *Courtesy of Syracuse University Library.*

Red Lewis, the first American to win the Nobel Prize in literature revisiting Berlin in December 1930, after receiving the award i Stockholm. (Beyond the balcony of the Adlon Hotel are the Branden burg Gate and Unter den Linden.) *Courtesy of Wide World Photo.*

At Dorothy's 1932 Christmas house party, Semmering, Austria, a few miles above Vienna. *Opposite, above:* left to right, Edgar Mowrer, Baron Hatvany, Christa Winsloe (Baroness Hatvany, author of *Mädchen in Uniform*), Red Lewis. *Below:* the party in one of its gayer moods. At left, Red Lewis; Virgilia Peterson is the dark-haired young woman in the background, between Marcel Fodor (with glasses) and Christa Winsloe (in trench coat and slouch hat); Dorothy is the second passenger on the sled, leaning against Lilian Mowrer. At right with camera is Edgar Mowrer.

This page: Red with unidentified companion in front of the Villa Sauerbrunn, Semmering, during the ten-day-long house party.

Red Lewis writing at Twin Farms in the 1930's.

In the mid 1930's with sculptor Jo Davidson. The bust was later presented to Dorothy by Mrs. James Roosevelt, the president's mother. *Courtesy of Lotte Jacobi.*

On shipboard with four-year-old Michael in early 1935, one of their few trips together during that period. *Courtesy of Wide World Photos.*

Above: Vincent Sheean and his wife (the former Diana Forbes-Robertson) arriving in New York from Europe in early 1938. They were to make their home a year later at Twin Farms in the old farmhouse. *Courtesy of Wide World Photos.*

Opposite, above: Dorothy at the German-American Bund meeting, Madison Square Garden, New York, February 1939, just before she was bodily removed for laughing and shouting "Bunk!" (Less than five years previously, she had been expelled from Nazi Germany by Hitler's order.) *Courtesy of Wide World Photos.*

Below: Dorothy in wartime England, August 1941, visiting the Czechoslovak troops based in Britain. *Courtesy of Culver Pictures, Inc.*

1941. Wendell Willkie paying tribute to Dorothy Thompson (foreground) at a dinner in her honor at the Hotel Astor. During the 1940 presidential campaign, Dorothy had dramatically switched her support from Willkie to Roosevelt. *Courtesy of Culver Pictures, Inc.*

1941. Red Lewis with actress Marcella Powers during a road tour of his play, *Angela Is Twenty-two*. *Courtesy of United Press International*.

It was on July 8, 1927, and I had been granted a divorce in Hungary the day before, and I thought I had never seen anyone as unhappy as I except he, with a face like one who has gone through war + "flammenwerfer," and a tongue so cynical + brilliant and he said "I have been looking for you for years. Will you marry me?" And I thought "I have been looking for you, too." Then always those years of intense pleasure + blackest pain. Still the crazy conviction that he loved me + it would all add up to something. But it was so quickly over for him, or maybe never began. On that first day he said "I will buy us a house in Vermont, this shape ⌐‾⌐ and looking down a valley. And he did. And insofar as we were ever happy we were happy there. Now, to sit in the Woodstock Courthouse, charging desertion···· and to feel nothing at all, literally nothing except some faint distaste. To have felt too much is to end in feeling nothing. Four years of loneliness + agony + work, all an odyssey. The last terrible remembering in London last spring. But now it is the ratification of something that has been over + done with + not even Michael, any more, reminds me of him. "Far + forgotten like a scene in canvas."

Dorothy's diary entry, January 2, 1942, the day her divorce became
final. *Courtesy of Syracuse University Library.*

visit to America with his first wife, the lovely red-haired Laura, and this party was in their honor. It was distinctly Dorothy's party, in that none of Red's chosen people, such as Philip Goodman or George Jean Nathan or H. L. Mencken, had been invited. Dorothy's concession to her husband's weaknesses consisted in asking several publishers. There was, I suppose, some whisky somewhere (Red became unconscionably drunk), but the only drink I remember was the "Bowle," the inevitable punch bowl, a vast affair in the middle of the dining-room table, with quart ladles, into which Dorothy had then, and for thirty years thereafter, the practice of injecting innumerable products of the earth. Chief of these, as I learned on that night, was tea — I distinctly remember that she told me no "Bowle" could be made without a solid lacing of tea to hold it together. There were liqueurs in variety (most of them German) along with the tea, and the juices were manifold. Anyhow, it was a powerful dish and highly appreciated by all.

We talked, argued, narrated. Time passed. I do believe it was about two o'clock when the very last of us, out of deference to Dorothy's condition (she was then prodigiously big with child) consented to go home.

As I learned the next day, she began to have pains an hour or so later and finally woke up Red to tell him so. He declared she had had too much to eat and drink but was willing, after a telephonic consultation with a doctor, to taxi her up to the Woman's Hospital at 110th Street. It was there that their son was born the next morning (June 20th).

On the following afternoon at four thirty, according to telephoned instructions from Red, I got into a subway and went up to the Woman's Hospital to see Dorothy. She was blooming — all pink and white and relieved — and she sat up in bed and harangued me.

"Here we are," said she, "in the year 1930, with every possible advancement of science already upon us in every conceiv-

able field, and yet nothing whatsoever has been done to miti-
gate or diminish the boredom of childbirth. It is not difficult
and it is not painful, at least it was neither difficult nor painful
for me. That doctor who said that a woman of thirty-six would
have trouble with a first child must have been an idiot. I had
no trouble at all. I scarcely even noticed. But the length of
the gestation, nine months, has not changed by so much as a
moment since time began. Evolution has scarcely affected it,
although it may have had a deleterious effect upon the mam-
mary glands. A woman must be gravid, like an animal, until
the unseen forces command the delivery. This is barbarous
and utterly unworthy of those wise and great men who rule
our universe. If they can make invisible waves bring sounds —
and some say, soon, pictures — over great distances, and if
they can take the heart out and put it back again, and if they
can fly to the moon as they say they intend to do sometime,
why in God's name can't they do something about the womb
of the human woman? Why must it be subject to the same
irretrievable processes as the inner organs of the horse or the
cow? Ingenuity and humanitarianism and the combined resources of chemistry, medicine, psychopathology and surgery
are baffled, set at naught, reduced to zero, by a mechanical
automatism as familiar to prehistory as it is to you or me.
What has been the practical use of all this progress through the
centuries when a woman is faced with her fundamental and
indeed quintessential function in the life of her species, which
is to reproduce it? One might as well be a Bulgarian peasant
inured to parturition in a furrow. I protest."

If these be not the precise words, they were something of the
sort — very near it indeed. I can see Dorothy now in her pink
silk nightie, pawing the air. I may not have every word of it
but I surely have the gist of the harangue, and its general
style, too.

When she ended up with "I protest" we both laughed and

she rang a bell. A nurse came in. Dorothy lifted an imperious and well-arched eyebrow. She really felt well that day. "Bring in the child," she said.

3

THE CHILD MADE NO DIFFERENCE, SO FAR AS RED WAS CON-cerned. I believe that Dorothy was at first persuaded, along with the greater part of humanity, that a baby sealed the union of its parents. She thought everything would be different after its birth. She was herself far more placid and content, during the first six or eight months of the baby's life, than I had seen her since their marriage. I have not told the story before, and do not intend to tell it now in any detail, but there was actually a moment not very long before the baby's birth when Dorothy felt she could no longer endure life with Red and asked me to drive her to the Roosevelt Hotel where she could take refuge while she worked out her plans for a separation. This was at about midnight or afterwards, when Red had gone into his periodic coma. (One never knew that he might not be up again in half an hour demanding attention.) I did as she asked. At the Roosevelt Hotel (then new, and, incidentally, named after Theodore, not Franklin) she was in fact registering when she came to the signature and realized what it might mean. Red was at the height of his fame and she was at the peak of her pregnancy. It would have been a dreadful little item for the gutter press, which at that period paid a good deal of attention to the Lewis family. She put down the pen, apologized to the night clerk of the hotel, and asked me to take her back to Tenth Street, which I did. We never mentioned this again. I have never forgotten one detail of it, just the same, because it showed the extreme uncertainty (what is called "imbalance" nowadays) of Dorothy's mind.

After the birth of the child she cheered up considerably and the transfer to Twin Farms was made in peace. Rapidly it became apparent that Red could not endure the baby. Through the years it was more and more apparent that he could not endure either this or any other child, principally because of the noises they made but also because there was in him some bitter and ineradicable protest against the perpetuation of a life which he did not truly feel worth carrying on. His nerves were by this time completely shattered, to such an extent that he suffered tortures from any accidental plop or bang, any of the quite ordinary noises of a farm or of a city street. I saw him cringing and cowering, and I remember very well the look of horror in his pale blue eyes when any unexpected noise reached him. Under the circumstances Dorothy made the reasonable arrangement — she put the baby and his nurse into the old farmhouse ("my" house) and lodged herself and Red in the Big House which was approaching habitability. Guests also (including me during this and the next two years) stayed in the old farmhouse.

Babies cry, of course. And, after they cease to be babies, they make noise. Very much noise. None of this was possible for Red to suffer. He was much too advanced into his own neurosis, and, quite possibly, into the world of his own imagination, to take into his being a raucous, sporadic and to him intolerable interruption. His whole essence rejected it. Dorothy, in conversation, understood this.

"Yes," she would say to me, then and for some subsequent years, "I know that Red is a genius and suffers far more than we do. I have done everything possible to give him peace and quiet. I have truly tried. But his demands are too great."

Perhaps they were. Still it must be recorded that Dorothy forgot them fifteen minutes after having acknowledged them. This was her characteristic throughout their marriage and also throughout her final marriage. She would nobly and generously state her obligation and then promptly forget it. So far as the children were concerned, she knew that they drove Red to the brink of insanity and yet her principles commanded her to give "playmates" to her own. Her child had been named Michael, owing to one of Red's youthful enthusiasms for English novels (in a period when every boy was called Michael in English novels). What Dorothy did actually, believe it or not, was to engage secretaries, chauffeurs, gardeners and cooks who had children or grandchildren, so that they could be "playmates" to her son! As a result, when she went gallivanting off to Berlin, Vienna and Budapest during the next few years she left Red with such a menagerie of infants, nurses, servants and overseers that the poor man was badgered into flight. This happened over and over again. The children drove him mad, and the more they drove him mad the more she augmented their number.

Dorothy did this with the utmost good will and in accordance with her highest principles. She believed quite passionately in social and political democracy, and to her it was always important that her son's playmates should be the children of persons employed by her. (Our beloved Marie, her cook for decades, was the grandmother of the best boy of the lot, Henry, who grew up with Michael.) She would have liked the children of the neighboring farmers to join in the fray, but, so far as I could ever tell, the neighboring farmers regarded us all with the gravest suspicion and I am not aware that their children were permitted to come to Twin Farms.

Dorothy's sister Peggy had one child, Pamela, who spent almost every summer on the farm and incurred the utterly unreasonable dislike of Red at one period. Pamela was a sweet, serious child with a true desire to understand what was going on, if this were possible. I can never forget her sixth birthday, when she sat on the swing on the front porch of the old house (where I also was staying) and told me about her age. I declared that I thought this was a very good age.

"I don't know," she said with a sigh. "It's pretty old, for a woman."

In that same conversation she asked me why I was clacking away all day long at the typewriter.

I told her that it was a form of work, called writing, by which I hoped or indeed was obliged to earn my living.

"But my Aunt Dorothy is doing the same thing," she said, "and so is my Uncle Hal. Does everybody have to do the same?"

I said that I supposed everybody had to do more or less the same if they happened to work at the same trade. She heaved another of her stupendous sighs.

"*Well*," she said, accepting I suppose, but still marveling and still unbelieving.

The years 1930–1935 on Twin Farms were indeed alive with children. Dorothy loved them but often left them. To give an idea of how they affected Red, it will be necessary to abandon chronology altogether and give later letters in which he really tells a part (but only a part) of what he felt. I can well remember more lurid and perhaps more precise descriptions, but this is what he wrote to Dorothy on one occasion when she was in Germany and he had fled from Twin Farms to New York. (Internal evidence, particularly the reference to the "Western trip," makes the likely year 1934, although similar conditions obtained in 1933.)

THE BERKSHIRE
21 EAST 52ND STREET
NEW YORK CITY

Wednesday, August 15

Dearest, if you ever go to Europe again in summer for more than five or six weeks, including steamer, I *shall* go to

England and see you now and then when you're free — or else I'll go off to some new and interesting place, like Norway, by myself.

For me, this summer since you left hasn't been a great success, except for most of the Western trip, and for seeing Wells. Another time, if you feel you must chase off so — and if you do feel so, then you must — we'll just open one of the Vermont houses for Mick, with a good nurse — perhaps better, a man tutor — and Marthe and Marie, and rent the other house or let it stand idle.

I came back from my trip to find the Old House simply lost, not to us alone but to Micky and Pammy, who were become mere excrescences in a house the porch & every room of which simply swarmed with four hearty, cheerful, well-mannered, and most God-awfully inundating Wallers, Mrs. and her three healthy young. One had to escape from them, simply run from them, even to talk to Micky. And they four, with Marie's grandson added, of course monopolized playlawn, bathing house, and woods. And while the kids certainly did keep away from the New House scrupulously, Mrs. Waller would brightly drop in, unurged, four or five times a day — for tea, for invitations, by God, to bathe at *my* bathing house, for discussions of obvious bills.

Now last winter Mrs. Waller in the same way got terribly on my nerves at Bronxville. You will — you must — remember that I was most dubious about her coming to Vermont for all summer. And I certainly never had it clear that her crew of kids were coming for as long as they liked — I'd supposed it would be a couple of weeks, at most. And, thus returning, I saw Mrs. Waller each day a little more the supreme controller; [. . .]

Certainly by the amount that I have sent and answered for you, she seems not to have given much attention to your mail. And it had been my supposition — perhaps I hadn't made it clear to her — that while I was West she would dispose of a lot of my letters which are adequately answered if the customer received a polite "Mr. Lewis is far away" letter from a secretary. She didn't dispose of one.

So I let the horde of Wallers go, with a polite explanation — really polite — that there seemed to be no use of keeping both places open, and with a month's salary. And I did close the house and since thus there was no need of Marian, I also let her go, with more than a month's salary. (Marian has worked pretty well, though she has simply refused to help care for the kids much and has thought, all summer, apparently, of nothing much beyond taking "her" new car and getting to a dance every evening. But still she's a good girl.)

The washing will, of course, be sent out.

When you come back, you will want a secretary. I'll get you a good smart one here — [. . .] and have her already to go up . . . and she can stay at the Allens'!!! I'll take care of all the bills and mail myself, whether I'm down here or up there.

I feel that Marthe and Marie love us all the better because I have thus removed a source of slight friction and envy. I have let Marie's grandson stay — though I certainly don't want it assumed that he is to come, any more than Pammy, every summer forever and forever. With the washing sent out, Marthe and Marie and Emily (who returns from vacation today) can beautifully take care of Peggy, Mick, and Pammy, especially as I shall be away a lot; and the only guests that are invited are Freeman and Judy. Peggy — with whom I talked all this firing over before doing anything at all — will see how the work goes, and may have some one in for the heavy cleaning once a week.

Alice seems to have been very good with kids, and she is staying on some days after Emily's return to clean up the other house sufficiently so that you can open it when you come — all bedclothes that sort of thing. (Old House will be kept dusted, ready for you.)

I'm sorry about the Wallers. But I couldn't have stood the place one more day with her and her horde monopolizing it. And if you will go off 3000 miles, I must use my judgment about *our* house, however bad . . . Sure, I'll trade with you, and never have Lou about when you're there if you want.

Between you and me, I have had, for an undomestic gent, rather a full measure of kids heaped upon me, this summer when I meant to be tranquil: Wells, Micky, Wells's friend Stephen, three Wallers, Henri, and Pammy — good God, is that only eight? — they seemed like a hundred; and occasionally appearing, playtime Lucias and Thayers.

I've never missed you so. I wouldn't have minded armies of kids, omitting Wallers, if you'd been there to talk to. I didn't want to invite many friends, with you away, because most of them are more fun if you are there too. Phil, Joe, a few like that who would have been agreeable with or without you, couldn't come.

Did I say above that Peggy will stay, more or less in charge, as long as she can — possibly till you come? I do love Peggy, but as a dinner companion, night after night, she's pretty unexciting — unless we're exploring Italy and daily trapping new topics of talk.

No, if you go again for any great time next summer, things will all have to be arranged differently — quite possibly with a house in England, for Mick and Nurse, as we thought of doing when in Bermuda.

I came down here day before yesterday. Phoned house today, and everything fine, says Peggy. Micky looks grand.

I do love you!

h

Mick, Pam & nurse comfortable at New House.

PS. Your letter from Cliveden, when you were alone there, was one of the loveliest things you've ever written. Atmosphere — Lord! I'll let you see it when you return.

The next example must be either from a month earlier or a year later, depending upon when Wells passed his entrance examinations at Harvard. (From the preceding letter we learn that Mrs Waller and her brood have been summarily dismissed, and yet she is predominant in this one, so the chances are that this letter is a month earlier than the preceding one.) The other should precede it, just the same, because it is a serious and detailed statement of Red's grievance at being left in a regiment of children and servants. This one, which I find to be, on the whole, more funny than sad, does not state the case but gives a very glaring example of it.

This letter is also notable for the appearance, in our narrative, of Red's secretary-chauffeur-companion-and-all, Louis Florey by name, upon whom Red relied for years in his escapes from domesticity. Lou, as we always called him, was a public stenographer — and more accurately, a copyist — with an office somewhere in the Forties (perhaps Forty-third Street?) in New York. Red had originally met him by professional chance when he was in need of a typist. That was in 1925, and Lou had earned the hearty dislike of Gracie from the beginning. He always called Red "the Boss," both to his face and when speaking of him, and was always willing to find a bootlegger or drive a car as well as copy a novel. When Red married Dorothy he had not seen Lou for some time, and it was in fact about 1931 before the eminently serviceable secretary came back into his life again. From that time on Dorothy, like Gracie before her, tended to blame many of Red's lapses (at least in part) on Lou's willingness to be of service. We shall see that the feud went on for years — and that Red's dislike for Mrs Waller, Dorothy's secretary at one time, was equal to Dorothy's for Lou. I knew Lou well and was never for one moment convinced that he contributed anything to Red's delinquencies. He did what he was told — yes. If he had not done so, Red would have found somebody else to oblige.

This letter — another flight — is as follows:

PECKETT'S-ON-SUGAR HILL

P.O. FRANCONIA, NEW HAMPSHIRE

Monday morning
July 17

The household got to be just a little too much for me, Saturday. Wells, in all sweetness I know, had invited the registrar of Andover, one Dr. Eccles, who had been very helpful to him in entering Harvard (he has passed all his exams, by the way) to drop in at Barnard, when he should be driving North for his vacation. He had just thought of our giving said Dr. and wife a meal, if I didn't mind. Well, Dr. phones and can he and his wife AND nine-year-old girl (in a house already simply lousy with children) come and stay from Friday to Monday? Poor Wells was aghast; but I backed him up — and stayed long enough to welcome Eccleses, hordes of Eccleses (and very nice they proved to be), to explain that I had previous engage here, and beat it. I had intended to send Lou back to New York on Friday, but I retained him for this trip, and I'll go back to Barnd today. This is a nice place, but it is not as nice as Barnard and, as I feared, it is very twittery with the incessant chatter of dreadfully Nice Women.

Pammy is better with Micky, but still pretty Godawfully bossy with him. I think he's getting to hate her — or dread her. I'm not sure we can ever have her again for more than a couple of weeks. She doesn't as you thought, really improve; she just, each year, shows some different aspect of her grim, selfish egocentricity, which cheerfully sacrifices her mother, Micky, or anybody else to her own sense of power. She made the house miserable in Semmering; she's more clever now . . . . . and thank God not in my same house . . . . . but I'm not sure but that I'll have to have her there, to save Micky . . . . . Probly I exaggerate, but I certainly am backed up by Emily and Mrs. Waller . . . . . tho they are also both exaggerators.

Well, Pammy will be gone by September first, I hope. And I am fond of Peggy. But no more Pammy for even a whole month, after this, ever, I think. Let Peggy farm her out, and come by herself.

* * *

It's curious how some tiny thing, material thing, brings the vivid thought of the Beloved . . . . . Like your bright, absurd rack of poker chips.

x

4

THIS HAS INDICATED, AT LEAST SUMMARILY, HOW RED FELT about children in the house. It must be used as a counterpart to those numerous letters which can be read both at Syracuse University and in the Yale collection in which he displays concern, anxiety or simple affection for his own and other children. There is no question that he felt warmly towards children in general, and his own in particular, when he was a safe distance away from them. In actual life he was inclined to pay a child a visit once every other day, as he did the infant Michael in 1930, and waggle a long finger at the baby's nose and go away again. I saw him do that often enough.

Two other recollections are vivid in my memory: one of

Michael's second birthday (June, 1932) and the other of some Fourth of July a little later, possibly in 1934 or 1935 (not after 1935, because I was then away from Twin Farms until 1939).

On Michael's second birthday, June 20th, we were under the great elm at the corner of the new room in the Big House, which had only that year assumed the character and dimensions it was to bear thereafter. I was staying in the old farmhouse and so was the baby and his nurse. For the birthday occasion, at teatime, we gathered under that vast old elm tree at the corner of the studio and there was a handsome cake for the child with two candles on it.

That elm tree, by the way, is only a stump now. Dorothy tried for years to keep it alive. It was cemented and wired and chained together by every device known to the science of trees, so long as there was a vein of sap or a flowering leaf left, but it had to be sacrificed in the end (about ten years later) because nobody could guarantee that it would not crash down upon the house in the night and destroy everything. The frail but magnificent old tree was in its senile splendor when Michael was two.

Everything went well enough until the moment came for the baby to blow out the two candles. Perhaps it was over-ambitious to expect him to do this — or even to understand why he should try. At all events, he was asked to perform the feat and failed. No doubt he did not realize that the extinction of the candles was the objective. We all showed him how to puff and blow (without ourselves extinguishing the candles) and he did likewise. The candles remained ablaze in the afternoon sunlight. Red went into an uncontrollable tantrum, utterly beyond reason or argument. He was almost (but alas not quite!) bereft of the power of speech. His rage was centered upon the child's inability to blow out the candles, although obviously many other things entered into it. After a painful interval he went stamping off to his room and the child, by this time in an equal extremity of hysterics, was carried away by the nurse.

On the Fourth of July, which was later (perhaps by two years), the cook's grandson, Henry, was chief of the small band of children participating in the festivity. We sat (that is, Dorothy and Red and I, for there were no other grownups present except the servants) on the terrace in front of the Big House. Underneath that terrace was another, reached by rock steps, with a wall where Dorothy had labored over the perennials; and beneath this was the big sloping lawn where the children often played, with a grove on one side and the big garden on the other and the pasture and valley below it. Here it had been arranged that Henry, Michael and Pamela should have their fireworks (with perhaps another child or two from the neighborhood) as a display for their elders and an excitement for themselves. They were, indeed, wild with glee over their modest resources, and their yells of nervous pleasure had begun to exhaust Red's patience before the first little bang exploded. As they went on, laboriously and noisily, he grew more and more exacerbated. Finally he got up, in something very near a state of screaming hysteria, and asked Dorothy to put a stop to it all. When she expostulated — the Fourth of July; they had looked forward to it — he vanished in a kind of agonized howl and was not seen again until dinner.

(At dinner, by the way, the children were all safely put away into the old farmhouse under adequate supervision; we usually ate at the long refectory table in the new room of the Big House, the Big Room with a wonderful view over the sloping valley and Mount Ascutney in the distance.)

These and many other episodes gave me a vivid notion of how little Red cherished the joys of parenthood, and yet the reader of his letters (many of them) might suppose him to have been a doting father. It was possibly one of his ways of reproaching Dorothy for her own absences — one can detect this in the first and longer of the two letters just now given about children. Through years when he never even beheld their son, he would still write to Dorothy about Mike or Michael or Mickey or Mikey or Mixy or whatever form he chose to use — he was fertile in invention on this as on other themes. His tone was almost always affectionate.

And indeed their tone, between themselves, was that of extreme affection and a deeply felt deprivation at the absence of the other. We know that Dorothy contemplated some form of separation from the winter before her child was born — she has said so often enough in letters of a later date — and it was indeed this year, 1930, the year of the sojourn in California, the pregnancy and the birth of the child, the year also of the Nobel Prize, that seems to have sealed their fate.

It *was*, however, the year of the Nobel Prize as well as of everything else. And the Nobel Prize in itself postponed, although not for long, their progress into a life of separate interests and divided time.

5

THE NOBEL PRIZE HAD BEEN A MIRAGE TO RED FOR MANY YEARS, a fountain in the desert, not because it could by itself solace his lifelong pain (that was not, in truth, to be solaced) but because it came from abroad and had the mystery and magic of a consecration. He had refused the Pulitzer Prize — and what an uproar there was over that, too! — and did not much like the idea of any prize given for one book over another. He did not even like the idea of judges authorized to make such choices, and for a good many years no book of his was ever submitted to the Book of the Month Club or any other such organization. The Nobel Prize was altogether different in its aura, its unspoken or unexplained meaning. It had been given

to writers who, with varying degrees of power, had always
served high purposes; some of these were great writers; the
prize itself was large (almost $50,000 in 1930); it had been
greatly coveted even by those who, in many countries, had
deserved without receiving it; and it had never yet been given
to an American. For all of these reasons Red had hankered
after it for years, but I suspect that the strongest element in
his desire came from the fact that he (if he got it) would be the
first American to be so honored. It would thus in some respects
set him apart from all others (above and beyond Dreiser, for
instance, whose work he deeply respected). It would be the
best possible reply to those critics, now diminishing in number
but still extremely vocal, who regarded him as some kind of
renegade or unworthy son of his native soil, a rebellious and
evil spirit because his picture of American life was not pretty.
All of these thoughts or desires, wishes or dreams, commingled
in his imagination, and it is very likely (almost certain) that
what it came to was a glimmering awareness of a far-off possibility which he never expected to be realized. He had spoken
of this possibility once in a while to close friends of his own
age — never to me — but we know that when it actually came
to pass he could not believe it. The Swedish Embassy in
Washington was only able to make him believe it by dint of
reiteration on the long-distance telephone to Westport, where
he sat stunned and incredulous at the dream come true.

Frank and Esther Adams — he was F.P.A. of the *Herald
Tribune* and subsequently of other papers, a legendary figure
of wit and light verse and even scholarship, famous beyond
most newspaper figures in those days — had a beautiful, big,
roomy house called Indian Hill, near Westport, which they
were not going to use in the autumn of 1930. Red and Dorothy
rented it as a compromise between Twin Farms, where it was
not practical to remain after late October, and a house or flat in
New York which they did not possess. (Mr Connett had given

them his house in Tenth Street as a codicil to their purchase of Twin Farms, but it was no longer theirs.) Dorothy had gone down to Indian Hill a couple of weeks early to get the house ready, leaving Red at Twin Farms, and already she was thinking of a long absence abroad while her baby — "the loveliest thing that ever happened to me" — would be cared for by friends. The plans were, so to speak, in flux, but it is quite obvious that Dorothy was thinking of some kind of separation as well as of her own budding career. This had been germinating in her mind since the ill-fated stay in California the preceding winter.

Compared to Twin Farms, in remotest Vermont, Indian Hill, near suburban Westport, was practically metropolitan, and Red did his usual grousing, but there was really little ground for complaint: it was a spacious, lovely house, and once he had all his own private belongings in it he was at home. (I always thought Red was most at home in a hotel room, but of that more later.) He moved down to Indian Hill from Twin Farms at the beginning of November and was there when the successive telephone calls from Washington convinced him at last (on November 5th, 1930) that he had won the Nobel Prize for Literature.

There followed, of course, an immense commotion. Interviews and photographs, photographs and interviews, declarations, denials and comments, were scattered across the press of the United States and of the world. There was an overwhelming body of opinion, much the greatest, which held that the prize was well justified, that it signalized the coming-of-age of American literature, that it was high time this had been acknowledged by the authorities at the University of Upsala, etc., etc. There was a dissenting opinion of considerable bitterness in (chiefly) the United States, holding that it was a backhanded compliment to our culture since all Lewis had ever done was to ridicule it, and us. Some few voices dissented on different grounds — that, regardless of America, Lewis was not a solid and great literary artist in line for this honor: Rebecca West in England and Ellen Glasgow in America were among these. (At the time I do not remember that Rebecca spoke up, but she has done so since.) Most writers of all nations rejoiced, or appeared to rejoice, in the event.

I have pored over literally hundreds of letters from all over the world on this matter. A very great many were found in my house in Twin Farms years later and are now in the Yale Library. Others, which came to Dorothy and were answered by her, are in the Syracuse University Library. I see her unmistakable handwriting on them: "Ans. Nov. 15," a strongly penciled notation which to me shows that she dictated answers for him, although to what secretary (out of that multitude they had!) I cannot tell. I was then in Paris and knew nothing at first hand of their travail. I know that they had a crowded and tumultuous but on the whole enjoyable time, helping each other through it, appearing together more constantly and more sympathetically (in the sense working it out together, feeling it together) than they ever could do again. I have no doubt that Dorothy helped him in preparing for the grand ordeal (it was an ordeal but it was certainly grand) in Stockholm. It was no doubt she who made up for him those lists of Swedish princes and princesses whom he was likely to meet, professors of the University of Upsala, Swedish writers who had (and who had not) received the prize, and other elements of a civilized attitude towards this great honor. She knew much more about the customs of the world in Europe than he did. She also must have been acutely anxious, not to say alarmed, over the possibilities of his ever-uncertain behavior. Some of his friends in America (George Jean Nathan, for instance) had freely predicted that Red would get drunk and disgrace himself at the most solemn moments, such as when he stood before the King to receive the prize.

Nothing of the sort took place. Red was resolutely sober and polite from the beginning to the end of the episode. He even went to New York and got all his "hickeys" (this is what he called those dreadful pustules on his face) removed by an electric needle before he went to Stockholm. I find this very touching. He loathed having his "hickeys" removed. It could only be done by a painful process and it took a long time if it were to be done thoroughly, completely. Generally, and indeed for years at a time if he had no urgent need to get rid of them, he allowed these things on his face to flourish: it was easier so. For Stockholm he was rehabilitated, stem to stern.

He and Dorothy sailed on the *Drottningholm* on November 29th and arrived in Stockholm from Stavangerfjord on December 9th. From then until the presentation of the prize (December 12th) they were engaged in official ceremonies at which Red, in spite of his nervousness and his profound provinciality (his rooted conviction that such grandeurs were not for him), acquitted himself very well.

His actual address on December 12th before the Swedish Academy, on having received the Nobel Prize, caused a tremendous stir throughout the world but does not, in retrospect, seem quite so remarkable as it did then. Most of what he said about American literature, culture and opinion was simply the truth and like all truth, once realized, can never surprise again. He took as his point of departure some remarks by Dr Henry Van Dyke, the eminent Princeton divine, who had objected to the Nobel award to Lewis as being, in effect, an insult to America. Red's irrepressible and sometimes irrational patriotism combined with his disgust for academic criticism to make a memorable address, suitable to the occasion and expressed with greater care than was usual with him. To his dismay, it was cabled to America and elsewhere in the truncated version common at that time, leading to many errors in print, and it was this highly distorted edition (straight out of the daily press) that his publishers, Harcourt Brace, used for the pamphlet they quickly got out on the matter. This, too, added to his growing list of grievances against Alfred Harcourt, with whom he was soon to part.

On Sunday, December 21st, the Lewises left Stockholm for Berlin after a round of festivities in academic, literary and royal circles. In Berlin with old friends the parties, although somewhat of a different category, began anew, and it was after one of these (with the Knickerbockers and others) that Dorothy collapsed into great pain and had to be taken to the hospital. This was on Christmas night. Acute appendicitis was diagnosed; the operation was the next morning; she was in hospital for ten more days. Red was, of course, a prey to great anxiety — his devotion to her was unquestionable, however oddly he showed it at times — but all went well and they were reunited in January for a short while in the mountains of Thuringia.

Then Red took off for London, although there seems to have been no imperative reason to do so. Again and again, in the story of Dorothy and Red, we encounter these journeys for which no explanation quite suffices, these absences without motive. My own guess is that her preoccupation with journalism and with journalistic friends was too much for him; it often was. She had made plans for a good deal of work (including another journey to Russia) which had to be revised because of her illness, but she still had plenty to do in Germany. Her interest had been vividly aroused by the Nazi movement, then not taken very seriously by most observers, and she wanted above all to talk to its leader. As usual, Red was delighted to see her working or about to work, but at the same time he felt extraneous to it all and wanted to get away — or so I interpret it.

Actually he said he had to be in London to see publishers. All his discontents with the Harcourt firm had now boiled over and he had quite summarily notified Alfred Harcourt of the fact. Alfred, without defending himself, and indeed almost as if he were already quite resigned to losing his most profitable author, acquiesced. The question then was where Red was to go next. Nelson Doubleday went to London to see him, and in the result (as had been on the cards since the preceding spring) he signed a contract with Doubleday, Doran and Company. It was actually not with Nelson that he was to deal most constantly in the next decade, nor yet with Dan Longwell (the promotion chief who also went to London) but with Harry Maule, the editor to whom he stuck for the rest of his life, both in the Doubleday firm and afterwards with Random House.

Obviously Red's publishing arrangements could have been made just as well in Berlin as in London. I can only think that Dorothy and Red were fonder of each other when there was an appreciable distance between them, when they could grieve over the separation ("how I miss you!" they never stop saying) without any of the rasping little dangers of propinquity. She already had, as we know, the gravest doubts about the permanence of her marriage, and her mind was set upon a career of her own — not really through ambition, as I have indicated before, but through that "sense of historic mission" which has been mentioned as a dominant characteristic. There were things she felt she could do and ought to do and which (she would have stated it quite plainly) she thought nobody else was doing or could do in the same way. If by doing these things — in one sense, her duty or her "mission" — she could also earn a living, she might feel herself released from the perpetual insecurity of Red's stormy sadness and his ungovernable temperament.

Two letters of Red's to Dorothy at this period (February, 1931) should be given for the sake of the record, in that they show his frame of mind in making the change from Harcourt to Doubleday. "Don" in the first letter is Donald Brace, Alfred

Harcourt's partner; "Saul" is from the Cosmopolitan publishing company; Rohwalt is the Berlin publisher; Oswald Garrison Villard (who had inherited the New York *Post* and sold it to Curtis) was the owner of *The Nation*. "Hal" is Harrison Smith, who had his own publishing house at the time. In the second letter Karlfeldt is Erik Karlfeldt of the Royal Swedish Academy, who had presented Lewis at the historic meeting on December 12th.

The two letters follow.

Thursday, Feb. 12

We're free of Harcourt. His letter has not come — I expect it in a day or two — but finally yesterday I decided I dared not wait any longer; simply couldn't tell where I was; perhaps Harcourt had blandly gone off to Florida & I wouldn't hear for another month. A cable was too difficult and brusque and would require their writing in return. So I 'phoned across the Atlantic. (Cost only thirty dollars.) I got Don; he was as sweet and forgiving as ever — I wanted to weep and almost did. "Why yes, Red, of course, if you want that, what can we do. We've returned both the Next Book and Neighbor contracts to you." (The Neighbor contract could be construed as a Next Book contract.) "We wrote you on the third of February."

So we're ready to go . . . slowly. I've talked it over with Villard (One needn't be *too* confidential now.) He favors Hal; he thinks Viking hasn't the origination (but I don't believe he adequately knows); he insists that Doubleday-Doran are unreliable (but the firm may have bucked up since Nelson took hold). Of course he regards Cosmopolitan Book Corporation as just being sold down the river, which is probably a sound estimate. What about Harpers?

Saul should be in Berlin this morning. Don't let him give you the impression we have gotten any nearer to closing. We have not. And I notice that his ideas about the book do not progress — just pay a hell of a big advance, spend a smashing lot advertising, print a handsome book and give a lot of deluxes away, and send out a lot of slips in routine Heart advertising — i.e., just $$$$$, which alone do not sell books.

I've let G. Wren Howard — Cape's partner here — know, and he's going to cable Jonathan, who's in NY, confidentially, so that Hal and Jonathan can talk it over. Then when Cape gets here, about March 1st, I can talk it over with him, later Hal in New York, NOT closing here in London.

Also Nelson Doubleday arrives here, end of this month. So I can't go back on the Europa with you. I've been thinking a lot of doing so. I don't merely miss you; I feel downright lonely without. Perhaps I wouldn't have felt SO lonely if I'd been working hard, but I've been rather loafing — looking at myself to see what I'm like. Moods. But I'm coming out of them now, beginning to work. But I would like to go with you. But I'd better not, with publixes coming. But I will work. But I'll get out of London & see some new place — not too far, so's can return for publixes. But I adore you.

Yes — as I wired you, answer to your wire with your gadding plans for Vienna & Brussels and God knows what other lewd and foreign cities — I have had a nasty but quite unserious cold, couple of days. I just stayed in, slept a lot and read in dressing-gown by the fire, and today I feel fine again. I've been out to try on — guilty secret — did I tell you? — four beautiful suits I've ordered, one a heavenly Harris tweed for the country.

* * *

News for you.
Waitll next page.

Oswald Villard wants you to consider being managing editor of the Nation beginning next fall. He is also considering Raymond Swing. Mussey has resigned as m.e., though he will stay on the staff. Frieda has been all busted up by the death of a child. Villard is crazy about you, and wanted to see you in Berlin — but now he'll miss you, and he is not going over Paris. There's no hurry, as he doesn't want to start things till fall. He returns to U.S. in early May. I take it from what he says he'll pay $7,500 a year, top-notch. Might be worth considering; certainly it would link you to America if later you wanted to do articles there, & sire, you grand American political dope while,

IS that a long letter?	grand American political dope while,
IS that news?	perforce, keeping
IS that a husband who adores his wife?	you in touch with
	European politics
	. . . Mick & me
	could live on Long
	Island.

Bury St.
16 February, 1931.

Dear Dorothy,

I hate to dictate letters to you, but if I dictate this one it will get to you much quicker. — I'm so afraid I'll miss you in Berlin — and it will be much more complete.

The letter from Harcourt was in exactly the tone I had hoped for, but hardly been able to expect. It runs as follows: —

"Dear Red I have your letter of January 21st. Of course,

we don't want to hold your next novel by the semi-compulsion of a contract. Here is the agreement for the 'next book' and also the one for 'Neighbor,' which I include so that your title will be completely clear. I've endorsed them 'cancelled by mutual consent.' If you will acknowledge their receipt and confirm their cancellation, this will clear the record until you find it convenient to return your copies with a similar endorsement.

"I know you have some idea of how sorry I am that events have taken this turn. You and we have been so closely associated in our youth and growth that I wish we might have gone the rest of the way together. If I've lost an author, you haven't lost either a friend or a devoted reader."

On the same mail with his letter came a reprint of Karlfeldt's address & my Nobel Prize oration. Unfortunately, the latter was taken entirely from the "New York Times'" cabled account, and was dreadfully inaccurate. I cabled immediately asking them to suppress the pamphlet, and they have obligingly cabled back that they were doing so and would I please send them a copy of my original address. I am doing that to-day. I had not realised how much the "Times" managed to garble the original until I fell upon the pamphlet and began to curse.

Esther's letter about Mickey was entrancing. That young man already seems to have the following of a matinee idol. I am glad you socked Lena Goldschmidt. She sounds like a nice person. I would like to chew her ear. No, I wouldn't. I am sure it would not be hygienic.

No special news, except that I seem to be beginning to work a little — a strange new phenomena. Saturday I drove down to Bechhofer Roberts' again. It was a really beautiful day, and we were able to walk in the sunshine. I thoroughly enjoyed it.

EXTRA SPECIAL. WIRE ME WHERE I CAN REACH YOU IN

PARIS. I AM SORRY AS THE DEVIL ABOUT SOUTHAMPTON. I
WAS MAKING PLANS TO GO DOWN. YES, I WAS!

You know all the things I would put in this paragraph if I
were not dictating it!

P.S. Lookit what you're missing! "The Ambassador of the
U.S.S.R. and Madame Sokolnikoff request the pleasure of
the company of Mr. & Mrs. Sinclair Lewis at a Reception of
the 25th February, 1931, from 9 to 11.30 p.m. During the
Reception a Russian Film will be shown (9.30 to 10.30)
P.P.S. Have you gotten that money out of Rowhold? If you
don't before you leave Berlin — well —
P.P.P.S. The two contracts returned by Harcourt Brace
& Co. are simply marked "Cancelled by mutual consent,
February 3rd, 1931. Harcourt Brace & Co., Inc. A. Harcourt,
President.

6

RED DID JOIN DOROTHY ON THE *Europa*, AFTER ALL, AND THEY
landed in New York on March 4th of that year to an ac-
companiment of interviews, photographs, accusations and denials, controversies and disputes, more uproarious than ever.
Red's address in Stockholm had stirred up all his old enemies
and created new ones. A target of his earlier arrows, Calvin
Coolidge, had sought to still all this by saying, exquisitely and

characteristically: "No necessity exists for getting excited," but it was a nervous moment anyhow, at the very outset of the Great Depression. Americans were in a controversial mood. To argue about Sinclair Lewis and his Nobel Prize was one way of exorcising a most uncomfortable demon of doubt and alarm.

The Lewises found their son healthy and strong at Westport in the Adams house where their friend Rose Wilder Lane had held the fort all winter long. Red was on the move, of course — Westport could not contain him — and a series of events took place that spring. One was his open transfer from Harcourt to Doubleday (which had been arranged but not announced). Another was his famous altercation with Theodore Dreiser at the Metropolitan Club, in which Mr Dreiser slapped his face twice; another was his vain effort to give the actual Nobel Prize (the gold medal) to the Yale University Library. He was, as he often told me, treated with contumely there by a young man, an assistant librarian, who obviously did not believe that he was Sinclair Lewis. Since Red and Hal Smith had been driving up to Twin Farms and merely stopped at New Haven on the way, I have always conjectured that they were somewhat lit by strong waters when they called upon the Yale librarian for this lofty purpose. Red was so incensed by his reception that he took his gold medal along to Vermont and (later) gave it to the State Historical Society at Montpelier, on a temporary basis; it is now at Yale.

All his comings and goings left Dorothy more than ever convinced that she must develop her own capacity for work, for a life independent enough to become separate if this were necessary. They were apart a great deal even in 1931, even before her journey to Berlin in November of that year for her Hitler interview. Their letters never cease to dwell upon how much they miss each other. But from now on it was evident enough that they were not destined to anything which could correctly be described as a life in common. Their interests began to diverge, too, as she became more absorbed in the international journalism (or its political material) which was to be her distinctive career at its zenith. Red had been drinking very heavily indeed, as he tended to do whenever he had no big piece of work in hand. His last novel was *Dodsworth* (1929), and there was not to be another until *Ann Vickers* (1933). He still had the labor novel in mind — he talked of it a great deal that summer — but it was never clear in his mind and he was forever being disillusioned or repelled by essential elements in it when he came to examine them closely. He did not actually begin to work on *Ann Vickers* until late in 1931, after Dorothy had gone to Berlin.

Thus it could be seen how the next three or four years were to divide them. Their protestations of love did not cease until much later, and there is no ground for doubting their sincerity: it would not be the first time that a man and a woman have been unable to live either with or without each other. Even so, it was clear that their love, if it were love, was fated to be mainly love in absence.

9

A Rather Strange Interlude

DOROTHY'S PROFESSIONAL SKILLS WERE ALREADY HIGHLY AP-
preciated. We can see how highly when we reflect that Oswald
Garrison Villard, an experienced man, seems to have considered
making her managing editor of *The Nation*. It was a remarkable tribute to the abilities of a woman correspondent.

She was now about to enter upon the decisive phase of her
journalistic ascent. When she left for Europe in November,
1931, she had it firmly in mind that she should have a comprehensive interview with Adolf Hitler, the head of the National-
Socialist Party of Germany, so as to determine what, if anything, he meant to the future. She achieved her purpose, and
the interview was afterwards expanded into the book *I Saw
Hitler*; all of this was duly admired in its time. But the after-
math, three years later, when Hitler in one of his tantrums
decided to expel her from Germany because of this almost
forgotten interview, was far more sensational than the original
work: it made Dorothy a heroine within twenty-four hours
and propelled her into that national and international celebrity
— not as Red's wife but as herself — which was to be her
native climate thereafter. These years and the two that followed were full of incessant movement for both Dorothy and
Red, and as we trace them over the map of the western world
it almost seems as if the two of them had made up their minds
to be everywhere at once, so long as it was not simultaneously.
She went to Europe in November and was back for Christmas

and then off again; he went to Europe in April (1932) and brought her back in May. Her interest in her own career was at the time backed, incessantly and in the most stentorian tones, by Red, who embarrassed her often in company by overpraising her merits. Most of the summer of 1931 and the summer of 1932 she had spent at Twin Farms, but he came and went, obviously in search of a subject, some very large, generic, inclusive and posterlike subject; no other would do for him; and the subject finally turned out to be that of the "career woman," feminist and reformer, *Ann Vickers*. On this he worked savagely for long weeks at a time, usually with Lou Florey as secretary; then they would vanish together to the south or the west, whether Dorothy was in the country or not. She had taken a commodious flat for them at 21 East Ninetieth Street (by this time they not only needed separate bedrooms but separate sitting rooms as well); she was in Europe a good deal of the winter (1931–1932) and in Vermont in the summer. It was of this period that she spoke when she told Professor Schorer (as is to be seen in his *Sinclair Lewis*, page 568) that when Red came to her room, late at night and drunk, he smelled of rotting weeds. This, of course, must have been at Twin Farms, since they were seldom together anywhere else.

Even so, I do not think she had fully made up her mind to leave Red. It was so supposed by many of their friends; she even said so at times (and often to him); there exist a number of flat statements to that effect in various letters, notably one from Philip Goodman to H. L. Mencken which is dated February 3, 1933. That winter, 1932–1933, was to be an exceedingly difficult one, but we shall also see that it brought a sudden recrudescence of her former hope and faith in their marriage. However brief this may have been, no reader of her diary could doubt that it was real. She even hoped for another child by him, and the early days (for a bit) seemed to have come back.

The whole concept of their 1932–1933 winter would appear, in retrospect, to have originated in their mutual desire to make this marriage work, to bring it back into being as it had been four years before, and to recall that which had originally brought and held them together. She thought of Vienna, of course (she always did), and perhaps in this one may guess some wish to exorcise forever the ghost of Josef; Red thought of Central Europe in general (not Vienna in particular, which he never really liked) because it was in Central Europe that they had originally believed in their love.

And, as it happened, Red had made a great deal of money just then. *Arrowsmith* had been bought in 1931 for a film by Mr Samuel Goldwyn, that great and good man, and Sidney Howard had written a scenario for it which resulted in a memorable production (Helen Hayes and Ronald Colman played the parts). *Dodsworth* was then commissioned for dramatization, also by Sidney Howard. And *Ann Vickers*, which was finished in the spring of 1932, was bought for serialization (August to November of that year) by *Redbook* Magazine. As I remember, Mr Goldwyn paid munificently for *Arrowsmith* and *Redbook* paid splendidly for *Ann Vickers*. This alone (without any other income and without whatever the advance was on the dramatization of *Dodsworth*) gave Red a lordly income in that year. The reason why I remember this so distinctly is that he never stopped talking about it. He was, of course, well aware that it was an exceptional year and that he was lucky to be the recipient of such emoluments. At the same time he was infuriated to think that he would have to pay heavy taxes all at once, because the money came all at once, and then quite possibly have no income at all for the next three or four years. He used to stamp up and down the floor and shout with rage against a tax system which thus penalized an author (or any other kind of occasional artist, dependent upon the whims of the public) whereas businessmen,

bankers and entrepreneurs in general had every opportunity
to spread out their gains and losses. Red's proposal, which at
that time had never been made in public, to my knowledge,
was for an equalization of income over a period of years — I
think he said four years — for persons like himself whose income was subject to such wild fluctuations. Some years later,
when Léon Blum became Prime Minister of France, and he was
of course himself an author (although never on Red's scale), he
did introduce legislation to this effect, spreading the irregular
incomes of artists over a five-year period. Later on, by various
Treasury regulations, the United States also made some ac-
commodation of the kind possible. At the time (1932) Red was
faced with the flat fact that he must pay on sums which, as he
well knew, would never come again.

And even so there was a great deal of money left for the
extravaganza which Dorothy and Red now embarked upon,
a sort of attempt to recapture (or possibly to purchase? — but
that would be too harsh) the vanishing dream.

They left together on the *Europa* on August 24th, 1932.
They had both been back and forth across the ocean many
times in the past twenty-four months, but seldom together; and
this was to be their last crossing together. They had already
taken a villa up at the Semmering, in the hills above Vienna
(they call them "mountains") and Dorothy went there directly. Red spent two weeks in Germany while she got the
house on the Semmering (Villa Sauerbrunn) ready. I have some
recollection — confirmed by indications in the correspondence
— that her old friend Eugenie Schwarzwald, that energetic and
philanthropic lady to whom Vienna owed so much, had made
the arrangements. Genia, she was called: to her Dorothy had
recourse for many years in times of trouble.

When Red arrived on the Semmering he was at first (as
usual) enchanted and then quite rapidly disenchanted. The
house was "a cuckoo clock in aspect," he wrote to Frere Reeves

in London (afterwards A. S. Frere, dropping the other name). It was "a Ritz" in comfort. But he wanted to go away. They went to Italy for three weeks. They came back. Then he went away alone, again to Italy.

Italy drew him very strongly even then. It was to become his final passion, or at least obsession, and he spent his last years there, trying to read Dante, trying to understand Italian music and literature. I have survived thus long to state, on a stack of Bibles, that he never was able to say the simplest Italian word correctly, much less a sentence, and that his comprehension of Italian music and literature was as near to nothing as twenty years of struggle would permit. Shortly before he died I heard him say a line or two of Italian poetry and could not have believed, until I heard it, what gibberish could be made out of it. The extraordinary thing is that Red, who was a sublime mimic, one of the cleverest and funniest anybody in our time has heard, could not say a straight phrase of serious import in any of the languages he imitated. What is more, he could not understand one serious word, grammatically and clearly expressed, in any language except English.

And this was, of course, one of the principal reasons why the winter in Vienna (there and on the Semmering) was a failure. Although Red had learned German as a boy, he did not truly understand it. Dorothy's friends all spoke German by preference and most of them had no English at all. They could all speak French, of course, but to Red this would have been equally incomprehensible. The result was that he found himself tongue-tied and deaf in the ordinary company of everyday, which, to him, was unendurable. That is one very important reason why he fled so often from the treasurable (and extremely expensive) surroundings which had been arranged for their second honeymoon.

For his "work" he took a flat in Vienna, but of course he had no work. (After a big novel he could not work for quite a while.)

He gave interviews and was photographed. He gave opinions. (On leaving New York he had told the ship news reporters that there was no use having an election in 1932, because Herbert Hoover and Franklin Roosevelt were both "fatheads.") But mostly he ran away; he got drunk; he mourned and sorrowed.

Dorothy's remedy for this was to contrive a really fabulous holiday party on the Semmering for Christmas, full of English and Americans and snow and sleds and skis and music and dancing and beer and wine and conversation. For this she took a whole annex (a *dépendance*) of the hotel, in addition to their own spacious villa. She brought over her sister Peggy from America, with the latter's daughter Pamela; she invited Robert Nichols and his wife from London (this poet was more appreciated then than now); she asked her own old friends, Mr and Mrs Edgar Mowrer and Mr and Mrs John Gunther; Virgilia Peterson was there, and also Prince Paul Sapieha from Warsaw, whom Virgilia married soon afterwards; there were Frere Reeves from London and Patricia Wallace (Edgar Wallace's delightful daughter) whom Frere was to marry. There were people driving up from Vienna. No doubt Genia was there from time to time — the Semmering is two hours from Vienna — and so were many others. Among them was Baroness Hatvany, the beautiful and talented woman who wrote books under the name of Christa Winsloe: her story, *Mädchen in Uniform*, had made the rounds of the world in many languages, and most recently in a film version which was highly successful. Christa was a guest throughout the ten days of the festival, and her husband also I believe; and it seems to me that Marcia Davenport and her husband were also there. I have been hearing about this party ever since it happened (I was working in Paris and could not be there); but it strikes me that every time I hear about it the name of some new guest appears. They may not all have been there at the same time, but at any given moment there must have been a horde. There were also five children (Michael, two and a half years old, had come over with his parents) and some nurses, and some of the guests brought servants as well.

Only recently I have talked with Lilian Mowrer in Washington about this momentous party and she says it was accursed, at the very outset, by the weather. Dorothy had planned a kind of winter festival in which everybody would be out of doors all day long, all healthy and sportive and not needing lunch. She had planned breakfast and dinner only, with plenty of time for the servants to clean out both the villa and the *dépendance*. With fog and rain and unpleasant cold (not the brisk kind) most of the guests preferred to stay indoors, where there was approximately nothing to do and both the conversation and the nerves wore thin. Red was for the greater part of the time in a mood of desperate depression. John Gunther (Dorothy in her letters always calls him "Johnny") was stricken by asthma. The drinking that went on was excessive, not only for Red but for many others. Dorothy had hired an orchestra and installed a bar in the *dépendance*.

One's imagination really boggles at the thought of such a party, lasting ten mortal days and nights.

Peggy Wilson, Dorothy's sister, has written to me that "Red couldn't stand Dorothy's friends." Whether he could or not, he does not seem to have made much effort. At the end of the ten days he seized upon Peggy and whirled her off for a tour of Italy, while Dorothy and some of the others followed Baroness Hatvany to Budapest. Everybody who was there remembers the party on the Semmering vividly; no two accounts agree, of course; but the result of the story, to me, has always been to make me glad I was not there.

2

WE COME NOW TO A SECTION OF DOROTHY'S DIARY WHICH IS best left in her own words without interruption. She wrote this in a mood of self-analysis, herself wondering why she had to do so; and yet in the many years that followed, almost three decades of them, she never destroyed the book, although we must in common sense think that she destroyed a good many others. (Her diaries, after the honeymoon, are very intermittent; generally she would start one and keep it for a week or so and let it go; there are five years at a time when she noted nothing down in such a book.) She must have been rereading this diary in the last years of her life because it contains some penciled notes made at that time. In this rereading she occasionally pencils out the last six letters of the name Christa, leaving it as the initial C.; yet even this is not uniform. Sometimes we meet the name spelled out, as we do in the letters. She wished this, as well as all her other surviving papers, to go to the Syracuse University Library, where it now is. There are intimacies at which one wonders; Dorothy, who was in life a reticent woman about personal matters, had every opportunity to omit them from her papers and did not. By almost innumerable indications we know that she intended these papers (those willed to Syracuse University) to be published. It seems best, therefore, to obey her will: the all-or-nothing principle, when all is said, was an essential part of her greatness, and whatever a friend's preferences might be, it is her will that rules. For obvious reasons, two initials in the first entry have been changed to [O.] and [M.], and two names to [X.] and [Y.]. All other names and initials are as Dorothy gave them.

The diary follows, otherwise verbatim:

Dec. 28.

So it has happened to me again, after all these years. It has only really, happened to me once before: with [O.] (Then I was twenty and [O.] was 37, and I see her still quite vividly. She wore a black broadcloth tailored suit with white frills and a *jabot* and big hat. She was very handsome, full-figured, and womanly, and I wanted to be close to her, to be like her. I took my fortnight's free vacation and went all the way to Northern Canada to be with her — she was at Gerryowen — just in order to, while exploring in a canoe, say: "Why, it's you — so near." Just to be near her. I fell in love with W. before it wore off, or went away, and all the time my feeling for [O.] was in the background. Sometimes I think I love her better than anyone, and there's a queer tenderness between us still).

I don't count [M.]. Then, so many other elements entered. (Are there similar elements counting now?) But one was curiosity and that plays no rôle now. I behaved awfully badly with [M.]. In the end I hated (and feared) her. Just the same I still remember when she pulled my cheek down to hers that afternoon in Berlin (Schiffbauerdamm 28) and her soft scented mouth —

Only I should like to have left it there. I should have left it there. The rest seemed such a perversion, a perversion of a love for a man. One loves men differently, and the culmination of love for a man, with me, is very simple. Those forms of sapphic love were like making love to . . . . being made love to by . . . . an impotent man. One sickens.

There's something weak in it and, even, ridiculous. To love a woman is somehow ridiculous. *Mir auch passt es nicht. Ich bin doch heterosexuel.* Even according to the very simple Freudian definition which determines the matter by the location of the orgiastic sensation. Like Marguerite in Faust, the *womb* throbs — not something else, more surface. All this petting is nothing without the deep thrust to the heart of one.

Well, then, how account for this which has happened again. The soft, quite natural kiss on my throat, the quite unconscious (seemingly) even open kiss on my breast, as she stood below me on the stairs — there were a dozen people

around — "Good-bye," she said, "*Liebes*." Anyone might
have done that, said that — Martha, or Frances. But when
I walked into the room at Wohlbebeng and she stood there,
still in her hat and jacket; it was seven in the morning and
I wore green pajamas. "Hello," I said and went to shake
hands. It was six years since I had seen her. But instead we
kissed. I thought she looked much older: much too heavy,
and tired. What was the sudden indescribable charm in that
too-soft face, and the heavy-lidded eyes. (The upper lid is
very arched, the lower straight). Anyhow immediately I
felt the strange, soft feeling . . . curious . . . of being at
home, and at rest: an enveloping warmth and sweetness, like
a drowsy bath. Only to be near her; to touch her when I
went by. She has a quite simple, unconscious way of kissing
the inside of one's arm — I say "She has a way" and she
only did it once. "Don't go away," I wanted to say. "Don't
go."

Her name suddenly had a magic quality. *C.* I wanted to
say it. To use it. I talked about her to others, to hear her
name. Like holding an amulet in your hand, that was what
saying her name is like. I love this woman. There it stands,
and makes the word love applied to any other woman in the
world ridiculous.

Jealously! It is absurd! I could laugh at myself . . .
except that I couldn't! Jealous of [X.]. Not a sign. [X.] is
beautiful, young, somehow glamorous, and unhappy. It's
the last that attracts my dear. They went away together. The
door of [X.]'s room stood open and the door of C's . . .
wide, open and empty. I went for a walk with [Y.] and in the
woods he turned suddenly and put both hands on my cheeks
and we clung together. His mouth tasted deliciously of love,
like the smell of semen, and I could have lain down with him
right there in the woods then and there as I could have done
for five years, except that we agreed we wouldn't . . . the

old leap of the heart and womb were there, and we walked along, greatly shaken, but even then the sweet wistfulness, the heart's reaching towards warmth . . . that remained . . . and as we walked my heart said her name over and over, and said: she went with [X.].

There's me. The me I know & the world knows which says all this is ridiculous & exaggerated. What's she to [X.] or [X.] to her — [X.]'s in love with her Pole, after all. But so am I with [Y.] and happily married too, and yet wanting that curious tenderness, that pervading warm tenderness . . . there are no words for it, only her name said over & over expresses it. Come back! Come back! I have the feeling that something will happen to me in connection with this, and that it will make me unhappy.

Jan. 2.

I have got to go on writing about this in an attempt to justify it. There's a critic in me these days . . . a creature created by experience, who takes me firmly by the hand, pushes aside the curtain and insists upon my looking forward, down the road. (The critic says, to be sure, Don't write in a diary, particularly with your careless habits. You ought to have a locked book like the Queen of Rumania & wear the key on a bangle: only I would lose the bangle). But I must try at last to understand myself, because if at forty one has no wisdom . . . in two years I'll be forty . . . then what has one?

We went to Budapest and there she was on the platform, in a black fur coat — lamb, with a high collar of sable and a brown tilted hat. She looked exquisite . . . beautiful and worldly, as I remember her.

The curious thing is how vividly I remember things about her, after all these years. Once at Lainz, in summer, there was a teaparty, which dragged on. She was going somewhere to dinner later and wore a white dress — some thin stuff, embroidered all over with small white beads. Consciously, I only thought: she looks beautiful. This never happened to me, then. But years afterward I bought a dress like that, because she had worn one. Another day we walked through the villa — it was an ugly house, with big bare rooms full of bad furniture and the usual imperial taste. When we went through her bedroom, the bed had been opened for the night, and the bidet pulled out. I was somehow shocked at the insouciant and quite unveiled presence. But I remark it now only because I remember it after nearly ten years. I wondered what sort of life she led. She had the animals which she loved and modelled in the garden. I could see her in tweeds, always walking alone. She seemed to me always lonely, repressed, and volcanic. Even then I wondered at her relation with Laci. I don't usually speculate about people — what they do in bed. I have inhibitions — and I hate that people should speculate about me — still many questions crossed my mind about Laci. I think he never understood her at all, but was fascinated by her . . . and still is. I hated his children and wondered why Laci who seemed not greatly to care for them inflicted them on her. L., after all, was my friend, and surely in those days I bored her; I belonged to the political side of the dinner table. The émigrés chattered and she listened to them polite and remote. I listened otherwise — professionally. But though all my connections were with L. . . . . . he was my friend . . . all my sympathies were with C. But, I thought, we shall never be friends. It's a different world.

We rode on the train together to Berlin and she told me she would get a divorce. Laci was going to marry B., who was twenty, young and "unverdorben," flattering to a man going on toward fifty. I thought: Laci is a fool: one doesn't throw away a wife like this woman, so distinguished and so sensitive. But Jews return to Jews, particularly Jewish men to

Jewish women. Suddenly, yesterday, in the midst of dinner, Laci said to me: "Now, as I hear C's voice I remember that when our love was young and I would go to her, she would say, 'Beloved, it is so good you are here . . . I have missed you and needed you . . . come close to me, darling.' She would say it," said Laci, imitating her admirably, "all in the same tone of voice, soft, running the words along evenly, as though she were saying 'I hear it is raining in Vienna and the opera program has been changed.' I tried to make love to her in the same tone, but I could not. I would try to say erotic things, flattering things, tender things all in the same voice, but always I had to raise it."

That was like [X]: "Aren't you *ever* excited . . ." when I was perishing of excitement. Stupid. But L. must have been stupid to her, otherwise. He was so bungling, yesterday, and made me bungling. Together we hurt her. It was about the money. I had asked Lyon to help her get out what she wanted and he said he would, but when L. told her so, triumphantly, she was wounded, and I saw that the fool had no idea of what was really going on in her mind. She expects from L. tenderness and protection. That she still has a claim to, she thinks, after the years. With what tenderness she always treated him! "L. wants a divorce, so I must give it to him. I feel very badly about it." I remember how she said it. How she worked for him when he was in prison. What she wants L. to say is: "C, what do you want to do, and I will help you do it. Don't worry ever about money if I have any." Give *her* a chance to be generous. She wants to act nobly and not haggle. The tone was all wrong.

Anyway, she walked away, and my heart was like lead. I could hardly speak during dinner. Literally I *ached* with chagrin & self-hatred. Immediately afterward she was kind and warm, and she put her arms about me, and the rest of the day was heavenly.

I put the incident down here as a record of my own

sensibility to this woman. What in God's name does one call this sensibility if it be not love? This extraordinary heightening of all ones impressions; this intensification of sensitiveness; this complete identification of feeling? It was so when I read her book and suddenly felt that I *must* translate it, because in its essence I might have written it myself. *I* was Manuela, as she is Manuela, and everything that has happened to her has in essence, and other circumstances, happened to me. This incredible feeling of sisterhood.

In the end I translate all my emotional states into replicas of an earlier, family relation. My love for Josef broke because with him I could not do so. He remained a strange & sweetly assaulting male . . . and no "blood relation of mine." The overwhelming sweetness and understanding in my relation with Hal is that he is close to me as my brother. "My sister, my darling!" Our son is of *our* blood, as near and known to me as my own hands and heart. I was afraid to have Josef's child — afraid that its eyes would be black and its hair thick and curling, and its ways not my ways. A little stranger. Michael has always been there. I played with my son in my own nursery.

(But Jeffers made Orestes say: "I have fallen in love outward!" Oh, I have tried and I have failed! Only if I renounced this pounding of the blood, this periodic delirium, could I know what Jeffers means. To be in love with no one, but with the world. But that's an illness, too. From now on I shall "affirm myself," and let the Freudians make the best of it. Affirm myself, and try, in the light of my own peculiar experience, to be wise).

At Hatvan, when the crisis about the money was over, the day was magical. The place suits Christa. I wanted (ungrateful guest) to take it away from the Hatvanys all together and give it to Christa. If I'd been God I would have.

Laci wanders about in the garden like a Deca-Dante (not my wit) in one of his several hells, but Christa belongs to land, animals, a wide house, unpretentious hospitality. I'd like her to be terribly rich because it would hurt her a bit but would do her good — and everyone else.

The house is beautiful: baroque and simple, a lovely warm yellow, just weather-stained enough, and the mossy-trunked plane trees in the big court between the house's two arms (I love a house with arms) grow beautifully and etch drooping shadows on the walls. The air was mild and there was a thin snow, insufficient to disturb the contours of the formal garden. We walked in the garden and then ate lunch. (But in the garden the contretemps with Laci occurred and lunch choked me). Afterward we went to the vineyard, the stables, and the wine cellar, and Christa went with me in the car. C. and Irene. The rest in a carriage.

(Oh, you baby! Oh, you love-struck adolescent! What a moment, during which it was decided who was to ride with whom! Believe me I laugh at myself. I am perfectly conscious that I am absurd. But do you think the self-mockery and the clear, rational consciousness helps one bit that curious, sweet, faint feeling. It does *not!*)

We came back after visiting the wide-horned white oxen in the stalls, and watching the sheep moving about the barnyard like undulant brown waves, and spending half an hour sampling wines in the wine cellar. (Pat had six glasses in front of her and looked selig). We walked, C. and I (and Irene, but I forget Irene) and talked of this and that and I was happy.

At the house again gipsies played while we had tea & talked, and the little maid & the coachman sang. C. lay on a deep divan and I beside her, and she held her cheek on her hand, and looked quite young, and translated for me: the song says:

And the song said: Other girls have flower pots in their windows.

Why have I no flower pots?

Because they are in the way when he comes through.

Or

"I lost my handkerchief in the cemetery. It was my best handkerchief. But I don't care about the handkerchief. Only I care for my sweetie whom I left there. I really am sorry about her."

They all seem like that — the songs — bittersweet and ironic.

C. began to look tired. But she had begun to look tired in the morning when L. and I talked of money to her.

I told her I should like to translate her book. She looked pleased — or was she? But I would do it very, very well. I know that. And would somewhat (perhaps) satisfy my intense need to do something for Christa. So I didn't mind even if I seemed *zudringlich*, because I *know* I would do it more carefully and lovingly than most, and care and love are needed to make a good translation. It's a very feminine book, too. And I know what it's all about, innerly, and that, too, is necessary in the translator, because the book is subtly and delicately written.

So then we had supper & left & went home.

We kissed each other & she called me "liebling" and said: "I will write to you & telephone, and you shall not get rid of me." And I felt full of beatitude.

I put all this down to look at it: The result: There is not the *slightest* indication that the extraordinarily intense erotic feeling I have for this woman is in any way reciprocated. I *feel*, of course, that it is — but the wish is so easily father to the thought. And if it isn't, I stand to make a damned bore of myself to a woman from whom, in the last analysis, I want only a warm friendship, and the opportunity to go on loving her no more articularly [articulately] than heretofore. —

I came home [to Vienna] on the night train. In the morning I dropped into bed in the Wohllebengasse and slept until 10. Then motored to the Semmering. Above Glognitz the sun was brilliant. Suddenly I was glad, glad, glad to be home with the party over. Hal was in his room. When I came in he was glad. I could see he was awfully glad. I stood a long time in his arms, loving his familiar feel and smell, rubbing my face on his face. What are you going to do? he said, and I said: First of all take a bath. So he said: Stop in on your way down. I stopped in in a dressing gown and nothing else and he said: Come to my bed. So I did and it was awfully good. Especially good, with me just too tired to expect it to be and suddenly it was there and very wonderful. Afterward — quite a while afterward — he said: Darling, I didn't do anything. Did you? And I hadn't. And I didn't. It would be nice to have a new child as the end-of-the-party. So I slept all afternoon.

I write all this out to be clear. Obviously there are two quite different feelings. I don't love Hal any less. Rather more.

Mikey came into my room at about six. "Mammy wead," he said, and climbed with his books into my bed. I kissed the back of his neck and he smelled delicious, like a kitten. "Mammy's pet," he said and grinned delightfully. I think he will be a terribly attractive male.

I have been very, very happy. And all the time, every moment, I have thought of Christa.

Jan. 4.

Standing above Buda looking down across the Danube, through the arches in the *Bastei*, Laci said: I will tell you the history of Hungarian architecture. What the Romans built, the Huns destroyed; what the Huns built, the Turks destroyed; what the Turks built, the Magyars destroyed; what the Magyars built, the Jews destroyed; what the Jews built, the Magyars are now destroying."

In all these countries there is a smell of death. And I think it was always so, and not just "since the war." The prerequisites of a genuine and profound civilization were never here. Andreas Ady said: The Danube was made to put half-nations and half-people in the stocks for shame. Laci said I should come and make a great tour and write a book about the last refuge of feudalism. It is incredibly strong still. Laci said: "What is reaction in other countries is progress here. Elsewhere capitalism means reaction; here it means progress."

Jan. 5.

Another nice day. In the morning letters, then a walk ending at the Erzherzog Johann, where we lunched. I looked at the ice rink, bought shoes & skates & shall try tomoro. Then home & wrote more letters & played with my boy. A quiet (and very good) dinner & a long talk with Hal who is sympathetic (but skeptical) about the idea of my writing a novel. We are very close together these days, tender, friendly, and always a little amorous — distantly. I read Joe Hergesheimer's article in the Post . . . . the one Lorimer wanted me to do. But I can't. I agree with what he says about France & Germany, and about our sentimentality and Galahadism (my words, not J.H.'s) but when he advises us to act in the same way as Germany & France then I protest. In the end the policy of these countries will lead to impoverishment, a lowering of the living standard, & war. The whole thesis of a *national* economy is exploded . . . has no reality . . . and in particular none for us. There is, actually, only a world economy — which doesn't function.

* * *

These years have robbed us of our Utopias. We've seen them all realized and are disillusioned with all of them. Communism is a stupid rule of a meanminded burocracy employing terror against every energetic and courageous individual, a contemptible glorification of the mass-man. Socialism is the rule of the "Bonzen" — entrenched burocracy mouthing noble formulas, like Adler addressing the relatives of the dead; fascism is the rule of the top sergeant and the half-educated, national socialism is the sick affirming their health — a lot of wavy-haired bugger boys talking about woman's function in bearing SONS for the state. The nobility is played out. Bethlen's a good example, taking money out of the treasure to "repair" or compensate himself for his lost estates, & deserting to the riviera with his mistress; or Windischgraetz forging franc notes; or Elizabeth Windischgraetz fornicating with a socialist. As for the capitalists and bankers, they are stuffed shirts, like Parker Gilbert, or poor fools like all the people who lent money to Europe, or are plain crooks, like [. . .]. "Where shall wisdom be found & where is the place of understanding?"

The reversion to our own hearts & souls, to the kingdom of Heaven which is within us.

Steiner says it will all be good for culture. But I don't think the reserves of this decaying economic order (vast as the reserves are) will reach that far. Culture usually, alas, goes with prosperity.

* * *

I read some in Guy de Pourtalès' Life of Wagner & found it enormously interesting. In my mind I was comparing Wagner's age — the period of the Napoleonic wars[1] — with now. Enormous similarities. Liberal uplift romantic movements like La Jeune Europe reminiscent of Clarté (Nous voulons faire une révolution d'esprit) etc. And, of course, general breakdown. Still the feudal order was stronger then,

---

[1] Richard Wagner (1813–1883) did not live in the Napoleonic era.

and it was based on *land*. The people at the top were essentially stronger than our people at the top can possibly be. *They* "sat & possessed" (sitze und besitze) but our Otto Kahns must *move* & possess . . . and their fortunes shift with them. All relative and dynamic.

Jan. 6.

The latest word for "planned economy" is technocracy. I don't believe in it. When we can't even make an administration for a city which will attend properly to traffic control and emptying the garbage, how do we hope to organize the whole of economic life? Who is going to do it? Even the church, which selected its apostles according to a far more rigorous standard than any lay body can impose — pledging them to poverty and to chastity, holding before them the vision of another world . . . could not escape corruption.

The lot of man is tragic and the cards are stacked against him. And "justice is not without us as a fact but within us as a deep yearning." Still, I suppose we have to hope and work for a better world, or drift into impossible cynicism and despair.

Jan. 6.

I went and tried to skate. I was too tight and cramped, and kept tripping myself up. "Relax," said the instructor, who was a personable young man though I hardly remember more than his mitts to which I clung like Prometheus to his rock; "gently, gently; no effort; you must let yourself be cartilage — above all let yourself go." I laughed out loud & he wondered why. I thought: that's the recipe for success in love & it's taken me twenty years to learn it. To be soft and receptive. All of grace & feminine beauty is in it. Anyhow, in a fortnight I shall skate decently, I am sure.

But did I suddenly develop a desire to skate because of

C.'s book? Because some time or other she must have skated?

We had tea at the Südbahn Hotel, supper at home, went to a movie "Under false flags" and afterward drank a bottle of wine in the bar. Hal was sweet.

I drowsed after lunch. I am full of languor. Hal, looking at me, said: "I thought I had married a serious publicist, a traveller, a conversationalist of parts, an economist, a reader of belles lettres. And what does she turn out to be? A cake-eater! A sleeper in chairs!" He only jeers at me when he is liking me a lot.

Over the wine tonight I thought of Fanchon,[1] & told Hal the story. H was enchanted.

Jan. 7.

At the rinks this morning I watched the two Pousine children from Vienna skating. The instructor said they are the finest juvenile skaters in the world. Slender, long-legged, fair youngsters, the boy in the traditional black tights and short, astrakhan trimmed coat, the girl in white tights & shorts and a brief white dress with a fitted bodice, they were almost exactly the same size and looked like twins although their mother (whom I met afterward in the garderobe) said that the boy was twelve, the girl thirteen. They came flying from the boards at the back of the rink, hand in hand, leaning far forward their feet flying behind them. That's the loveliness of skating — the gesture of Victory, as though the body were carried by the exposed breast, the wide flung arms the thrown back head, and not by the feet at all. It is as though they were propelled by breath, by soul!

Suddenly the boy lifted the girl high, his hands at her little waist, and then they were off, dancing together, she spinning at the end of his arm: now they skated with feet

---

[1] Fanchon Arthur, who had gone into a nunnery.

spread and calves turned out, their bodies flattened against
the wind: now entwined together, with only two legs between
them — he holding her foot, she his — now drawing away
behind them: now pirouetting: now low on the ice their little
feet dashing from under their crouched bodies. And everything they did was with exact precision, with a completely
synchronized rhythm, and they were so happy and exhili-
rated that their eyes and teeth continually flashed.

Afterwards, in the garderobe, I saw the little girl changing
into a warmer and simpler dress. Her mother pulled the
white frock over her head, and her little body emerged, as
thin as her brother's with just two tiny buds of breasts.
Her brother had withdrawn to a corner of the rink and was
practicing a broad jump on skates. He would run, stop, and
leap clear and straight into the air, feet together, and land
as much as two yards away, erect upon the shining blades.
The little girl was excited by this: "Das kahn nicht jeder
tun," she bragged. "Ich auch nicht: bin zu feig . . . ."
She paused a second, "nicht eigentlich *feig*, aber ich möchte
es doch nicht tun." Her pride was of a woman toward a
lover. I wondered what would become of her. Would she
ever find again a man, so black and slender to her slimness
and whiteness, so commanding and so responsive, so articu-
lated with her every muscle, so other and so part of her?
Would she ever, in love, move to music with such music of
blood and music of sinew, with the other there moving the
same way, or would she always, always, love best in the world
the male just like herself only male, moving beside her on the
glittering waste, past the applauding people, while the
radio's waltzes played for their flying bodies. The two of
them were set off, apart, quite alone in the crowd, alone
because of their peculiar and consummate skill, and peculiar
and consummate beauty. And I noticed that whenever —
after the exhibition was over — she floated away, he was

after her, swiftly, and whenever he glided away, she followed him, her long pale, childish legs seeming to trail after her narrow, eager body.

"Will they become professionals?" I asked the mother, who was a little, round, jolly woman.

"Lord, no," she said. "They are, thank heaven, good students . . . skating is just for sport, for pleasure. Both of them will study medicine."

* * *

My skating is atrocious — my left ankle is so weak that I cannot take a long glide on it. It wobbles disgustingly. But I shall keep it up. My son is better off than I was, because he lives in a world which has discovered that people have bodies. I begin to discover sensual pleasures at a time when I should be abnegating them for things of the spirit!

Anyway, I hope Micky will ski & skate, swim, ride, and play tennis, expertly and beautifully.

Since the second of January I have discovered in myself a gentle languor which reminds me, portentously, of another time. I wonder if I *am* enceinte. It began that way before — a sweet laziness and gentle tiredness. And if I am, will I be glad? I should like to have that long-legged red-headed girl that I imagined Michael would be. But — But — But —

Anyway, I won't have an abortion. My whole being rises up against that.

I am not sure that having a child, actually bearing a child, isn't, for woman, the only entirely satisfactory sexual experience. It is a kind of terrible ecstacy accompanied by a feeling of great expansion and power, and terrific heightening of all impression and experience. The pain is secondary — as it is in the first embrace, when one strains that piercing agonizing blade to one. "No, no, beloved (fainting) do not go away. Stay! Stay!" So in childbirth one falls upon pain, fights with it, exultantly, the air full of flashing blades: covered with blood and wounds, one is, and furious and profane. It seems to me that as my child was born I was full of agony and full of laughter. Then I remember that there was an earthquake, some cosmic catastrophe; the world opened up and all the stars fell, and I died. And when I woke again the world had never, never seemed so sweet.

Jan. 9.

Wrote to Percy Lubbock re the Villa Medici which we might take for March and April.[1]

At Sacher's tonight where Hal & I dined happily alone (after one act of Kreisler's Sissy, which I enjoyed but which bored Hal).[2] I told Hal of one scene which I see from *The Tulip Box*.[3] My heroine is being delivered of a child. The wind is blowing the white hospital curtains into the room and she, in great pain, finds all sorts of memories flashing thru her mind. The curtains blow: Oh, wild west wind . . . I fall upon the thorns of life, I bleed . . . one too like thee, tameless, and swift, and proud . . . And . . . . my head is bloody but unbowed. But why west wind? No sun that afternoon . . . north, perhaps, and anyway, it's all too romantic. Unmodern. Today one dies (only one doesn't . . . the childbed mortality is higher in fiction than in any civilized country . . . Hergesheimer, Mt.Blood . . . . from Hergesheimer to Hemingway. Do all writers who begin with an H kill their heroines in childbed in the Hemingway manner? So. aloud: "The romantic tradition is dead, don't you think, Doctor?"

---

[1] They never did. The Villa Medici belonged to Lady Sybil Lascelles, subsequently in marriage Cutting, then Scott, then Lubbock, but it was and is a national monument of Italy, with vestiges of Botticelli painting in one gallery and many other noble remembrances; it would have been beyond even Red's temporarily swollen resources.

[2] *Sissy* was a musical comedy by the violinist Fritz Kreisler.

[3] *The Tulip Box* was Dorothy's novel, never written.

"Save your strength, Mrs Lewis. You must save your strength."

"How deep the source, how inexhaustible." More poetry. Either one has strength to spend, to waste . . . go away, darling, and don't look so funny. It's not so bad. Only — ouch — oh, darling, do go away . . . . to spend to waste or one cannot live at all oh my God oh my God oh Jesus Maria Christus and all the saints. What do they do in the tenements, doctor, women in labor? Where I live in summer in the Vermont hills they've never heard of anaesthetics in childbirth. At most a whiff of chloroform. What do they do, doctor?

Save your strength, Mrs Lewis, please save your strength.

Or in the tenements. Women are confined in the presence of the whole family, aren't they, doctor? And there is something so hideously obscene about birth. "Als bewegung unaesthetisch" — do you remember what Heine said, doctor? Or do you? (That's Evelyn Waugh). Only Heine spoke of something else. Something terribly obscene.

I suppose that's why chars are so much fouler mouthed than any men oh my dear loving God excuse me, doctor, but I feel profane. Tell me, do more women scream or swear?

Please, Mrs Lewis, it is foolish to talk. You must save your strength.

Foolish to talk and foolish to think. Dear Doctor you talk like George Jean Nathan in The American Spectator. The place of woman . . . . The modern woman . . . The feminist . . . who dares to talk even at a moment like this. Must it go on, doctor?

I don't know whether I can stand it. How do you know until it's all over how much you can stand. I don't want to stand any more. It's enough oh dear loving God it's enough give me something . . . quick quick . . . . damn it. I can stand a lot more of this. Any pain in your head is worse, is worse.

Dec. 22.

A propos the talk last night with Barbara:

There is no possibility of an elite existing except in a society where minorities can exist. The *characteristic* of an elite is that it has other standards than the mass. Ortega[1] says: If ten or twelve men died the whole of modern physics would vanish. In Germany the first sign of the continued existence of an *elite* is the protest of the protestant pastors.

German Nazi-ism is not an elite movement but a mass movement, led by mass men who have no reverence for the machine which they take over by violence no realization of the process by which it was created, no historicity and who have no hestitation in imposing their mediocre opinions upon everybody including their betters.

3

DOROTHY'S DIARY FOR THE YEAR 1932–1933, OR THE ONLY PART of it we know, stops here. The cheap and sleazy notebook in which it is written contains only blank pages after this last entry. And this last entry — written in December, eleven months after the rest of it — seems to bear no relation to what has preceded. We do not know who Barbara was or why this sudden return to the diary, after such a long absence, was necessary.

Dorothy's diaries (after the honeymoon) are all of this inconsecutive, hit-or-miss character. Years would pass without a single entry in such a book, so far as we know (I do not pretend to guess what she may have destroyed). A typical year would contain a few entries (1942 and 1945 are examples) and then nothing: blank pages. As she grew older a diary was a form of good resolution for her, something connected with the

[1] Ortega y Gasset: *The Revolt of the Masses.*

first of the New Year, something soon abandoned in the rush of daily life.

But this diary of the party on the Semmering and the visit to Schloss Hatvan in Hungary is far more revealing than any other document Dorothy has left to us. We behold, in awe really, and at times in consternation, the search for love (it is no less) on the part of a woman nearing forty and by no means inexperienced, yet desperately innocent at heart and in many ways untouched, virginal. How she turns first here and then there — ! It is so unlike her own serene and competent exterior that most of her contemporaries (those who were at the famous party, for instance) would be astounded at it. Never again did she put pen to paper, so far as we know, to tell such secrets of the heart; never again did she dwell upon the vague and contradictory impulses, unknown or unknowable, which overwhelm sense and brain alike in the emotional jungle of the human interior. Interiority was not, if one may so express it, her field of investigation, or even her realm of being: for the most part she dwelt outside, resolutely outside herself. Here for once (and remember, she kept this little shabby, sleazy book for decades) she was all within, bewildered indeed and afraid to be happy, but at all events enclosed and indwelling.

And another thing worthy of remark is that Phil Goodman's letter to H. L. Mencken, written from Vienna on February 3rd, 1933, to tell Mencken that Dorothy is determined to divorce Red, comes on the very heels of the rapturous diary here reproduced. There is not one hint of any such thing in the diary, and yet at this very moment the rumor began to appear in all quarters and was (as in the letter from Goodman to Mencken) authenticated by persons who had just been hearing it from Dorothy herself. She had evidently recovered from her rapture (perhaps on finding that she was not pregnant, after all?) and Red's bad temper and his dislike for her friends may have played a great part in making her think (as she had already

thought for almost three years) that her marriage could not be
saved. Certainly the winter in Vienna-and-the-Semmering had
not saved it. Phil Goodman's letter to Mencken says, point-
blank, that "this was the earful Lily and I got last night."
(I.e., from Dorothy.)

Red had gone to London, ostensibly on business connected
with *Ann Vickers*, which had appeared in America in January
with a success unknown since before the depression. (Its
great run inspired the hope that it might be breaking a cycle
of four years' failure in the publishing business.) He wrote
lovingly from London, but sailed from there later in the
month (incognito, at least in principle) on the semi-cargo
steamer *American Farmer* for New York. Dorothy went first
to Munich and then to Portofino to Christa's house. She was
concerned chiefly about the treatment of the Jews in Germany
and was planning a series of articles for the *Saturday Evening
Post* on this subject; her career had now really begun to fulmi-
nate and was, within a year, to reach its explosion.

She had, I believe, achieved with Christa precisely what she
said in this diary that she wanted: "a warm friendship, and the
opportunity to go on loving her no more articulately than heretofore." They were together in Munich and in Portofino for
the spring, and Dorothy brought Christa back to America and
Twin Farms in May; Red was absent most of the time, and
the two women returned to Europe in midsummer for a while.
When Dorothy returned (it was a wild summer of coming and
going) Red presented her with a new house as a headquarters
in New York: it was in Bronxville, and in the most purse-proud
part of Bronxville, at 17 Wood End Lane. It was a present
to Dorothy, from the beginning: a propitiation? a confession?
a lament? She never liked it, and later on rented it to me,
which disposed of the matter: on an icy night in February,
1941, I succeeded somehow in burning it down, and all dwelling
within it (my wife and children, their nurse, the servants and

myself) narrowly escaped incineration. This house had a back garden conterminous with the back garden of the Kennedy family (Joe Kennedy was ambassador to London when I lived there; his son, as is known, became President). The Bronxville house was supposed to take the place of a house in New York, which it did not; it was too far from Manhattan for most business or social meetings; it was not far enough to be country. It was, more than anything else, a symptom of Red's restless and ever-growing despair.

That year of 1933 and the next one, 1934, really were a feverish muddle for both Dorothy and Red, or perhaps it should be said that their muddle grew worse, became incomprehensible, became really final. Their letters never ceased to express love, longing and bereavement, but one wonders, one really wonders, what they meant. They meant, I suppose, an aspiration, a sigh for the might-have-been, a wish for the never-was; it was a concerted make-believe which may, indeed, have been their only real point of agreement at the time. I do not doubt their sincerity. I only see their letters, as now so mercilessly exposed, and contrast them with my own distinct recollection of their half-controlled hostility when I saw them together. For I did see them together, on a very few occasions, and it was not good to do so: earlier or later (much later when they had frankly separated and met as friends) the climate was more propitious.

Mostly, however, I saw them separately. Red had taken it into his head to use a hotel, or the hotel business, as a sort of symbol for the aesthetic impulse in the American character — the desire to create beauty. He was worrying away at this idea even earlier, but in 1932 and 1933 (after the publication of *Ann Vickers*) it rose to domination, and resulted in a novel called *Work of Art*, published in January, 1934. He used two brothers for his contrast of characters (the plowman and the poet, so to speak, much as Eugene O'Neill had done in the

early work called *Beyond the Horizon*). The novel was, I
thought (and have heard no other view), unsuited for publication. It represented the least valid of Red's gifts, or indeed
the most glaring of his deficiencies, which was his sense of
poetry. *Beyond the Horizon* was a very immature work but I
well remember how uplifted (as by Shakespeare or Keats or
Wordsworth at his best) it made us all feel in our first youth.
Red, trying to do the same sort of thing, failed because the
sense of poetry was not in him. The *knowledge* of it, yes: he
had memorized it by the million kilometers, and he could imitate almost any sort of poetry in English with extraordinary
skill, but he had no real sense of poetry as he had no real sense
of music. He never really wrote a musical or poetic passage
in the mammoth books of his best achievement: and it was
not for lack of trying. For poetry, music, languages, etc., he
was an imitator, and even an imitator of genius, but any child
could tell that it was not the real thing. It is therefore unfortunate that he undertook to create a novel in which the sense
of poetry (or of the creation of beauty) was central to the
theme.

Nevertheless, he did, and just at this time. As a result he
frequented hotels all over the country, taking off on a jaunt
whenever he felt so inclined, staying here a week and there a
week. In New York he occupied a penthouse apartment in the
Hotel New Yorker, which was then new or relatively new. I
think he knew the manager, the affable Mr Ralph Hitz, and
obtained from him considerable information about the operation of such an establishment. How many hours I wasted
in that penthouse apartment! Red would call me up at any
hour of the day or night and command my attendance. If it
were possible to do so, I obliged. My juniority was extreme,
not only by the sixteen years between us but by my own sense
of his power and eminence as a writer. Aside from all that, I
was also fond of Red and he knew it. There was something so

earth-born and yet iridescent in his best moods (something like, say, Niagara Falls) that I was always constrained to silence over his worst phases, and his headlong rush of kindness (when it came) obliterated every vagary of his tortured temper. So he would call me. And I would go. (This was in 1933 chiefly, and in the winter only, as I went back to Paris in the spring.) There would be Lou Florey, always, answering the telephone and making the calls (as well as doing anything else Red's oscillometer indicated). There was, that year, Harry Maule, because he was, I think, attempting to get some kind of work schedule out of Red on the forthcoming novel. Harry had become Red's editor; he was afterwards, and for life, my own editor; when he left Doubleday for Random House in (about) 1940, I followed him there, as Red did eventually. His dry, quizzical, antiseptic manner was always out of place in the madhouse Red created about him. Harry was the voice of common sense, reason and, to some extent, even decorum. He was obliged in self-defense to do a certain amount of drinking during those years, because it was impossible to spend any time with Red Lewis without doing so, but he was the master of his soul. He was patient, unbelievably patient, and could spend many hours at that penthouse on top of the New Yorker Hotel, but he was never out of touch with his secretary and I well remember how, in the midst of the most awful brawls, he would be in the corner quietly talking to his office on the telephone.

Aside from Lou and Harry, who were endemic, the New Yorker penthouse gave leg room to an ill-assorted gaggle of guests. George Jean Nathan, who always treated Red with a tolerant and amused contempt, came there sometimes. (I have always thought that the surest proof of talent is its condescension to genius.) There were times when the "rank and fashion of the County Clare," as the drunken publican says in *The Playboy of the Western World*, could have been seen weaving in and out of that nondescript cubicle with its square forms and seriatim furniture. It had rather a Stonehenge look, or rather as Stonehenge might have been after it had been ruined the tenth or twelfth time, before it was dug up: it was all square and in blocks, prehistoric without touching upon history at all, and through the big windows there was an unrivaled view of the Hudson River and of the sky above it. Grand Rapids had moved to a roof in Manhattan: that was it, but the setting could not impair the blue heights in which it swam.

Red thought nothing of leaving the sitting room–drawing room–receiving room for an hour or so, with or without notice, and taking his usual nap in the bedroom. Not everybody was accustomed to his habits in this regard, and the more sensitive guests had a tendency to go home. He was always deeply injured when he came back to the party and found that such a catastrophe had been allowed to occur. He was fierce to the point of savagery with anybody like Harry or me if we dared to stir. He could not, of course, be quite so Caesarean with his other guests. If I am not utterly mistaken, Miss Lillian Gish was one of those who, on one occasion, took Red's withdrawal as a signal to depart, and when he came back into the room half an hour later he upbraided me for permitting this deprivation. Lillian was then, as now, an object of adoration, and once she got into Red's clutches he never wanted to let her go. She was so much stronger than Red!— but he never knew it; her fragile and timid silence, her few chosen and diffident words, her imaginary bonnet-and-shawl in the air above us, counted for so much more than Red's excursions and alarums. I don't think either Scott Fitzgerald or Ernest Hemingway ever came to this hell hole in the sky; if they did, I was not present. I never saw Dorothy there either.

Baroness Hatvany (Christa Winsloe) was instinctively akin to Red, co-conscious with him, as only neurotics can be with each other; no sentence had to be completed really, because each knew what the other intended to say. I think they liked each other very much. I have this impression, however, chiefly from what he said; I do not remember having seen them together, and I was not at Twin Farms when she stayed there. (Obviously I must have seen them together in New York, but all recollection of it has gone.)

I did see Christa with Dorothy and others, notably, as I remember, Ben Stolberg, the Marxist or ex-Marxist intellectual who carried such weight with both Dorothy and Red at that period. (He deflected Red for one whole year from the native-American-radical idea of the labor novel into a pseudo-European Marxist interpretation of the drama.) The one and only thing I ever had against Christa was her habit of dropping into German, or even into Viennese dialect, at the very crux of the matter she was talking about. Whether it was a funny story or a deeply serious idea to be presented, she would reach the climax and then abandon English (which she spoke perfectly, with only a burry, furry bit of accent) and go into whichever German accent or dialect happened to suit her best. She was as much at home in the sharp Berliner talk as in the soft Viennese drawl, and either one was Chinese to me. My German was never good (it has grown worse with the years) and the dialects have always been beyond me. At these points the only person in the room who knew what Christa was talking about (and, mind you, at the peak of her discourse) was Dorothy. Dorothy would then laboriously explain what Christa had said in Viennese (or Berliner or Münchener) and the point would, as usual, get blunted. The laugh, if the discourse had called for a laugh, had been exclusively between Dorothy and Christa.

This sounds ill-natured, which I was not then and am not now towards this charming lady whom I scarcely knew. She was beautiful, witty, knowledgeable, and truly sensitive, almost too sensitive. She could pass without transition from tears to

laughter and back again. If anything moved her to pity or
terror she would say "Ach, Gott!" under her breath and it was
a prayer. She had a liking for generalizations of the most
sweeping character but she would abandon them within a few
seconds — unlike Dorothy, who would really pursue any generalization to Ultima Thule. One night when I was in a restaurant with Christa and Dorothy (and others whom I forget)
there was some worthy citizen who asked her how she liked
New York (where she had been only for a week or so, and for
the first time). She said she had all sorts of conflicting and
irrational impressions, things clashing and banging against each
other in her head, but she was only sure of one thing, that New
York was *gross-städtisch*, and that it was probably the most
gross-städtisch of all the great cities of this world. She referred
to Kafka's *Amerika*, in which I think he uses the same expression (the book was less old then than now). I was very impressed both by the modesty of her response (that she had
nothing to say of New York except this impression) and also
by the immensity of the generalization, which would seem to
mean that the quintessence of the urban-metropolitan disease
is in New York. (I suppose that is what Kafka meant too, but
Christa was not really talking about Kafka: she felt it herself
and it was obvious in her earnestness.)

We then passed off into a discussion of how to put the word
"gross-städtisch" into English, and settled, I think, on "metropolitan," which has precisely the same dictionary meaning and
nowhere near the same complex significance. The overtones
are totally different.

Christa was a true charmer, in the truest Budapest-Vienna
way, but for the sake of the story we are telling I think I must
say that I never saw her as quite such a dazzling creature as
Dorothy did. She was beautiful, yes, but neither young nor
slim; her clothing was, I thought, for the most part unobtru-
sive; her conversation was limited to the subjects which
(however great and various they may be) can only be discussed

by those who have the habit of doing so. In other words, she had no ordinary conversation that I could see. Put her down alongside a total stranger at a dinner party and unless he had a twinkle in his eye (corresponding to her own) I could guarantee a disaster. What I mean is that Dorothy saw her as a *grande dame*, a woman of the world, a fatal and irresistible woman, whereas in fact she was not. She was that goulashwoman produced on the Danube, neither an aristocrat nor an intellectual nor an adventuress, but some sort of vivid combination of them all, with a special writing talent thrown in to make it more exceptional.

As a "woman of the world" I think Christa could not compare to other Viennese aristocrats who were Dorothy's own friends in later years. And — even beyond that — in the ease and indeed mastery of social situations, the ability to deal with any and all — there is the simple matter of tact which I have mentioned before: she spoke an unknown language when she reached the point of her story. English was as easy to her as it is to you. But she funked it at the high point of whatever she had to say; she invariably fell back into dialect, or, if it were really serious, into classical German.

I am not elaborating an objection to the Baroness Hatvany, because I had none and have none now. I am only trying to throw light upon one element of Dorothy's character and intellect. It is this: her extreme susceptibility to the Danubian pretension. She always thought, to the day of her death, that persons from Vienna and Budapest and their environs were more cultivated and perceptive than all others. She thought "culture" either belonged on the Danube or could only be consecrated there. It was, I suppose, Josef Bard who created this misconception, but there is no doubt that it governed her unconscious to the very end. She judged Italian, French or even English writers by the value given them on the Danube (we saw this earlier, about Pirandello); and every quality to be observed elsewhere was enhanced if it were found there.

This is one of the many ways in which I was always in disagreement with Dorothy. What Vienna and Berlin were to her, Paris and London were to me. The young American in Europe (really young, I mean, which could be at any age — I was twenty-two) acquires a second home if he stays a while. ("J'ai deux amours, mon pays et Paris!") If I were to have picked out a fascinating woman of the world, beautiful and intelligent and above the battle, to put at the masthead of the ship, I should certainly not have sought for her in the Danubian regions. To me the most beautiful women have been generally English and the most truly chic women have been French: it may be banal but it is so. With Dorothy the Josef-hypnosis never faded, and her one altogether admirable woman, with beauty and intelligence and chic, was Budapest-Vienna.

Christa was great fun, just the same: nothing I say is to detract from her. It is said merely to explain Dorothy.

In 1934 Baroness Hatvany went to the Salzburg Festival and saw Ezio Pinza for the first time, singing *Don Giovanni* under the direction of Bruno Walter. She was moved to write an eloquent essay on the subject, of which the manuscript is in the Syracuse University Library. She also took off, and we never saw her again in these regions, although she wrote to Dorothy at great length from many places (Chicago, Los Angeles, San Francisco) where Ezio was singing. He must have been rather rude at times. Christa prided herself on her Italian, but often when she spoke it Ezio would say to her: "Speak English." I think myself that it was because her Italian was better than his.

4

RED AND DOROTHY WROTE TO EACH OTHER CONSTANTLY DURING these years, and there are some letters, out of the whole mountainous mystification, which ring true to the intention if not to its fulfillment. Dorothy's are longer and more numerous: they are also, in general, more "composed," more conscious of composition, more given to narrative, analysis and description. Husband and wife are alike in complaining about the absence of letters, or their slowness in arriving, just as they are in the constant assertion of "I miss you." Thus we have Dorothy, from Vienna on March 13th, 1933:

> My beloved, I have a very bad conscience that I haven't written which isn't appeased by the fact that you, presumably, haven't either. And if you say that you were on the ship, then I say that on a ship is a fine place to write every day to your girl and post the letters when you get off. And that I was *not* on the ship, but in the German inferno.

(This was her trip to Nazi Germany, a very mild inferno indeed at that time compared to what it became later.)

Another letter at the same period begins:

> Darling, darling, whether you get any letters or not, or whether or what, please believe that I love you always and will till I die (which at the present moment seems remote.

In these and in many others we get no hint of quarrel or misunderstanding, although Dorothy had spoken to a variety of friends about her intentions. There does come, in the letters of only a few days later, from Christa's house at Portofino, a part of the truth. There are a good many of these letters, enough to indicate that probably Dorothy wrote to Red every day even though all the letters have not been kept. Christa had gone ahead to Portofino to get the house ready and settle Michael and Hammerli (his nurse) into it; life is all arranged; many German writers of quality, already in self-imposed exile from Hitlerism, live in the neighborhood; the landscape is wonderful, the days uneventful, work going well. Dorothy writes often of Christa, but not at all in the vein of the diary. On March 30th she says:

We are having a lovely time here together — she's the most sympathetic woman I have met in years and years. As for your last admonition to me — do you remember it? — have no fears, I ain't thata way.

A letter of five days earlier (March 25, 1933) is in another vein — sadder, perhaps, but more germane to the actual situation. It is given in full:

Torre di Giorgio,
portofino mare
Italia Levante
March 25.

My dear, my dear:

Your two letters from New York came only today which makes me think that my long one to you must have been greatly delayed. Hal, I couldn't write for two reasons; in the first place, in Germany, I could think of nothing but what I saw, and I was on the move from nine in the morning until twelve at night and then dropped into bed utterly exhausted. The other reason is that I have never never felt so cut off from you emotionally as I have been in all this time. I think for one thing I was ill for a time after you left. I had that miscarriage and after that I was sick every ten days, and prostrated. I had to go to a doctor finally, who gave me some medicine and some treatments and I am all right now. But perhaps it was that which made me so depressed. I felt as though you did not care for me any more; that last fortnight in Vienna weighed upon my memory. I felt as though our marriage were somehow going on the rocks. And I had no emotional strength with which to try to pull it off. Your going back to drinking spirits was part of it. You yourself had said, you know, "If I go back now on my own decision it will be very serious." It seemed to me that our life together was falling into exactly the pattern of your life with Grace; that it would move in the same direction and to the same denouement, and that nothing I could do would help to stop it. Then, your own letters were curiously remote and cold. They did not bring you to me; rather the contrary. These two which came this morning . . . they are sweet . . and you might have written them to anyone. I thought: I must save myself; I must really, now, save myself. I really tried hard not to love you; I confess it. I have been too hurt in my life, Hal, before, to dare even to think of being hurt in the same way again. Only it wouldn't be the same way now, but much, much worse . . . .

Only, and this is the truth, and I suppose the only truth, I do love you. I love you too terribly. I know now that it is all a self-deception . . my trying to think that I could get along without you . . I, too, find in you the only security I have in the world . . we've got to go on together, forever, and be kind to each other . .

Oh, sweet, be loving with me.

d

We have already seen the rest of the comings-and-goings of that year. Dorothy brought Christa back to New York and later on to Twin Farms. Red, in his unceasing quest for a subject of work, and influenced no doubt by the skill and effectiveness of Sidney Howard's dramatizations, was beginning to think longingly of the theatre. Just then, at the end of 1933, he made the acquaintance of Lloyd Lewis in Chicago. Lloyd Lewis, who was an expert on the American Civil War as well as a writer for the Chicago *Daily News*, had actually met Red two or three times before he spoke of a subject which aroused the latter's immediate interest: the anti-slavery men known as Jayhawkers in Kansas. Red was fired with the wish to write a play. (The wish was already there, I think: now he saw a subject and a collaborator.) Having finished his novel *Work of Art* in September, Red now moved to Chicago for a time to work with Lloyd Lewis on the play, with Lou Florey in attendance for the typing.

The letters which follow, written from the Blackstone Hotel in Chicago, are very characteristic of Red. They are spoof, quip and jape, but some sort of suggested or implied meaning could always be found in Red's nonsense, and as often as not without his conscious intent. So often, indeed most of the time, when he was in this mood he did not seem to be saying anything beyond froth and bubbles, and yet afterwards it seemed to carry at least a hint of reason.

THE BLACKSTONE
SOUTH MICHIGAN AVENUE & EAST 7TH ST.

Chicago,
November 14, 1933

Dear Dorothy:

I venture so to call you for I have heard Red speak of you so often under that name. Will you please come and take your husband away from here? What he is doing to my boy, Lloyd, is just nobody's business. He is certainly raising hell with my poor husband, who, up to Red's arrival was an Archbishop of the Catholic Church. They have now closed down Michigan Avenue because of his misbehavior; Lloyd has been fired from the *Chicago Daily News;* the *News* has also fired Eddie Mowrer; and I no longer dare to go to my job on the Hearst paper here. Can't you do something?

Yours sororily,
Mrs. Katherine Lewis

November 14, 1933

Mrs. Sinclair Lewis
17 Wood End Lane
Bronxville, New York

Dear Madam:

We apologize for troubling you, but is there any possibility you will come West and take your husband out of this hotel. He has practically ruined our business. He and his cousin, Mr. Lloyd Lewis, who was recently in the hospital, which seems to me much the best place for him — go striding up and down the halls of this hitherto respectable hotel shouting out such foul phrases as "God damn you General, I'm going to kill all the southerners."

We set our hotel dick on them but your husband killed him with what he says is a Civil War sabre. We then ordered these two gentlemen out of their rooms — which cost too damn much — but they have barricaded themselves and we see no way of getting rid of them except through your helpful auspices.

Will be glad of anything you can do in this matter, and beg to remain, Madam,

Your most humble obedient servant,
Otto Schemmelfpenniger, Mgr.

November 14, 1933

My darling,

It is eight o'clock in the morning — I thought of telling you it was six o'clock in the morning except that you might get the goods on me later. But I really have been working since six this morning, in the last throes of the play. I think I shall have it done in about four or five days.

I am as worried as hell about Lloyd. He has a stomach ulcer and he looks so pale and thin.

When he comes on east I want to have him out at the house with every care taken of him. Katherine will not be along, which will simplify his domestic problem.

I think it was terrible of you to fire Johann. That was very thoughtless. He had promised to show me the best gambling dens in Westchester County and to introduce me to the very sweetest Nazi agent, who would finance my new trip to Germany, where I am planning to write a book called "Heil Hitler."

And then you put this on the bum! A hell of a wife you are.

Among the letters of this period, so numerous and indeed so similar, there is one which might have been written by either Dorothy or Red. They had by now acquired the same dialect of separation. Furthermore, the letter (undated) is signed "Tiny," which is one of the many names Red called Dorothy. There is not really a doubt in my mind that it is from Red, but that is a matter of handwriting only. It follows:

Barnard

June 28

Thursday

Talking to you on the phone yesterday, to Bronxville — lovely — it made me believe in modern inventions. But last evening, the valley so lovely under the full moon, the farther hills gray shadows mysteriously sliding one into another, that I was homesick for you. I've never loved you so much!

Tiny

I O

The Career

ON AUGUST 25, 1934, DOROTHY THOMPSON WAS EXPELLED FROM Germany by decree of the secret police. Since she had already visited Germany five times since Hitler's advent without trouble, the chances are that such drastic action in her case had been delayed by the uncertainties of the new regime — that, and the difficulties attending any clear decision in a case so notable.

For Dorothy had already become established, particularly in the last year or so, even though she was not yet famous. She was an American, a woman, and the wife of a world-renowned writer, all of which complicated her status as a political journalist. Moreover, no action of the kind taken against her had yet occurred in the year and a half since Hitler's seizure of power. Nowadays the expulsion of a foreign correspondent from almost any country causes no astonishment, but thirty years ago it was an event almost unknown. Dictatorships themselves were still practically unknown, and their full development in tyranny was still to come.

As a result Dorothy's expulsion caused a great deal of excitement and anxiety. It seemed a foretaste of the future, as indeed it was. Nothing of the kind had seemed possible only a year before. The decision taken was indeed so serious that there is no room for doubt that Hitler himself made it. It involved policy, both internally and externally, and no lesser authority in that regime would have risked taking it without the Führer's order.

The police officers waited upon Dorothy at the Adlon Hotel, where she was living, and gave her the request to leave within twenty-four hours. The document was dated August 24th.

The New York *Times* correspondent, Frederick Birchall, wrote a long story about these events, which appeared on the front page of his own paper in America and in numerous others. It is remarkable for the caution with which he approaches the word "expelled," which had hitherto not appeared (either by word or deed) in the doings of governments. The first paragraph of Birchall's story reads:

> Dorothy Thompson, magazine writer, special correspondent for the Saturday Evening Post, who in private life is Mrs. Sinclair Lewis, wife of the novelist, left Germany tonight at the request of the Hitler government. Since the request was backed by an intimation that if she did not go within twenty-four hours she would be escorted to the frontier, it may be said that Miss Thompson — or Mrs. Lewis as she is best known to her friends — has been expelled — politely it is true, but nevertheless expelled.

Birchall goes on to say that practically the entire Anglo-American press representation in Berlin went to the Nord-Express to see Dorothy leave, bestowing on her a great sheaf of American Beauty roses. They had all understood at once that this action inaugurated an entirely new system of dealing with the foreign press under a dictatorship, involving many others besides Dorothy.

The reasons for her expulsion were clear: she had spoken ill of the Dictator in her interview of 1931, widely printed, and in the short book called *I Saw Hitler* (1932). What was not at all clear was why the Third Reich had done it like this. Even now it is hard to guess why the Nazis did not do it earlier, except on the general hypothesis that they wanted to go slow in all things during their more tentative period.

Certainly it was a foolish thing to do at any time, since it did Hitler no good and aroused an uproar against him even in circles which had been trying to withhold judgment, or the expression of judgment. Hitler's contempt for the western democratic press, so often shown thereafter, had not yet been allowed to appear blatantly; there still were advisers in the Wilhelmstrasse who retained a little control. But this episode served notice of the time to come, and it would have been absurd to expect the western press to be anything but wary and suspicious as a result.

So far as our story is concerned, the expulsion from Germany made Dorothy into a heroine, and the more the details were forgotten the more the central phenomenon emerged. That she had been politely and indeed ceremoniously deported was forgotten, for example, and that (on request of the American embassy) an extra twenty-four hours had been allotted her — such softening circumstances did not count: she had defied Hitler and been expelled for it at the imminent risk of her life. That was the general impression given, not only in America but in many other countries, and from that time on Dorothy was known to most of her contemporaries everywhere. Like Byron, she awoke one morning to find herself famous.

2

HER CAREER UP TO THIS POINT HAD BEEN FAR FROM NEGLI-gible. Before her marriage to Red she had been a valued foreign correspondent for the Curtis newspapers, and after her marriage she began to write for magazines. It may be useful to tabulate what she had written in this way between her marriage and her expulsion from Germany. The facts come from *The Reader's Guide to Periodical Literature*, volume 8.

In 1929, her first year in America after marriage, she pub-

lished a series of newspaper articles on the effect on Canada of
prohibition in the United States: these were signed "Mrs
Sinclair Lewis" with her own name in parentheses. She also
published two articles in the *Pictorial Review* called "The New
Patriotism Is Peace" (January) and "Is America a Paradise
for Women?" (June).

In 1930, the year of pregnancy, California, Twin Farms and
recuperation, she published nothing.

In 1931 the *Pictorial Review* published two of her pieces:
"At the Court of King Gustav" in April and "Peace on Earth"
in December. The year was notable for her first contributions
to the *Saturday Evening Post*: "Poverty De Luxe" (May 23)
and the two-part "Something Must Happen" (May 2 and 9).
In that year the *Literary Digest* (April) published a "Portrait"
of her.

By 1932 the contributions to magazines, especially the
Saturday Evening Post, have become regular. The list:

"The State Dictates: the economic evolution of Germany"
(S.E.P. Feb. 6).
"The Gray-Squirrel Complex" (S.E.P., Feb. 20).
"Water Under Bridges" (S.E.P., April 9).
"Our Stake in Germany" (World's Work, May).
"All the King's Horses" (S.E.P., Aug. 6).
"Gangway for Mars" (S.E.P., Aug. 20).
"Why Call It Postwar?" (S.E.P., July 23).
"Will Gangs Rule the World?" (S.E.P., July 16).
"The Militant Disarmed" (S.E.P., Sept. 17).
"Election! What For?" (Pictorial Review, November).

This makes eight long articles for the *Saturday Evening
Post* — they were very long in those days and involved much
work — in a single year, besides two other pieces. The year
1933 was less productive, because of the Semmering party,
illness and travel, but it produced three for the *Saturday Evening Post:*

"Back to Blood and Iron" (May 6).
"Room to Breathe In" (June 24).
"What This Country Needs Is — " (August 19).

In 1934 she wrote four more for the *Saturday Evening Post*, entitled:

"The German Liberals' Flight into Egypt" (March 31).
"The German Revolution, a Continued Story" (Sept. 8).
"Knox of the Saar, a man on a volcano" (Nov. 10).
"The Great War of Words" (Dec. 1.).

There were, in addition, two articles for *Harper's Magazine*, rather more reflective and less journalistic, one called "A Wreath for Toni" in July and the other "Goodbye to Germany," in December.

Magazine articles about Dorothy, or Dorothy and Red, were also more frequent in 1934. There were three in September (after her expulsion from Germany, but probably in print before that event). One was a "Portrait" in *Newsweek*, one was an article in *Home and Fireside* by Emily Kimbrough called "The Sinclair Lewis Place in Vermont," and the third was a piece entitled "They Stand Out From the Crowd" in the *Literary Digest*. In the *Pictorial Review* for January, 1935, Dorothy was named high among the "women of the year," an annual selection, sharing honors with Mary Roberts Rinehart.

Now, from any point of view this is a goodly showing of work. Every journalist knows that the *Saturday Evening Post* made serious demands upon its contributors in the field of foreign affairs, and eight in a year is, or was, an achievement. At the same time the recognition that comes to a journalist through magazine pieces is long, slow and limited, although the payments are good; and to attain any kind of influence with the widest public something besides this is needed. Such work reaches a public inured to discussion, interested in the subjects, prepared to argue with the author — in short, a fairly well-informed audience of fairly prosperous men who already know something of the points at issue. That is essentially, and always will be, a limited public.

To penetrate into the mass of American opinion and stir it up — or, in another dimension, to reach out horizontally towards disparate groups, regions and subcultures — something far different is required: a sort of magic independent of the journalist's craft (or the politician's). Even in journalism it requires what is called "leadership," not at all the same as being understood: a personality-gift, the gift of being heard even by those who do not understand but will, when necessary, take your word for it.

This was the gift now about to befall Dorothy, mainly as the gift of Adolf Hitler.

She was ready for it, and the moment her chance came (within a few months) she rose with meteoric suddenness into the position of an American oracle, one of those very few who have the corporate, general permission to tell people what to think. Her natural aptitude for the task was enormous — her tendency towards doing it was pronounced even before she received the national accolade — but there have been few or none in the whole history of American journalism who made such use of the power of opinion in an immense crisis. To prepare America for war while it was still possible to win may have been, and surely was, the task of others, but the assistance rendered by Dorothy was very great. As we shall see, those directly responsible for the war on our side (Roosevelt and Churchill) were keenly aware of this, and she did not lack for appreciation among other leaders, but when the crisis was at last over — as so often happens — the people themselves needed her no longer, and a long, gradual decline set in from the pinnacle on which she had dwelt for about a decade.

The story of that decade is in itself unique and merits the telling in every detail, but it is not altogether our story. Where it concerns us most is in its effect upon Dorothy's marriage to Red Lewis, which, already shaky in every respect, was soon to become a hopeless simulacrum and to dwindle away, leaving hardly a trace.

For the ironic fact is, of course, that Red, who had been the most enthusiastic supporter of Dorothy's career since they first met, found himself unable to endure it when it came — it was so much more than he had bargained for; it had such grandiose aspects (the President on the telephone and the senators on the doorstep) and such curious little wounds for his *amour propre*. He hated to be identified as "Dorothy's husband," which, according to him, was a common occurrence. I never heard anything of that kind in New York. Perhaps it occurred elsewhere — in the Middle or Far West, for example: Red was constantly moving from pillar to post, and he may well have run into persons who were well aware of Dorothy (from the radio and the newspapers) without being sure of who *he* was. He had a horror of being known as "Mr Dorothy Thompson," and in one way or another this phobia was made known to all of his friends. Speaking of the whole period 1935–1940, that is, from Dorothy's sudden explosion into fame until the beginning of the second world war, there was a distinct difference between Dorothy's public position and his. Red was, of course, known to all readers of books; no other writer of the day was so widely known. But Dorothy was known to the corner druggist, the taxi driver, the hairdresser and the headwaiter; people who had probably never read a book in their lives quoted her familiarly from day to day; she was as national (as much a "star") as any baseball player or film actress. The characteristic of "stardom" in American life is that it glitters tremendously while it glitters, but is obliterated totally when its day is done. Only recently I have found (while writing this book) that although practically every American knows, more or less, who Red was, the younger people have no notion of Dorothy.

Every friend of Red's must have tried, at some point or other, to make him see the difference between a permanent historical reputation, such as his, and a dramatic meteor such as Dorothy's had turned out to be. Perhaps he did understand, but even so he was uncomfortable — and, I must say, most unreasonable — about the entire situation. Dorothy herself spent a vast amount of time trying to convince him, not only of the difference between the ephemeral and the permanent (which in his depths he knew very well), but that *she* knew it, and that *she* did not overvalue her public triumphs as against his lasting achievement. The correspondence on this subject, later on, would be downright funny if it were not also pathetic.

I may tell one little story which perhaps (we may hope!) Red never knew. Dorothy told it to me to illustrate the difficulty that this situation created in their expiring marriage. It was along about 1937, as I remember, when for some days their paths crossed and they were housed at the Beverly Hills Hotel, in California. Dorothy went to the hairdresser's and found herself, at the end of an expensive treatment, without any money to pay for it. (She never carried money — one of her secretaries gave her a single dollar when she went out of the house, to ensure safe return; if she carried more she often lost it.) She said to the hairdresser that her name was Mrs Sinclair Lewis and she was staying in the hotel and wanted the bill charged to her room. The young lady explained that the hairdressing establishment did not belong to the hotel and that this could not be done. Dorothy, in search of a solution, suggested that somebody might telephone the hotel cashier and say that Dorothy Thompson wanted ten dollars (or whatever the sum was). The young lady seemed startled.

"Are you Dorothy Thompson?" she asked.

"That's my name," said Dorothy.

"Well, why didn't you say so?" the girl replied. "Of course you can charge it."

This whole situation, ludicrous though it may seem to us now, was really painful at the time. It gave rise to innumerable jokes and "funny" stories which were repeated throughout the country (like all the Roosevelt jokes at the same period, or the Kennedy jokes today). And of course Red was always being badgered, during his ceaseless travels, to say something or other about his all-too-famous wife. On one occasion (I think in Kansas City) he was confronted with a newspaper rumor to the effect that Dorothy might be the Republican candidate against Franklin Roosevelt in the next presidential election.

"Fine, fine," said Red (and I can imagine how sourly!). "Then I can settle down and write a column called 'My Day.'"

On another occasion the reporters asked him something about his wife (where she was or when he had last seen her — they really were merciless about it).

"I had a wife once," says Red, "but she vanished into the N.B.C. building and has never been heard of since."

Since Dorothy was heard almost incessantly on the radio at the time, this quip made Americans laugh a good deal, and was repeated for months or years afterwards.

We have gone ahead of our story, in the strict time sense, so as to show some of the ways in which Dorothy's resplendent career put the finishing touches to her marriage. These anecdotes and episodes refer to the entire period between 1935, when Dorothy began to write her column for the *Herald Tribune*, and the divorce. There were dozens of others (true or false) as Americans of the older generation will remember. Even the false or made-up stories had a vestige of truth about them, because that to which they referred was essentially true. 'Tis true 'tis pity; and pity 'tis 'tis true. Nobody wanted Dorothy to shine more than Red did (he was indefatigable about it for years) but when it really happened it was more than he could endure.

3

THE BASIS, OR PERHAPS MORE ACCURATELY THE SPRINGBOARD, for Dorothy's ascent to astronomic heights was the column she wrote for the New York *Herald Tribune* from 1936 to 1941. The first contract began March 16, 1936; the last expired on April 30, 1941, and was not renewed.

The name of the column, chosen after long discussion, was "On the Record." It was not originally conceived as a political idea — indeed it was supposed, from the beginning, to be a personal expression on almost any subject the writer might find conducive to thought. And there was a wide range of subjects in Dorothy's field of interest. She never held herself to politics alone, either national or international. In the first years some of the very best of her columns — enjoyed from coast to coast — were half-humorous and half-serious efforts called "Grouse for Breakfast," which developed out of Red's talk at the breakfast table. Even when she no longer had breakfast with Red — or anybody else: for thereafter she breakfasted in bed — she still used this useful device for a kind of writing at which she excelled.

She also retained, to the very end, her interest in family and household matters, although these subjects, after a while, were more often used for her monthly page in the *Ladies' Home Journal.* In the list of her magazine pieces at the beginning of this chapter it can be seen that her earliest published essays were on the sort of subject — *Kirche, Küche und Kinder* — which women are supposed to cherish. "Is America a Paradise for Women?" for example, in the *Pictorial Review* in 1929, was the kind of thing she could always do with skill and warmth.

Furthermore, with her zest for life and her intrepidity on all subjects, she would attack or extol a popular idol in any field (Walt Disney, Toscanini); she would assault popular fallacies or absurd forms of advertising or anything else that seemed to her worth the trouble; she would praise a book or a play if she saw fit; she used to make lists of her favorite people or stories or scenes. One of her most diverting efforts along about 1939 consisted, as I well remember, of an outline for an "ideal party," to which she named the guests and gave her reasons for wanting them. This kind of thing, which sounds more like a popular magazine than a newspaper, was immensely readable to a vast public and contributed much to her national popularity, although it is not part of her historic significance. The point is that all these writings on all these various subjects, done with the verve and dash characteristic of her at her best, helped to conquer that public of many millions which constituted the source of her power. She could never have acquired such a public through politics alone — everything else contributed to it, too; and we may well imagine, knowing Americans as we do, that her own legend and even her marriage to Red were elements in the conquest.

However, when all is said, it is through and in politics, both national and international, that Dorothy takes her place in the history of the time. She won her public by a combination of gifts and interests (many nonpolitical), but what she did with this power when she obtained it was of direct political importance. She was profoundly interested in government itself, although this was not easily translated into the language of newspapers and radio; it was like a reserve force which she maintained within herself to give weight to lesser considerations; she could call upon Hamilton, Jefferson, Montesquieu, Tocqueville or Spengler, without specifically naming them, because she read them often and deeply. Any book which Dorothy had really studied (such as Spengler's *Decline of the*

West) was impossible for anybody else to read afterwards, so copiously did she comment, argue and expatiate in her marginal notes and interlineations. Her copy of *The Decline of the West*, or of *The Federalist Papers*, or of numerous others, always looked to me like two books: one by the author and the other by the reader. This gave substance to her thought even when it was translated into very much simpler language.

But above and beyond her deep interest in government she cared about the real and present danger, as she saw it, both to the United States and to the western world. This was the passion of her work and gave it an incredible intensity at times, more like a crusader's call to arms than like anything normally known in journalism. It is for this, of course, that she is best remembered, and for which she became best known among thoughtful people in her own lifetime. *Delenda est Carthago!*

She was vowed, with an absolute sincerity for which my observation offers no parallel, to the destruction of Adolf Hitler and of the system of thought and action presented by him to the infinitely deludable German people. Dorothy really loved the German people (to excess, I always thought) and raged against all that would deflect their gifts and ruin them in the end. She also loved the institutions of the United States, England and France, comprising, between them, the laboriously accumulated and always threatened treasury of human freedom and self-respect. Dorothy is the only person I ever knew who could recite every single word of the Constitution of the United States, the Declaration of Independence and the Gettysburg Address without faltering. Even I might do the Gettysburg Address, but the others must surely be beyond the powers of all but schoolchildren working for a prize. She could say these words because they dwelt within her, not as if she had invented or originated them, but as if she had been impregnated by them at some time before time, so that she was they and they were she. There have been times when I have gone to Dorothy in something approaching despair (as, for instance, at the outbreak of the Korean War) and been restored to faith by the way she had of saying the life-giving words of the past. She knew them and could say them, in a clear, beautiful and unhesitating voice, outside of which, however dark the shadows, there was no real place for doubt.

This quality was called "fanaticism" and even "hysteria" by many of the time who did not feel that Hitler was a real danger to our own country and did not care about any other. The shortsightedness of the 1930's will ever be a marvel to students in generations to come. Hitler's plan was not only obvious, but was loudly and repeatedly proclaimed. He explained it in an enormous book, *Mein Kampf*, which was not translated into English until the decade was nearly over and found few readers even then. The Nazi songs and slogans were treated very nearly as jokes in the United States: hardly anybody realized that they were the most serious things in the world. On lecture tour in 1938 I found that persons in the audience disbelieved even the actual words of Hitler when I would read them out from his own public utterances or from his book. They refused to believe. And yet he made it so abundantly obvious, step by step: conquer first the West and then the East (Germany's neighbors) and then the whole world. He declared it, provided for it and very nearly achieved it. The commonest slogan of his followers was: "Today Germany is ours, tomorrow the world." And yet there were important elements in the United States, even as late as 1940, which would not accept the idea that we were part of that world.

They were not Nazis. They were simply stupid, lazy and unwilling to face the struggles and sacrifices which history demanded. Many of them truly believed that it would be quite easy for us to let Hitler conquer everybody else, if he so desired, and leave us alone. Many others thought (as Colonel

Charles Lindbergh said in public speeches) that it would be
useless to oppose such a mighty force as Hitler presented. The
idea that Germany was irresistible gained cogency throughout
the decade and reached its climax in 1940 when everything,
except the single island of Great Britain, had acknowledged
defeat or (in the case of Russia) acquiescence. It often seemed
as if Hitler was right in saying, as he often did, that Americans
would be "too late to count" and that nothing mattered except
the present power of the German army.

It was against this situation that Dorothy pitted her ostensibly feeble — and in reality very great — forces as journalist,
writer, speaker, woman and patriot. What she did "can never
be overestimated," as Winston Churchill put it, but actually
while it was going on there were a great many who thought her
overwrought, importunate and even hysterical. Her great
friend Mrs Longworth, the author of so many witticisms of
the period, is credited with saying: "Dorothy is the only woman
in history who has had her menopause in public and made it
pay."

Even that remark, by the way, had no effect on Dorothy. I
asked her in 1940 if she had ever heard it, and she said of course
she had, and laughed and added: "Alice is so funny." So far
as I was ever able to see, she cared nothing whatsoever about
such things, the slings and arrows: she was unutterably determined, and wherever the supreme purposes of her effort were
concerned, she was selfless. I thought then and think now that
she would have been perfectly willing to sacrifice her own life
at any time if by doing so she could preserve humanity and the
humanities from the dark forces, the tyranny of blood and
hatred, the domination of the devil. Essentially she saw it
just like that: the decisive, if not perhaps the ultimate, battle
between good and evil. Hitler was quite possibly not the con-
cise and inconclusive devil; there could be other devils; but at
the moment in time, and the place where she stood, Hitler

was the operative incarnation of evil. (He was, as Professor Einstein so gently put it, among the "forces inimical to life.")

I agreed with her immeasurably, more than words can say. This is perhaps the principal reason why our friendship was (in spite of many other disagreements) indissoluble.

Now, of course, this was all very hard on Red. He had betrayed a dislike for political argument, abstract discussion, journalistic excitement and table-pounding from the earliest days; now this dislike was not only betrayed but asseverated, enforced as a rule. Many is the time I have heard him say "No more *situations* or I will go to bed." Ultimatum. Generally he pronounced it *sityashuns* in order to make it seem more contemptible. *Sityashuns* referred to events on the continent of Europe, in general, and in particular to events in Central or Eastern Europe or to anything connected with Adolf Hitler. Neither Dorothy nor I could possibly avoid talking of such things at that time. Most of her friends were, roughly speaking, in the same frame of mind. If Red could get through an evening with Dorothy and me, or Dorothy and Gunther or Dorothy and Shirer or any of the others, he did so by imposing his own will and forbidding the discussion of that which most dominated our minds. In his later novel, *Gideon Planish* (which I never read) he evidently vents his spleen in a caricature of a journalist who, according to Professor Schorer, is supposed to be me or possibly Shirer, an expression of a resentment which was, to my judgment, a little peculiar in the first place. He never wanted the talk to pass from his control — that was it — and somehow or other the menace of Hitler was derogatory to his self-esteem. As he used to say, "If I ever divorce Dorothy I'll name Adolf Hitler as co-respondent."

Red's strange dichotomy about Dorothy's career and her larger interests can be illustrated by an excerpt from her diary in November, 1935. At the time she had not yet begun her column in the *Herald Tribune*: that was four months in the

future. She had, however, become so much an object of interest, since her expulsion from Germany, that she was constantly
invited to talk in public gatherings. Her aptitude for public
speaking had been strong, natural and unforced; it was growing with her absorption in her subjects; and it was soon to
make her one of the most eloquent speakers of her time. The
occasion seems to have been something of a feminist nature —
women's work, in one way or another. It shows well what I
have been trying to say — that Red wanted her to shine but
could not endure having her do so. The pertinent part of the
entry:

November 18, 1935.

After the talk at the dinner last night Red called me up. His
voice was excited. "Listen," he said, "that speech was magnificent." All afternoon he had sat and brooded. "You will
have to choose," he said. "I can't stand this. You live and
move in another world than mine. I haven't a wife." And
I felt horrible. When I got to the dinner, I was on the verge
of tears, and the strain was great anyhow . . nine speakers,
and to keep them inside time, to a minute. Mrs Roosevelt
was footling.[1] Club-woman at its sentimental worst. I kept
remembering Alice L.[2] imitating her. Alice is cruel, of
course. Still, she was right. Mrs Reid[3] good; intelligent;
only careful, as all people are who speak not for themselves
but for someone else. "For the firm, or the institution."
Fannie[4] was crisp and to the point. Right. Women aren't

[1] The President's wife did not speak as well then as later; but in any case she and
Dorothy did not fervently admire each other.
[2] Mrs Longworth (Alice Roosevelt, daughter of the 26th President of the United
States) was first cousin to Eleanor Roosevelt.
[3] Helen Rogers Reid (Mrs Ogden Reid), the moving spirit of the *Herald Tribune*, of
whom more later.
[4] Fannie Hurst.

good enough. Women are worms. But then, afterward, Red, with the excitement in his voice, happy. I couldn't tell him "You old idiot, the reason you liked my speech was because it is just you speaking." I couldn't because there were a dozen people in the room, but I wrote him so from Rochester. I love him with my soul. There must be a soul because otherwise, what in the world *do* I love him with? I feel as though we had been born in the same nursery and quarrelled through all our childhood, and studied together, and argued, and talked each other down in school, and fought and made up . . He's the only man I have ever known in my life that I really understand. Even why he drinks so. Only it hurts my feelings that he does . . makes me feel inferior . . one ought to have more charm than a whisky and soda, one thinks. Actually, there's not enough of one sort of tension between us. Too much alike. Not interested in exploring each other, because we know what we will find. With his talent, his voluptuous gifts, I could have written all his books. Alter ego.

This passage evokes two comments: first, that she is already beginning to call her husband "Red," as others did, and second, that when she says "I could have written all his books" she means that she could have done so if she had been equally gifted. In other words, there was nothing mysterious to her in his work — nothing she could not imagine doing herself if she had had the necessary skills. This was, and remained, a kind of definition with Dorothy: if she could imagine doing a thing herself, if it were in her nature to do it, she regarded such work as being comprehensible not only in result but in origin. She said of Rebecca West's work, "I might have done it myself if I had been clever enough." Of Virginia Woolf's work: "I know that I could never in this world have done anything like it: it begins in mystery." The distinction between what she *might*

have done and what she never *could* have done was essential for
her and (in spite of a good many early efforts) it put the whole
of poetry outside her limit, no matter how ardently she loved
it. Even Edna St. Vincent Millay, whose verses she could
recite at astonishing length, and whose personality had made a
deep impression in the very earliest days in Budapest, seemed
to her a creature set apart (in spite of familiarity) by this
mystery, the poetic fountain.

So, all told, when she refers to Red as Red, the name we all
called him, and says she might have written his books if she
had had his "voluptuous gifts," a great milestone has already
been passed.

4

DOROTHY'S FIRST COLUMN IN THE *Herald Tribune* WAS
published on March 17th, 1936, under the name "The Corporations Tax Bill."

The announcement of her engagement was made by the
newspaper in a display advertisement on the day before, illustrated with a photograph of such haughty beauty that one has
to look twice to be sure it is Dorothy. (It reminds me of
Georgiana Duchess of Devonshire as seen by Gainsborough.)
In this display announcement it is mentioned that she is married to Sinclair Lewis. That name does not appear again in
connection with her column or other public work.

"The Corporations Tax Bill" was, in a way, Dorothy's
extremely astute way of throwing down the gauntlet. By
writing on this subject she served notice on the public at large
that she did not intend to confine herself to subjects deemed
suitable for women. She begins her column by saying that she
knows little of the money system but has been studying all the
authorities diligently (and she names some of them). She finds

that they are in disagreement and that there is, in effect, no authority, and that she is left bewildered, more or less as Professor Einstein had confessed himself to be. Thereafter she proceeds to consider the proposed bill (a tax on corporation surpluses) from the point of view of common sense. She believes such a bill should have been the product of long study by the best available minds, instead of hasty improvisation. She concludes: "We are as a people timid in thinking but reckless in action."

The column is long — very long by the standards of today — and so were many others during that first year or two. They all show thought and careful preparation as well as the characteristic élan of Dorothy's best years. She worked hard, but it was part of her magic that she managed to conceal the elbow-grease from the casual reader. Somehow it all sounded like the reflections of an educated, urbane and world-conscious mind. For this, and perhaps also because she was a woman, this work made an immediate impression which grew with every week through 1936 and 1937. Her columns appeared on Tuesdays, Thursdays and Saturdays, in the right-hand corner of the first page of the newspaper's second section — a wonderful place for the prose of opinion rather than news. Walter Lippmann's column, on alternate days, occupied the left-hand corner of the same page.

The columns of the early months foreshadow, in subject matter and even in some elements of style, the whole of Dorothy's work in journalism. She was to grow much more positive in expression later on, although she never stated anything in print with the downrightness that made private argument with her such an exhilarating battle. In the beginning she made her points rather gently, sometimes by indirection, sometimes with considerable subtlety, but always with such clarity (as newspaper writing demands) that the reader could think for himself, *afterwards*, what she wanted him to think.

A few of these early columns may be named, since they give an excellent idea of the stuff of her thought — the stuff which was, with evolution and development and emphasis, her lifework.

On April 9th she wrote about "Fishing in Politics," a subject which I well remember provided one of Red's favorite breakfast diatribes years before. It says nothing is so sacrosanct as a fisherman; it would be as easy in America to attack motherhood or baseball as to attack the virtues of a fisherman; President Roosevelt has gone fishing; is this the answer to everything? It is good-natured, skeptical and salutary fun-making. At one point she inquires: "Where is the evidence that the President ever caught a fish?" The impression left when she has finished this quite amiable essay is that Mr Roosevelt ought to have had better occupations at that moment in time.

(It was indeed an ominous moment: Hitler had reoccupied the Rhineland in March; Mussolini was about to annex Ethiopia, having conquered most of it; the League of Nations was paralyzed; Japan was supreme in Manchuria and thinking of further conquests.)

On May 2nd Dorothy wrote, with warm approval, of "Secretary Hull's Program," and on May 5th, with acid disapproval, of "The Cracker-Barrel Bill." This was a law restricting the activities (ostensibly, anyhow) of big chain stores in favor of small operators. It had been hastily put together and passed with only two days' debate. Dorothy said, as she did of so much hasty legislation in those days, that it should have been the object of about two years' study before it was even drafted.

On May 7th she wrote about "The French Elections" (those which had just put the Popular Front combination into power with Léon Blum as prime minister), deploring the sharp division into Left and Right with no middle surviving. On May 9th she wrote on "Muddling — but Not Through," which considered the decline of British prestige on the continent of

Europe after the successive crises in which nothing had been done (the annexation of Ethiopia, in defiance of Britain and the League, being the latest).

On May 12th she wrote about "Words Without Song," by which she meant the Republican opposition to the Social Security bill. With all sympathy for the destitute, the unemployed, the victims of the tremendous depression which had not yet ended, she thought the Republicans were not making a good enough case against a bill which would, she felt, be a burden to those whom it was intended to aid. (Many of the loopholes she saw in the law were stopped up later, but she never really thought it was rightly drawn.)

On May 14th her subject was "Poker Game in Geneva," about the poor old League of Nations, then quaking with nerves over Hitler and Mussolini as well as Japan. On May 16th came "Disunion in Vienna," an extremely illuminating discussion of the relations between the chancellor of the day, von Schuschnigg, and Prince Starhemberg's semi-Fascist organization.

Of these early columns, which created her entire subsequent career, one of the most important was called "The Constitution and the People," published on May 21st, in which she says that Franklin Roosevelt's concept of government will not continue to be possible unless there are changes in the Constitution involving some change in the powers of the Supreme Court. Against this, she feels, the American people will be overwhelmingly opposed, and she gives her reasons, which are not legal but moral. She believes the people do not really trust or respect most governmental elements, which they know to be hollowed out by personal ambition and corruption. They do respect the nine old men of the Supreme Court, whom they know to be appointed for life, immune to politics, chosen from the most eminent jurists and essentially above the battle. This security the people will not forego. She puts it thus:

"It is a brutal thing to say, but it is, I believe, true: The

Supreme Court is the only branch of the Federal Government which is universally respected."

The weakness of the claim by any political administration to enlarge its own powers at the expense of the Court is a moral weakness; only by removing a great deal of administration from political control — by vastly enlarging the civil service — could a government (any government) hope to make such a claim prevail.

Now, of course, Dorothy was by no means alone in these views. (Professor Arthur Schlesinger, Jr., says they were held in the very beginning of the Roosevelt administration.) But by now four years had passed; some extremely large, comprehensive schemes of social and economic control had been made into law and even put into operation, only to be abolished by Supreme Court decisions. What had been a view of probabilities, or an estimate, had now become aching political reality. In this situation Dorothy's opinion (that the people would not tolerate tampering with the Court) proved to be correct, and Roosevelt yielded with a good grace when he saw that he must; it must also be said that she did everything in her power to influence events in that sense. She returned to the subject as often as she felt it necessary or intelligent to do so, and there can be no doubt that she played a considerable part in the outcome.

A further column of that spring — on May 28th, 1936 — shows another of her recurrent subjects, the literature of hate, race against race, religion against religion, etc. It was based partly upon a hate-murder in Detroit and partly upon Dorothy's own mail from the general public, which had already become voluminous. She gives examples and expresses her own horror at the growth of such feelings within the American democracy. The name of this column is "It Can Happen Here."

Red Lewis' novel, *It Can't Happen Here*, a remarkable super-pamphlet written at red-hot speed and intensity, had appeared the year before and was still a best seller. As has been remarked often before, its vision of a native American fascism (although inspired partly by Huey Long and others) came into being as some kind of result of their marriage. Much though he disliked "sityashuns," Red could not help becoming aware of them in that house, and his contribution to the awakening of the United States certainly owed something to Dorothy. Professor Schorer even says that the book "would never have been written if Sinclair Lewis had not been married to Dorothy Thompson" — quite possibly true, but, like most things in the genesis of writing, hard to prove.

There is another of Dorothy's columns in that same month (on May 30th) which foreshadows many later ones. It is called "The Issue." The presidential elections and other preoccupations of the hour take second place in Dorothy's mind to the fundamental issue, which she phrases as follows: "Are we for freedom or are we for the totalitarian state?"

It has seemed useful to touch on these various expressions of Dorothy's first months as a columnist because, essentially, these were her themes and, through the changing years, she never abandoned them. An atmosphere of crisis had begun to spread from Europe to the United States, far away and safe as most of our people felt themselves to be; there was a growing uneasiness, a desire for some light upon the dark and confusing world of the predatory conquerors, whose real nature, now being revealed by events, was at first almost beyond credibility for Americans. In the world of 1936–1940 Dorothy became a necessity — if she had not existed she would have had to be invented — because of a demand from the people themselves. Within a year her *Herald Tribune* column was being printed in every city or town of any size in the country and her voice began to be heard from coast to coast on the National Broadcasting Company's network. With this she combined as much lecturing as she could fit into her schedule (the demand was inexhaustible) as well as, after 1937, a monthly page in the *Ladies' Home Journal.* The amount of work she did, all at concert pitch, was a marvel to her colleagues, and without an extremely sturdy physical constitution and a stern power of will she could not have survived it. She was partly sustained, I have always thought, by a conviction that what she was doing was valuable to her country and to the freedom of humanity — a "sense of mission" as they call it. Old friends (John Gunther, for example) are thoroughly in accord on this; John says that long ago, in very early days in Vienna, she already had this "sense of mission" and that it was clearly discerned by analysts whom she briefly frequented. Now, of course, success and all its rewards must have played a part, but the essence was there from the beginning.

Red could have only a part, and not a decisive one, in such a career. Quite aside from his worries over being overshadowed (over being "Mr Dorothy Thompson"), there was really not much time left for him, or so he felt. He wandered more restlessly than ever, and by 1937 he had ceased to be, in any intelligible sense, Dorothy's husband: he was, sometimes, a visitor, but seldom even that.

Before he went out of her life he was responsible for a handful of Dorothy's columns which are know and remembered even now under the name of "The Grouse." The first one, "Grouse for Breakfast," appeared on October 9th, 1936, and drew such laughter and applause from all parts of the country that Dorothy was moved to write others in the same vein. Clearly they are her own work and only vaguely based upon Red's breakfast conversation; and yet, here and there, they irresistibly remind me of Red; whether he ever said these precise things or not, he must have said a good many things in the same vein. The first of these columns, although it is extremely long, is worth reproducing in full. Here it is:

ON THE RECORD
BY DOROTHY THOMPSON

Grouse for Breakfast

"Good morning. Have you got the papers? What's in them? How is the campaign going?"

"The Giants are three up."

"Don't be silly. I mean the political campaign, of course."

"The political campaign? I am decreasingly aware of a political campaign. Do you call it a campaign when two large hostile forces are retreating in the same direction?"

"The *same* direction?"

"Yes. Toward a liberal-conservative position. In other words, toward United States. I am not, young woman, interested in this campaign. Furthermore, I do not wish to discuss situations or conditions. I hope you have noticed that it is an exceptionally beautiful day. Your dahlias froze last night, but the asters did not. Can you explain that? Why do dahlias blossom last and freeze first?"

"I want to talk about the campaign. You act as though there were no issue."

"There are many issues. But the chief one is whether there are more nuts in this country or stand-patters, whether there are more lookers-back upon lovely yesterday or more gazers forward into a betinselled future. If the nuts have the more influence the present incumbent will remain. If nostalgia is tops the contestant will succeed."

"So you think the present government is nutty?"

"As nutty as this glorious autumn. It is thoroughly nutty. The D.A.R. ladies, I observe, are perturbed about its radicalism. They seem to think we are headed for communism, Fascism and atheism. I understand that the financiers are certain, or some of them are, that we are bound for bankruptcy. You will permit me to reserve the opinion that we are headed for ebullient prosperity, I fear, with its usual unpleasant accompaniments. Already I am being informed by those who call themselves my brokers that the moment has come when fortune awaits me in the stock market, with no contributing effort of mine. But the government is nutty."

"Now, look here, you can't just throw off snap judgments like that. How is it nutty?"

"Lord, it's full of the kind of soft-headed benevolence that doesn't become any person over the age of ten. Noble, aspiring, Junior League attitude. Uplift. Knows nothing of the nature of man. The human race, my child, has one chronic disease. That disease is the gimmies. It is endemic, epidemic and chronic, and woe betide the government that cries aloud in the market places 'Come ye, come ye, eat, drink, without money and without price, eat and be satisfied.' Because they come ye. It is a trait of the human race that it is never satisfied, never has been and never will be."

"There are many unemployed and many destitute. Even now."

"Naturally and of course. Let them be fed and housed. But what an idea that the government create work for every seamstress, paleontologist and hod carrier! Work is work. Succor to the poor is something else again. Aid to the unemployed is still something else. All mixed up, because of nuttiness. Having rendezvouses with destiny. Reconstruction of society by dancing on the green. It's arty."

"I did not know you felt so strongly."

"I do not feel strongly. But since you have directed my attention to this theme, which does not particularly interest me, I am polite. I suggest that you consider the fact that next to 'The Shooting of Dan McGrew' and 'Off Agin, On Agin, Gone Agin, Finnigan,' the favorite poem of the American people and almost the only one that the average

American can quote is 'The Psalm of Life.' Now the point
of that poem is that if we strive with appropriate earnestness
we can leave large footprints in sand. My knowledge of sand
is that no footsteps imprinted in it survive the first tide.
And the tide is inevitable. Note also the line 'Let us then be
up and doing with a heart for ANY fate.' That's us. Old
America rushing gallantly forward with an eye to any fate,
no matter what that fate is. Making, in fact, a rendezvous
with it."

"Since you feel so deeply, I presume you will vote for the
Republicans."

"My enthusiasm is insufficient to propel me to the polls.
There are fewer bees in the Republican bonnet, but there are
more moths. I do not suffer acutely from nostalgia. I do not
long for the good old times and the eternal simplicities,
particularly when they are preached by as astute and self-
protective a crowd of citizens as we possess. Besides, the
challenger is a mystery. Apart from two old ladies who
have been dug up to testify that they taught him school, and
my old friend, Bill White, he seems to have passed unnoticed
for forty-seven years. And for some peculiar reason that
seems to be an asset. It does not move me. Not to action."

"Nonsense. He is Governor of a great state."[1]

"Nonsense nothing. Tell me the name of the Governor of
Nebraska."

"Then I can only conclude that you are one of those
revolutionists who will fearlessly risk ten minutes of his cross-
word puzzle time to cast a "protest vote" for Browder,
Lemke or Norman Thomas."

"Your instinct for error is something for Freud and Walter
Pitkin to investigate. Thomas represents Social Democracy,
which flowered perfectly, and got frost-bitten, in Germany
and Austria. Lemke is not a candidate. He is an actor in a

[1] The Republican candidate, Mr Landon, was Governor of Kansas.

play written by Huey Long, financed by Townsend, directed
by Coughlin and still ably press-agented, although it expired
a month ago, by Gerald Smith. And Browder, the Communist, announces that Moscow no longer intends to absorb us,
but is zealous to support us as part of a popular front, along
with the Siamese Nudist Junta, the Finnish Bath Cult, the
interesting movement for the independence of Hollywood
under Upton Sinclair and Will Hays and all other forward-
looking efforts. In fact, the Communists have become altogether too loving — as Zinoviev recently discovered."

"Just another totally destructive thinker. I suppose you
think you could have picked some better candidates."

"I do indeed."

"So. And whom would you pick?"

"I would pick a man of learning: a man of authentic
learning. Some one who has some time or other gone through
serious mental discipline and has got out of it the kind of
freedom, courage and wisdom that such mental discipline
gives a man. Some one, also, who is a doer. An executive.
But not a business man. Nobody with the buying-and-selling
mentality. Some one who knows the world, the big world,
and has had to compete in it. Some one who has had wide
experience in getting on with many sorts of people, in con-
ciliating and adjusting."

"I suppose you think the country is teeming with such
people."

"Not teeming. But they exist. There is, for instance,
Mr Robert Hutchins. A scholar. A historian. A lawyer.
A gallant soldier. Dean of the Yale Law School at twenty-
nine. President of the University of Chicago at thirty.
Modern but not cracked. Turned a great institution upside
down to adapt it to modern needs, and didn't break any eggs
in the process. Has to be a financier. But not as an end in
itself. Has to get on with all sorts of people. Genuinely

superior man. Now, imagine picking a President because he's
just a home-body; just a practical, common-sense fellow like
you and me. I no more want an average man like me
governing this country than I want my cook to make coffee
just like mother used to make. If she can't do better than
that I'd fire her."

"You seem to me utterly frivolous. Do you think there is
nothing wrong with this country? Don't you think we need
a program?"

"There is nothing wrong with this country. It is Western
man's best break in history. But there is lots wrong with us.
We Americans have delusions of grandeur. And the program is to get over it. All this talk about waste and extravagance . . ."

"You kick about it yourself."

"Sure I do. But how can business in this country kick
about waste and extravagance and keep its face straight?
Hasn't business earnestly carried on a conspiracy — an open
conspiracy in the advertising columns — to persuade every
American family that a $1,500 income will support a $700
motor car and a $100 radio? All this talk about borrowing!
Hasn't every American individual been financing himself on
the instalment plan? Get what you want and pay for it
tomorrow? Boondoggling! Is that thing up in Maine — ?"

"Passamaquoddy?"

"Passamawhat? Is that a crazy idea? Well, and was the
Ford peace ship a crazy idea? The Florida ship canal? Yes,
and how about the Florida boom? Did Roosevelt make that?
Ukuleles for hillbillies, although maybe that's Republican
propaganda, but, anyhow, how about the hillbilly dames who
buy artificial eyelashes and spend money for that awful stuff
women put on their fingernails to make 'em look like Lady
Macbeth directly after the killing? Conspicuous waste.
That's us. And who invented Hollywood? Who pays

Walter Winchell? Who press-agented Anna Hauptmann? Who supports Aimee Semple McPherson?"

"You are pessimistic this morning."

"I am not. I am optimistic. This country is apparently foolproof. It must be."

There were more of these Red-and-Dorothy concoctions, all in more or less the same breezy manner with Dorothy as interlocutor and the Grouse opinionating freely. "More Grouse for Breakfast" (February 3, 1937) was on Hitler — "your King Charles' head" the Grouse calls him — and "Ruffled Grouse" (February 17, 1937) is on the Supreme Court. Its opening sounds quite a bit like the real Red in some of his moods. It goes thus:

"There is one certain remedy for a headache," said the Grouse crankily. "It is cheap, instantaneous and guaranteed. That remedy is decapitation."

"I fail, as usual, to follow you."

"I refer to the President's way with that bothersome old lady, the Supreme Court. He says the Supreme Court has, and is, a headache. He proposes to cure it. But he is a busy man. It's a long way upstairs to get the aspirin, and the doctors disagree, anyhow, as to just what's wrong with Auntie. So he has jumped into the kitchen for a cleaver, and the sure and lasting cure. Nice fellow, the President. Can't bear the sight of long drawn out pain."

The Grouse appears again on April 5th, May 12th, June 28th, September 10th, December 6th and December 24th, during the year 1937, and for the last time on May 30th, 1938. They sound less and less like Red as they go on; in fact Dorothy saw him less and less, and the whole device of the breakfast conversation was wearing thin. Its popularity (it never failed to produce floods of "fan" letters) was the only reason why she kept it up as long as she did.

In one of them, however, under the date of May 12th, 1937, there occurs a passage which I distinctly remember having heard Red pour forth at breakfast seven or eight years earlier. It must have stuck in Dorothy's memory as it did in mine, and when she needed it, there it was. She decided to have the Grouse talk about the English in general ("The Grouse on the English" is the name of the column) with special reference to the coronation of King George VI. A good many of the reflections in it, although couched in the same colloquial and grousy language, sound more like Dorothy than like Red. But then, towards the end, the Grouse starts imagining what England would be like "if they ever established communism." He makes up a version of the Court Circular: "Comrade the King was pleased to receive today . . ." And so on. Once at Twin Farms Red had actually done this improvisation and it was very funny indeed. Such remembered bits, no doubt, occur here and there throughout the "Grouse" series, but on the whole they are certainly Dorothy's own doing: that is, she is both parts of the dialogue, expressing, by means of this device, ideas of her own in something less than the formal editorial manner.

And with the Grouse, Red Lewis, too, disappears from Dorothy's public work as he does from her life. Their effective separation, not made public, dates from 1937, and although he visited Twin Farms after that (notably in 1939, when my wife Dinah and I lived in the old house) it was as a friend.

5

DOROTHY'S CAREER GATHERED MOMENTUM AFTER 1937, AND IN the great crises of 1938 (Czechoslovakia, Spain and the Munich

Agreement) she was a molder of opinion, a power in the land. The intensity of her preoccupation with the events in Europe was such that she often forgot every detail of ordinary life, and it required three secretaries to keep her going through the engagements and efforts of the day. She used to tell me (and often) of the great hurricane of September, 1938, which coincided with the Munich crisis. She was in New York, incessantly writing and speaking; like all of us, she was filled with horror at the prospect opened up by Hitler's victory over the democracies. In this desperate mood, and working many hours every day, she was unaware that the great hurricane had taken place. On the second night, seated in the N.B.C. studio awaiting her turn at the microphone, she heard a news broadcast which spoke of the great damage done to New England by the hurricane, and mentioning Vermont as a state which had been hard hit.

Dorothy's son and his nurse, along with other servants, were up at Twin Farms. She made an immediate effort to telephone them but found that all the wires were down. Her fears can be imagined; she got up to Twin Farms as soon as her work would allow, and in the meanwhile she made lavish use of the telegraph; but while the hurricane was actually going on she had been oblivious to it. As it turned out, many trees were lost at Twin Farms but the houses were undamaged. The episode remains as an extreme example of concentration on work — extreme, but highly characteristic of Dorothy, then as at all times.

From then on it may be said that Dorothy's career *was* her life — there came, in the end, a kind of autumnal happiness in her last marriage, outside the limits of our story, but the career dominated even then, and its necessities were always the ruling consideration. There came a considerable change when, in 1940, she felt compelled to switch her allegiance from Wendell Willkie to Franklin Roosevelt and in the result her contract with the *Herald Tribune*, expiring in 1941, was not renewed. This episode, as strange in history as in journalism, was accompanied by much bitterness, since Dorothy had played a great part in forcing Mr Willkie upon some very reluctant Republican politicians. Her role at that time, for the sake of chronology as well as of logic, belongs in the next chapter.

But what is one to say of her career as a whole?

It falls, to my way of thinking, into two categories, that of history and that of journalism. As a journalist she lasted a long time, made a great deal of money and influenced opinion for some twenty-five years or so, even after her decline had become pronounced. There was never a time when she did not receive a great deal of mail from the public, although after the war was over it no longer had to be delivered in special trucks. There never was a time when she could not, at will, telephone any president, king or prime minister on earth to ask a question and receive an answer. She did not abuse these privileges but she had them. Pope Pius XII came somewhere near to consecrating Dorothy's greatness in her profession when he said to her, at the end of the war: "I know you are a Protestant, my daughter." She said: "Why, Your Holiness? Because of my rudeness?" (She had been pounding on his desk and weeping because of the German orphans she had seen.) "No," said the Pope, "because you so greatly overestimate the powers of the Roman Catholic Church. And for your tears, I bless you, my child."

That was journalism. It was good and great and lasted a very long time — quite possibly she was the greatest journalist America has known since the first batch, Hamilton and Jefferson and Madison. She certainly was far and away beyond Horace Greeley, her predecessor on the *Herald Tribune*, who so profoundly misunderstood Abraham Lincoln and was of no assistance to our woeful struggle between the Northern and Southern states. Such diverse personalities as the old King of

Arabia (Ibn es-Sa'ud) and Chaim Weizmann, our beloved friend who was the first President of Israel, valued her friendship and her understanding. Bill Donovan, concocting his schemes and plotting his plots at the heart of the American secret service, relied greatly upon her. Any number of foreigners thought of her as the most secure and dependable voice of the American people: her friends who conspired against Hitler on July 4th, 1944, and were hanged for it, are the proof.

This, all this, whether in print or by the living voice on the radio, is still journalism.

There remains history. What was Dorothy's power, what was her greatness, in the history of the United States and of the world?

It was that she, more than any other private person in the most powerful of all countries, awakened our people from slumber and prepared them for their ordeal. Day after day, year after year, she called upon them to awake and fight, and told them what the enemy was. Franklin Roosevelt never dared, until the actual outbreak of war, to say the things Dorothy said. He may have wanted to do so — I think he did — but he was bound by an oath of office and the obligations of the presidency. He said to me in March, 1938, when I asked (after dinner) if I could attend a press conference of his on the following day: "Come if you like, but I warn you I can't say a thing. They'll all ask about the Czechoslovak crisis and I can't say one single word. My lips are sealed by the State Department." Dorothy's lips were never at any moment sealed by the State Department.

Intrepid, intelligent and free, she fought her good fight. In that sense (I am speaking historically) her career ended at Pearl Harbor, only three weeks before her divorce from Sinclair Lewis. It is the limit of our story. After that she had still fifteen years to go in journalistic achievement, but historically speaking, her service to her country and to western humanity had been accomplished. She had done more than any one creature, by the judgment of experts, to prepare us for our tremendous task. I am not at all surprised that Sinclair Lewis felt bewildered and afraid before the tornado of her destiny. Her effect upon action was, by 1940, absolutely terrifying, and as we all know it made Red's hands tremble when he spoke of it. It is a misfortune — nobody is to blame — that the greatest of American journalists should have been married to the greatest of American writers. Such things ought not to happen.

We may conclude this summary of Dorothy's career by two letters, both outside of the limits of our story (they are from 1944), which are kept at Syracuse University. The first:

10, DOWNING STREET,
WHITEHALL.

16 February, 1944.

My dear Miss Thompson,

I have just seen the article about me which you wrote in the "San Francisco Chronicle" at the time of my illness last December, and I should like you to know how touched I am by this tribute.

During these hard years you have worked tirelessly in the Press and on the platform to make people understand what is at stake. In so doing you have achieved results which give us all cause for admiration, and have rendered services to both our countries which it would not be easy to over-estimate.

Yours sincerely,
Winston S. Churchill

Winston's severe pneumonia in the Western Desert in late 1943 (after the Cairo Conference) had evoked a kind of prayer from Dorothy, to which he here refers: it was in a great many newspapers, of course, but he seems to have seen it only in the San Francisco *Chronicle*.

The second letter is from the President after his election for a fourth term, a phenomenon to which Dorothy had very strongly contributed (as she did to the third, indeed, as we may soon see). It reads:

THE WHITE HOUSE
WASHINGTON

November 27, 1944

Dear Dorothy:

Now that one phase of the fight is over with I cannot delay longer telling you how much I appreciate your valiant support. I know that it took courage and a resolute spirit to oppose the powerful interests which it was necessary for you to oppose in declaring as you did your confidence in the administration's policies and purposes in the field of international relations. There is a great task ahead before we can defeat our enemies and achieve a lasting peace. I shall need your understanding counsel and your continued support through all of the struggle until the goal we seek is reached.

Very sincerely yours,
Franklin D. Roosevelt

II

The End of the Story

WE MUST GATHER UP A FEW STRANDS OF PERSONAL HISTORY AT
this point, including that of the narrator. I had left America
in 1934 and did not return until 1938; in the interim (1935) I had
been married to Diana Forbes-Robertson, known as Dinah; we
lived in Ireland, France and England, and we did not see Red at
all. (I do not think he came to Europe very often in those years.)
Dorothy came to see us in Paris and at a house we had at Saint-
Germain, outside of Paris. She was full of the abdication crisis,
having come from London, and bubbling with stories and various amusements. It was not funny to us and we did not get on
too well just then. Even so, I was able to perceive an enormous
change in Dorothy's position in the world — she was in constant demand by cabinet ministers, ambassadors and the like,
who knew (far better than I did) what her powers had become.

In February of 1938 we went to America; for my wife it was
the first time, and, since she was very young, it was quite bewil-
dering to her. I had been upset by a visit from Ernest
Hemingway, who had come to Saint-Germain some months
before and had said to me: "You stay here and be comfortable,
kid: I'll go to Spain for you." I did not want anybody to go to
Spain for me, least of all Ernest.

On our fourth night in New York — I can date it precisely
because our first, arranged from Paris, was Lynn Fontanne and
Alfred Lunt in *Amphitryon 38*, for which Thornton Wilder had
done everything without even telling us that he had the first

night of his own play, *Our Town*, on the same evening — and
the second, a Saturday, was Thornton's own play which he had
not mentioned, and the third, a Sunday, was sleep and recuperation — Red Lewis asked us to a party at his penthouse on
top of the Hotel Wyndham, on Fifty-eighth Street opposite the
Plaza Hotel. He had a collection of actors and actresses, chiefly,
along with some writers and other New Yorkers. I learned,
very quickly, two things: first, that Red was completely and
irretrievably stage-struck, speaking of current Broadway suc-
cesses as if they were the works of Aeschylus and Shakespeare;
and second, that he was definitely separated from Dorothy.
He made it clear without saying so too brutally. He said that
she would be coming in later, and that she lived on Central
Park West.

Presently she did come in. She was almost too gracious to
the actors and actresses (after all, she must have felt that they
had hypnotized Red). She got me into a corner after a while
and asked me, point-blank, what I wanted to do.

"You are at a point," she said, "when you must decide.
What is it?"

"It is Spain," I said. "I want to go to Spain."

"Well," she said, "you've made a lot of money now and I
don't see why you don't just buy a ticket and go."

"No," said I. "Not like that. I must have credentials, a
reason for going, some papers to show when I get there, and
some periodical of some kind which will print my dispatches
after I have gone there. I can't do it for the North American
Newspaper Alliance, my old reliable, because they have engaged Ernest Hemingway for the same job. I don't know what
to do. The *Saturday Evening Post* and others who want things
from me don't want Spain."

"You must go for the *Herald Tribune*," she said imperiously.
"Do you know Helen Reid?"

"No," said I. "How in the world could I know her?"

She reached for the telephone which was on Red's desk in the corner of the sitting room and then and there (although it must have been midnight) called up poor Helen and said I wanted to go to Spain and needed credentials and she thought the *Herald Tribune* ought to supply them. Helen said she would see me at noon the next day.

I went, saw and was conquered. To this moment I think Helen Reid is one of the most remarkable women in the world. She governed her empire for many long years with an iron hand in a velvet glove; numerous were the persons who did not have intelligence enough to see that she was doing it. She had been in her youth the social or private secretary to Mrs Whitelaw Reid (Lizzie), at the American embassy in London, where she met for the first time Franklin and Eleanor Roosevelt, on their honeymoon, as she has since told me. She married Ogden Reid, the only son and heir of the Reids, who was the principal stockholder of the New York *Tribune*, the rockbound Republican paper which Whitelaw Reid (or his wife) had bought from Horace Greeley. This newspaper bought out the New York *Herald* after Frank Munsey had ruined it, and the combination was the *Herald Tribune*, which for a good many years, while Helen reigned, was one of the best newspapers in existence.

Her precise title changed from time to time, but has no importance. (President or executive or managing editor or chairman or other meaningless words.) She was, in fact, the spirit of the paper. The stockholders, mostly in the Mills family (the elder Mrs Reid was a Mills of the California gold-mining family), were at times restive. Unanimity was not always attainable among them. Nevertheless she ruled, but with what diffidence! Never has a sovereign been so deferential to her subjects. Along with this irresistible manner (irresistible because it was natural) she had an intelligence equal to that of Franklin Roosevelt or Dorothy Thompson in public affairs. She knew what was what. So few do. Or did.

Helen gave me what I wanted and I went to Spain, not once but several times that year. To Czechoslovakia (for the crisis terminating in the Munich Agreement) I went for John Wheeler of the North American Newspaper Alliance, since the *Herald Tribune* was already represented in Prague. After the Munich Agreement I was certain that war could not long be delayed, and I packed up wife, child and nurse and brought them all to America, leaving our Paris flat to the mercy of the events. (The Germans occupied it but did no damage, perhaps because it was plainly labeled as American property under the embassy seal.)

Here I came again into the orbit of Dorothy and Red. They were not together at all. She was at the very peak of her concentration on the Nazi danger and he was immersed in his stage ambitions, first as a playwright and then as an actor. I remember one party of his, in some temporary habitat during the winter of 1939, where nobody except Dinah and I spoke ordinary English — they were all talking about theatrical productions of this, that or the other thing unknown to us. Dorothy no longer appeared at Red's parties, or he at hers. At that moment they were living on opposite sides of the Park, a gulf which, to New Yorkers, can never be bridged.

Dorothy thought it might be a good idea if I took the old house at Twin Farms for the summer. We had one child and there was another coming; it seemed right. She said we could stay as many months as we liked (the weather suggesting May to October) for a thousand dollars. We did.

2

THE FIRST VISITOR TO TWIN FARMS THAT SUMMER (THE FIRST who sticks in my memory, anyhow) was Wendell Willkie, who came with our old friend Alexander Sachs, the economist.

Willkie was a large, jovial man who had a wealth of human kindness and comprehension and, I should guess, forgiveness. He was handsome in a square, straight, supremely American way, and his voice was even more midwestern than my own. (He was from Indiana and I am from Illinois.) He was a lawyer for a public utilities company and in some way or other, by some litigation against the Federal Government involving a constitutional principle, had aroused Dorothy's interest. At the time I had no idea whether he was a Republican or a Democrat — I hardly knew which was which in the parties, since my interests had been overseas for so long. I also did not know, until his visit was over, that Dorothy had determined upon getting him into public life.

There is doubt in my own mind that Wendell wanted great offices. I believe it was Arthur Krock who first suggested him for the presidency (February 22, 1940). Oren Root made the first letter campaign that spring, and the *Herald Tribune* gave it editorial support. Dorothy also came out strongly for him in 1940.

In 1939, at Twin Farms, all this was still to come. Wendell had never been in politics and had no political characteristics, skills or aptitudes. On that visit I doubt if I ever heard him say a political word, in the partisan sense. He was against government interference in private industry — clearly, plainly — but it seemed to be a philosophical point of view rather than a partisan one. He also had an almost superstitious belief in technological advance, achievement, supremacy. These are the only "political" opinions (if such they be) that I remember. Mostly he was the best of friends and companions.

Just at that time a wicked horse planted his hoof on my right foot and I was laid up for several days. (The horse, a single-footer unknown to me, was from the stable in Woodstock and shied unreasonably on the brink of a precipice in the hills south

of that town; I was not thrown, but dismounted so awkwardly
that the frightened animal stamped on my foot.) Wendell came
to see me, from the big house to the old house, and sat by my
bedside and talked to me about horses, men and international
affairs. Never could I forget his kindness. When I said I had
thought vaguely of going down to Mexico City for a few weeks
at the end of the summer he said he would call up this one and
that one (all the stupendous heads of colossal corporations,
such as the Standard Oil Company); he did so; and when, in
August, I did go to Mexico, I was astonished at the hospitality
his merest word had evoked. I was in Mexico when the news of
the Nazi-Soviet Pact crashed upon the world; knowing it to be
the certain guarantee of immediate war, I got the first plane
back to Twin Farms.

Wendell's stay at Twin Farms (it was about a week, I think)
belongs in this story because of the enormous part his presidential candidacy played in Dorothy's evolution. From this
point of view I think I should tell a story, trivial in appearance,
about his last night on the farm. Dorothy had acquired, for the
occasion, a vast steak which she herself cooked on a charcoal
broiler. In such high moments she dared the ire of her cook
(old Marie) and went into the kitchen to poke and push. She
had firm principles about cooking.

We had this meal in the Big Room, also called the studio
(formerly the barn) which Red had originated years before.
There were only Dinah and I, Dorothy and Wendell, to eat a
quantity of sizzling beef which would have delighted a squad-
ron. When it was all over Wendell said that he disputed the
theory that steak cooked over charcoal was any better, or
indeed any different, from steak cooked over an electric stove.
He said that the engineers of his utilities company (the Com-
monwealth and Southern) had conclusively proved, by the
most extensive tests, that the only thing that counted in cooking was the degree of heat, plus the rate at which it was applied.
The source of the heat was irrelevant.

At this we all burst into expostulations and rebellion. I remember shouting at him: "But it *tastes* different, it *tastes* different! Won't you admit that it *tastes* different?" I do not believe that we ever convinced him. When he went away he sent Dorothy (as a sort of bouquet or bread-and-butter letter) a magnificent icebox as a souvenir. I think it is still there.

The second visitor of that summer who clings in memory is Red himself.

He came as a friendly visitor, perhaps even as a ghost. His room had always been kept in the Big House exactly as he had left it, and he was always welcome there. ("I will go away if you wish," Dorothy had once written him, "but your room is always here.")

He did not like it much. By this time it was utterly impossible for Dorothy to speak for ten consecutive minutes without bringing in the subjects that governed her mind. We were on the very brink of war; almost every day brought some new evidence of the insolent confidence and the boundless temerity of the Nazi-Fascist combination. Country after country had fallen to them; others were brazenly indicated as their prey. Dorothy's whole existence was bound up with these events, against which she fought like a Trojan, but Red could not bear to hear them discussed. On many an evening he would say: "Any more sityashuns and I go to bed." And inevitably, unconsciously, fatally, Dorothy would be back at it within a few minutes. She meant no harm; she could not help it.

I believe that Red's happiest moments during that stay (which lasted about two weeks) were those he spent in our house, his own old house, learning his lines for two plays in which he was about to act at a summer theatre in Maine. These were *Ah, Wilderness!* by Eugene O'Neill, and *Our Town* by Thornton Wilder. He said his lines to Dinah and she gave him his cues (not the entire réplique but enough to keep him going). She was well accustomed to this, having been born in an acting family, and had done it often with her own elder sister, the

exquisite actress Jean Forbes-Robertson. She was sympathetic
to Red anyhow because she shared his horror of the endless talk
about international affairs, and also, naturally, because she
found his desire to perform parts on the stage an endearing and
comprehensible ambition. The rest of us thought it an aberra-
tion and a waste of time. Dinah took it seriously and even
went up to Maine to see him do it a little later; she said he was
not at all bad, although by no means professional.

It was a strange summer, clouded with premonition. In
September (just as I returned from that brief visit to Mexico)
the Germans invaded Poland; England, then France, declared
war. The Polish campaign, with the Russians meeting the
Germans halfway, was brief and sickening. The future was
grim indeed.

3

THE "PARTING" OF THE LEWISES — DOROTHY'S WORD — SEEMS
to have taken place in the early spring of 1937. There is a
letter of April 29th of that year, from 17 Wood End Lane in
Bronxville, which makes it clear — and we have also the diary
entry of January 2nd, 1942 (the day of their divorce), which
says they have been apart for four and a half years.

At the time, however clear the situation may have been
between them, it was not a matter of public knowledge. They
entered upon a period of rather intermittent friendliness for
another two years or so; also, as we have already seen, Red was
a visitor at Twin Farms in 1939, more than two full years later.
In February of that year, when Dorothy drew nationwide
attention and admiration by attending a meeting of the
German-American Bund (the Nazi organization) in Madison
Square Garden and being expelled from it for laughing, Red
issued a statement in which he said (among other things) "I am

proud of my wife, Dorothy Thompson." Such gestures now, in retrospect, may seem generous or loyal, but cannot alter the obvious fact that they ceased to be husband and wife considerably earlier.

Dorothy's letter of April 29th, 1937, from Bronxville, is immensely long. Even so, it should be given in full, since it illuminates the whole subject as nothing else could. It bears a note at the top, penciled in her handwriting: "On our parting." The year "1937" is also added in her handwriting. I assume these notes to have been made on the carbon copy long years later (in 1958 or 1959) when she was going over all her papers with a view to using them in her projected autobiography. The copy at Syracuse is a carbon copy of the original. It reads:

17 WOOD END LANE

BRONXVILLE, NEW YORK

Bronxville,
April 29.

Oh, my darling:

I am writing this letter without knowing where to address it, or how to reach you. I shall have to wait to send it, until I hear. It probably won't be very adequate, because I have not slept for two nights, and that makes one dumb. But it has been turning over and over in my mind.

When you stood there yesterday with the collar of your polo coat turned up against the back of the head you looked so like the photograph that Yvonne took of you in London at the time we were married that my heart contracted. There were so many things that I wanted to say to you, but I could not. Seeing you standing there made me go back, to find out why you should be standing there now, and saying goodbye to me. I thought of a great many things: the kind of people we each are; the hurts that we have done to each other and never talked about. Resentments accumulate; they aren't liquidated as they come up; they grow and grow and then suddenly there are too many. You have said many bitter things to me, but you have said them under alcohol, almost always. You never said them when you were cool and sober. After a while I thought they only existed in a feverish brain, as huge, exaggerated caricatures of something that you no doubt felt, but which certainly wasn't just what you said. But you were quite cold and quite possessed when you talked with me Saturday. The shock was very hard for me. It was harder next day and harder next day and harder today. A sort of delayed shock.

Now, tonight, however, I am quieter, and the hand that seemed to be clutching at my heart and squeezing the blood out of it is somewhat relaxed. I am at home, and soon I am going to go to sleep. Horace gave me some dope which he says won't hurt me or leave a hangover. And before I go to bed I want to say some things to you that are true for me, whether they are true for you or not.

I love you. I love you in just the same way as I did when you first set foot in my apartment in Berlin ten days ago.[1] Then I had the feeling, "This is the man I have been looking for all my life." Now I think, "That is the man I always wanted." I had from the beginning the feeling that we belonged together. That we really deeply understood each other, even though in the things that two people who love each other should find words for, we were both singularly inarticulate. I felt a sense of oneness, of destiny, as though you were some other part of myself. I will never, never forget how you looked, or how I felt, that first night. I felt a terrific indignation. I thought, "My God, how he suffers." I had suffered pretty brutally myself, and I was still suffering pretty brutally, but suddenly I wanted to say: Let's stop suffering. Suddenly I felt oddly gay.

[1] Meaning ten years ago.

There isn't anything rational about this. I wasn't even "in love" with you in the usual sense of the term. I didn't, anyhow, have an overwhelmingly physical desire to sleep with you. That was nice enough, too. Very nice. But you said to me once, half whimsically, half apologetically, "I exist mostly above the neck." Well, I understood that. So do I. There is a love of the body and of the body alone, and the Church, which knows a thing or two, calls it Lust. And I'm not so set against lust as the Church is, but lust never yet caused me to lose my head. But there is a love of the imagination. And it can be fatal, for women like me. People like you and me build up images, sometimes, and fall in love with them. I once did that with a wavy haired and senti-mental boy in Budapest. One fine day I woke up and my intelligence, which can be damned cold, told me that his existence, his very existence in my life, was a pure fabrication. I had made an image which I worshipped. I hated to see my work of art destroyed, and indeed, broke my heart over it. You did that with Grace. She was a fairy princess to you, and you damned near made her into one for herself. She went around dramatizing your own image of her, until sud-denly you caught her doing it, so your image was broken, and that broke your heart, too.

But this thing with you, was the real thing. I knew it immediately. You used to sing to me about a lady fair and kind was never face so pleased my mind . . I did but see her passing by . . and now I love her till I die. Well, that was true of me. There was never face so pleased my *mind*. I loved the shape of that face, the tall and narrow skull, the thin, silky red-blond hair, the long, adventurous hands, the narrow feet, the almost absent thighs. I loved the mer-curial moods, the darkness and light, the hilarity and the agony. Then I loved them, and I love them now. All sorts of men have crossed my life in the last ten years. Some of

them liked me. One or two claimed they loved me. Lots of
them I have liked, had real affection for. But you were my
man. I know this sounds like Frankie and Johnnie and a
Mae West film, but kitch [kitsch], as you have often remarked, is often true. Babies and kittens are kitch. I am,
therefore, in a not very classic way, the very picture of
Penelope.

When I married you, I didnt do it because I thought I
would be happy. All my intelligence — that cold part of my
mind — warned me. I knew that I wouldnt be happy, in any
ordinary sense of the word happy. Happiness is mostly just
the absence of pain. I knew that you would make me a great
deal of pain. But always, when I was with you, I felt that I
was alive. You were, and are, a constant, living experience.

But everyone must have rest. One must have anodynes.
God knows you have one: alcohol. And one recognized by the
poets. Said Wilhelm Busch: "Wer Sorgen hat, hat auch
liquoer." For a while I shared that anodyne with you, and
more than you yourself are probably in a position to remember, since you were usually at the time farther gone in it than
I. Just the same I have been very drunk with you, on
occasion. No such urge as yours drove me to it, and every
intuition of my nature revolted away from it. But I couldn't
live with you, every minute, wholly. No human organism,
which is sensitive and differentiated could stand eternally so
charged and electric an atmosphere. And work has always
been my way out. It is so quiet, so impersonal — my work,
my kind of work — and so demanding. Now, when you tell
me that my work has ruined our marriage, *that* statement
falls on deaf ears. I *know* that it saved our marriage for the
past six years. It was, for me, the outlet, the escape, from
something too intense to be born [borne]. Too "devouring."

You don't know what you are like, Hal, when you are
drunk. I am not attacking you. Go on and read further.

I want you to *see*. This restless, dynamic, overcharged, demanding personality which is you, becomes intensified to the point of madness. It is energy completely explosive and completely off the track. In our early marriage it dragged me with it, until I vomited from revolt that I couldnt control. I tried to stop you. We had crazy fights about liquor — don't you *remember*. I saw it destroying something — however temporarily — which I loved with all my heart and all my mind. And it was destroying me. I didn't want to be destroyed, because I believed that I was as essential to you as you were to me. I had to keep myself — for you. And I kept myself by constant baths in the cool air of work, in the cool, impersonal, intellectual, unemotional air of an objective world. I am grateful to work. Next to you, I love it best of anything. It has saved me twice in my life from utter shipwreck in emotion.

Now, as I write to you, I know that you know all this already. I suppose that it is why we talk so little to each other intimately. Because each knows the other knows already. I know all about you, my darling. I know what is eating you and always, periodically, has eaten you. It is the fear that your creative power is waning. You are a creative genius, and you constantly have to reaffirm your power to create. Times come when the "virtue," to use a biblical phrase, goes out of you. And until it comes back you are — spiritually speaking — like an animal in heat and impotent. It's a brutal phrase, but it's the most brutal thing I have ever seen. And the awful, terrible thing for one who loves you is that one cant do anything about [it].

All my intelligence tells me that there is some madness in it. Sometimes the woman who loves you as a man is thoroughly furious with you. "Who in hell," I say, "does he think he is. He has written a whole shelf of books and four of them, certainly, and probably more, are classics of American literature already. Or five, or six. One would be enough for a normal genius," I say. Nice words "normal genius." "*Some* time," I think, "the man will be old. Some time, he will have to resign himself to sit under the vine and ruminate on the past. He isn't God," I think, "and even God's part in creating the universe is universally conceded by the pious to have been over in seven days."

Well, your part in creating the universe of words, obviously isn't over, so you go through this cycle of creation, then oblivion, then the long and agonizing emptiness, and then creation again. And the lesson that I've learned, and maybe it isn't the right lesson, and you can teach me a better one, but the lesson is that all I can do is to sit by. If I get caught up in the cycle, I shall be ground to bits in it, and what will you do with a battered and dismembered Dotty? And in spite of all your recriminations, I honestly think that it matters to you, and apart from this business of creation, matters more to you than anything else, that I do sit by. And I think, whatever you may rationalize about it, that you know, that I see, and feel, and am innerly with you in the whole process.

This business that you have built up now in your mind about me and you, about being the husband of Dorothy Thompson, a tail to an ascending comet, and what not, is only because you are, for the moment, stymied, and you have been many times before. I know that it is an obsession with you, but I also know that it will cease to be an obsession, the moment you have again done a piece of work with which *you* are satisfied. Good God, Hal, you are one of the best critics living, and you know *exactly* my worth and limitations. So do I. I am a first rate peripatetic brain picker. I have taste, some energy, and a pretty good sense in spotting quality. That's why I am a good brain picker. I write the English language with rather more literateness and expressiveness

than the average journalist, thanks to an early affinity for
the English classics and thanks, even more, to having lived
with you ten years. That ten years has been a cure from ten
preceding years of writing cliches, which I havent recovered
from, but I am making progress. For the rest I have the
courage of my somewhat limited convictions, I dont care
what Ogden Reid thinks, and being, like yourself, a moralist,
I consistently appeal to peoples' better instincts, and that is
refreshing in a world filled with bitter little assassins of
character. That sums me up in journalism and is a recipe,
apparently, for "success." It's decent work, comparatively
speaking, and that ends it. And the lady and gentleman
morons who cant find anything better to do than to make
comparisons however invidious, like to play up that I, too,
in spite of being married to you, can write — and how. But
do you think that any man who knows American letters
believes any of that nonsense. It embarrasses me and it
embarrasses them. Hal Smith, or Raymond Swing, or Raoul
de Sales, or Carl Van Doren, or John Gunther — to take
some journalists in — do they any more think of comparing
me with you than they would compare themselves? Well,
you know. Frances Perkins and Wilson! My Wilson isnt
President of the United States and I am not Frances Perkins.

So funny. You go away and you say you will go forever
and suddenly I dont see how I can even write my column.
If you wont read it, if you wont like it, or dislike it, or crit-
icize its punctuation . . . then why should I write it at all?
For money, because I like work . . but the little pleasure,
the proud pleasure of being praised by you . . that was
always the fun in it.

Darling, darling, darling, there's only one thing in which
I am a really superior person. I have a really superior capacity for love. I love you. And that's the truth and that's the
last word. Go away for six months, or three months, or six

years, or three years, I shall sit at home, in *our* home, and be there when you come back to it.

All this I wanted to say to you as you stood there with your collar up around your ears, but you were in a hurry, and I was full of tears.

4

THE FOREGOING LETTER DIFFERS FROM MOST OF DOROTHY'S IN that the syntax, punctuation, etc., are more careless than usual and there seems no effort to "write." All the commas, scattered very nearly without attention to where they might fall, are an indication; so are the interrogative sentences without a question mark; so are the numerous "donts" and "cants" and "isnts" which bear no apostrophe sign for the missing letter; and on the whole, we may see without trouble, the letter is an outpouring of emotion, even though written on the typewriter. At the last moment it appears to us that Dorothy, who has been watching the shipwreck of her marriage since 1930, tries to save it by a sort of negativism that was not really in her nature — the posture of Penelope, forever waiting for the husband. From the style and manner of the letter we can tell that it is utterly sincere, with the sincerity of the historic moment which passes in special emphasis (in hard truth felt as such) without the possibility of return. For, of course, Red never did come back.

The letters between them in 1937–1939 are increasingly painful, as the climate of "casual friendship" wore thin and disappeared. It was not really possible for Red and Dorothy to meet at occasional parties in a friendly manner when their emotional entanglement was not yet wholly past. Moreover, each had formed other friendships, perhaps even attachments, of one sort or other, unshared and possibly resented. Red was more and more engrossed in the theatre and its people. In 1937 he wrote a play about Dorothy, lamentably entitled *Queenie*, but the leading actresses to whom it was submitted (notably Helen Hayes) did not want to play it on the stage and it was never produced. Dorothy herself wrote an anti-Nazi play in 1938–1939, about refugees from Germany, which was eventually produced (1940) without success. Her career in political journalism progressed apace: after the great crises over Czechoslovakia in 1938, ending with the Munich Agreement — a period when she was speaking over the radio almost constantly — she was at her peak. From 1939 to 1941 there is nobody in public life to whom she can be compared, either in politics or journalism: next to Franklin Roosevelt himself, she seems to have been accepted by the people as the voice of wisdom and duty. She was called, quite currently, by a sort of national nickname, "Cassandra." I never thought the appellation was right, really, since the Trojan princess was a prophetess of doom, and Dorothy never gave us doom without an escape hatch. What she told us, in essence, was that we were doomed unless we woke up in time to fight the appalling danger of Hitler's conquest. I always thought a better name for her, if we had to have one, was Boadicea, the warrior queen of ancient Britain.

In 1937 and 1938, when they occasionally met, she wrote Red some long letters which for the most part were never sent. He wrote to her (briefly) on money matters or, from time to time, to accuse her of self-pity. Her long, long, unsent letters need not be given in full, but there are two — one about her son and one about practical matters — which have some pertinence to the story and must be quoted. The practical letter (after a long emotional passage much like the letter given just now) reads:

You suggested sending me $1,000 a month. I shall need it this next month. After that I shall try very hard to put it aside as a reserve for either or both of us. As you know, I don't get my whole income from the Tribune, except in quarters. The regular income is about $800 a month. The L.H.J. pays another $500, so that I have $1300. My flat and service and secretarial and other office expenses, takes around $380 more of that, but the secretarial help is being negotiated, and presumably will be settled so that I shall not have to pay more than $20 a week out of my own pocket. But I dont know when that will be. I shall try to get back the rental of the flat over the summer. The $380 is: $220 for secretaries (all of Miss Walker's salary and $5 of Margot's), $100 for flat and service, and about $60 for incidentals such as light, gas, phone. Anyhow, when I tote up the extra travel and books and taxis and things essential to the column, I actually have never had anything like $1,000 a month of my own money. I have a continual struggle with the H.T. over money.

I know you wonder what I do with my money. If you like I will send you an itemized list of expenditures since I returned from Europe. You will see there are, first, a very heavy expenditure of things connected with work; then clothes; more than I need, no doubt. And I have paid more bills than you think — I mean household bills.

Just now I had to go out of the library because the carpenter came to fix your desk — as you ordered it some time ago. Bill Lucia is doing some painting, necessary if the place in Vermont isnt to be a mess — ordered last year. The door has finally been put on the little furnace room to keep nursery noises out of the library. Are we both crazy?

I only beg you one thing: Don't do anything rash or hasty about Vermont. You have loved it very much, and you have been very happy there and very productive. (Also unhappy, I know, but happy, too). There is something about places where one has loved and been loved. Michael was conceived there, and there I came with him. I dont want to read my emotions into you, but I love that place. It is the place you promised me the day we met, and it is my home. And the child's. It was the place that brought Wells back to you. It is, in some way, the best expression in life of both of us — beautiful, comfortable, hospitable, and unpretentious. A great many people besides ourselves have been happy there, my darling. I am superstitious. I think it's lucky. I could walk out of this house tomorrow and shed no tears, except that I find it handsome and comfortable. But I dont love it, and any other place not so handsome or comfortable, would do. But I would sacrifice a good many things to keep Vermont, and even as I write about it, I feel how much I love you . . . God knows how . . but how close I am grown with you. Oh, my dear, I'll never get you out of my heart, or my mind, or my blood.

There are indications that this letter, written from Bronxville, must be from the spring of 1937. It bears the notation in Dorothy's handwriting: "This was not sent," a note made over twenty years later.

It calls for comment in one respect: the money matters. Every sum mentioned seems small in comparison to the recollection I (and many others) retain of Dorothy's life in New York and Vermont. How could she run two big houses (Bronxville and Twin Farms) as well as a New York flat, with two secretaries, a child's nurse, two or three house servants and at least one gardener, and dress herself and travel, on the sum she names ($1300 a month)? Obviously Red had been contributing — paying a good many bills; he may have thought he was paying them all — but if he were to send her $1000 a month, as he evidently proposed to do, she still would have had only $2300 a month for an expenditure which, it seems to me, must have been more than that.

The answer I get, after contemplation of the letter, is that she had simply forgotten some of the sources of her income. She was lecturing in that year (she did every year for two decades). She was also on the air, although not as constantly as later. That should have provided a considerable sum. The figure $500 a month from the *Ladies' Home Journal* seems small: it was $1000 during most of the subsequent years until it became $1500 at the end of the war. The *Herald Tribune* figures show payments of $40,000 a year to Dorothy at her peak, only shortly after this. Of course the figures I have obtained, which give her a gross annual income of well above $100,000 after 1938, are not applicable to the preceding year, from which this letter seems to date; but on the whole it seems likely that her income even then was larger than this letter would indicate.

The one about Michael dates of 1939 and was also never sent. An excerpt will show the tone:

> More importantly — I cannot conceal it from you — I am deeply concerned about Mickey. The child is in wretched condition. His urine still shows albumen. He still walks badly. I called in a *great* specialist — Professor Lichtwitz — and he says that Michael suffers from an endocrine disturbance. [. . .]
>
> I have finally decided to send him to Arizona, to a very small school where he can live in a cottage with his nurse, and associate with other children and be out of doors, which he seriously needs. It will cost $250 a month — I can't send him alone — and, of course, his being that far away, so young, is a great care to me. I have investigated the school as well as I can — there aren't many where a nurse can stay, or that take such young boys. I feel that I should go with him, but obviously I cannot. He will leave on Tuesday, and I feel as though my heart were being torn out.

Another undated letter which was never sent surveys the whole failure of their marriage and contains this passage:

I deceived myself but never wholly. Underneath I knew. I knew ever since the baby was born, and since my pregnancy. You wanted to love me but you didn't love me; the will to love is not love. So my belief in your love for me was only the reflection of my love for you. I loved you but I did not trust your love for me. You loved Grace at the beginning, and maybe you loved Catherine Sage, but me you never loved, so not loving you had to admire, and I not getting love from you sought admiration from you as some second-best thing. And Grace was really right: I was always chiefly oatmeal. Healthy for a while, only one can get damned sick of it, especially if it ceases to be cheap. I should have known from a previous experience that you cannot love a person into loving you back. You can only make him (or her) dependent on you; a comfortable thing to have about, with resentment if the comfort is withdrawn. But that's not love.

Red's letters were rare and unsatisfactory, it would appear from some notes Dorothy makes on her own. Here is an example (1939?) written from the Hotel Mayfair in St. Louis on Sunday, February 12, on the typewriter:

Dear Dorothy:

I, too, have written you many letters which I have never sent. They have, mostly, been protests against your not only permitting yourself to wander through a great fog of self-pity, but even to enjoy this hysteria.

When, in your last letter, you say "I wish I had never set eyes on you, I wish I had never married you, and I wish with all my heart that I could forget you exist," then — even allowing for exaggeration — you really do make it clear why you never write.

You also finally make it obligatory for me never to write to you again, except for the most formal business letters.

I have been making no money at all, but I enclose a check for $300 for Micky, and I hope to send you, each month, this much or more.

h.

There are a good many letters in 1938 and 1939 about financial arrangements, a trust fund for Michael, etc., etc. In 1939 Dorothy was notified through Red's lawyers that he wanted to make over the Twin Farms property, acres and houses and all, to Dorothy; he had already given her the Bronxville house, from the beginning, as her own. The values assigned to these properties may have been rather high, as I believe they were, but the lawyers accepted them: Twin Farms was said to be worth $150,000 and the Bronxville house $50,000. There was no other financial settlement made on Dorothy then or later, but only (in the form of a trust fund and later allowances) for Michael.

During these years verging on 1940, while Dorothy was preoccupied in that great world where she held such a place now, Red was so engrossed in the theatre that he hardly noticed anything else. He had become fascinated with an extremely young actress, Marcella Powers, whose struggles at the outset of a career furnished him with both a novel (*Bethel Merriday*) and a play (*Angela Is Twenty-two*). The play actually had a production and a long road tour. One of Dorothy's many unsent letters to him refers to this phase of their existence, during which he evidently asked her (for the first time) for a divorce. She has dated it in her own writing as 1938, although on internal evidence it looks more like 1939 to me. It follows in full:

Hal:
   If you think it's wicked — go ahead and divorce. I won't oppose it. I also won't get it. For God's sake, let's be honest.

You left me, I didn't leave you. You want it. I don't. You get it. On any ground your lawyers can fake up. Say I "deserted" you. Make a case for mental cruelty. You can make a case. Go and get it.

What is "incredible" about my not writing? What is "incredible" is that I don't rush into the divorce court and soak *you* for desertion and "mental cruelty." I don't write because I don't know what to say to you. You have made it clear time on end that you dislike me, that you are bored with me, that you are bored with "situations and conditions. And reactions." You don't like my friends. You don't know my friends. You resent my friends. Shall I write you that I think Hamilton Armstrong has done a brilliant piece of journalism in his last book on the Munich conference? Or that Graham Hutton is in America and has a fascinating tale of Britain? Or that Peter Grimm has ideas on the Housing policy? Or that Gustav Stoelper has introduced me to Rietzler, who was the man who smuggled Lenin and Trotzky into Russia, and has just, at long last, left Germany? Are you interested in Alex Sachs' memo to Lehman Brothers on what Mussolini plans in Tunisia? Or in Fodor's letters from Riga? Do you want to know what Raoul says about Bonnet? Or what Edgar writes about Moro-Giafferi and Grynzspan? You are happy. Happier, you write, than you have been in years. I congratulate you. I am glad that you are happy. I happen not to be. I am not happy. I am not happy, because I have no home; because I have an ill and difficult child without a father. Because I have loved a man who didn't exist. Because I am widowed of an illusion. Because I am tremblingly aware of the tragedy of the world we live in.

I do not "admire and respect you." I have loved you. I do not admire your present incarnation or respect your present attitude toward anything. I did not like "Angela is 22" because I think it is beneath the level of the author of "Arrowsmith" or of "It Can't Happen Here." I think it is a cheap concession to a cheap institution — the American Broadway Theater. I do not admire the people with whom you surround yourself. I am horrified, on your behalf, at the association of your name with Fay Wray. Why haven't I said so? Out of tact! Out of the feeling that a great man may allow himself indulgences. Out of the desire not to hurt someone who is sensitive. But I am a bad liar. I cannot pretend that I think Jack Wildberg is a "prince." I don't. I think he is a racketeer.

When I am with you I depress you. I am depressed. But I would rather be depressed than pretend that nothing really matters. I don't write to you because I can't lie to you. Maybe it is because I respect you, or maybe it is because I respect myself — somewhat. I think you have thrown down the sink the best things that life has ever offered you: the love of friends; of your wife; the pleasure in your sons. Your home. For what? For whisky and art? Where's the art, at long last? Or the whisky?

You say I am "brilliant." My dear Hal, I am "brilliant" faux [faute] de mieux. I am a woman — something you never took the trouble to realize. My sex is female. I am not insensitive. I am not stupid. I do not love you for your wit, or for "nostalgia" — my nostalgia antedates our marriage. I loved you, funnily enough, for your suffering, your sensitivity, your generosity, and your prodigious talent. I shall not reiterate my feelings, nor insist that I still love you. I do not even know you — the you of the present moment. I shall certainly not pursue you, I am a woman. If you want my friendship you have got to win it. If you care for anything more, you have got to woo it. If you don't — then you, be honest, as you advise me to be — and break this relationship finally and completely. Forget that I exist. Forget that Mickey exists. Wipe him out as a responsibility. Wipe me out as a memory. Be happy! Be free.

I, however, am not free. I can neither wipe out my memories nor, above all, can I forget you, since you live with me, as the chief, perhaps the only tie I have to life, in the reincarnation of yourself in your son. You have fathered a child, violent and frail, gifted, [. . .]. Born to grow up in this tragic century. A [. . .], lovely, nerve-wracking, expensive child. [. . .] And he lives now, today, way off from here, in Arizona, and I go into his room and play with his toys, and ache with loneliness and loss. He is dearer to me than my life, and he makes life almost intolerable, and the bond that binds me to his father is "wicked." And I do not write to his father . . because if I do, I get a pedantic and old-maidish letter full of my faults. My faults are, as a matter of fact, much greater than you dream. There are things in my heart that you do not dream of, things that are compounded of passion and fury and love and hate and pride and disgust and tenderness and contrition things that are wild and fierce . . and you ask me to write you conventional letters because you are in "exile." From what? From whom?

Give me Vermont. I want to watch the lilac hedge grow tall and the elm trees form, and the roses on the gray wall thicken, and the yellow apples hang on the young trees, and the sumac redden on the hills, and friends come, and your two children feel at home. Who knows? Maybe some time you might come home yourself. You might go a long way and do worse. As a matter of fact and prophesy — you will.

d.

There were some minor matters at this period (1938–1939) in which Red offended Dorothy, such as telegraphing his whereabouts to Emily Carter, the maid, instead of to herself. He also canceled her power of attorney over his various accounts; in this case the offense was that he did it by formal notification to the bank and others concerned, not to her. In other respects he seems to have been correct enough: about money, for example, he was generous, considering that his stage ventures were not only unprofitable but often downright costly to him. The only dispute I remember between them on property or possessions had to do with the books at Twin Farms, which by 1940 were inextricably mixed. It would have taken a detective to separate what was Dorothy's from what was Red's, and yet he wanted his books. Some kind of division was made, but it was on rather slapdash principles, and chiefly by secretaries. Years later I found books of his on the shelves there, and distinctly remember, for example, a copy of *The American*, by Henry James, in the flyleaf of which is written: "Harry S. Lewis, Washington, 1908." This is twenty years before he married Dorothy.

5

DOROTHY'S PUBLIC CAREER, WHICH SO STRANGELY IRKED AND depressed Red Lewis, reached its peak in the years 1940–1941. Whether the career "ruined the marriage" or not, as he sometimes said, or whether it was her indispensable anodyne against the failure of the marriage, as she often said, it certainly had a profound effect upon their relationship; we have seen plenty of proof. The career now entered a phase which deserves the word climacteric, because the world itself had moved in Dorothy's direction. That is, the events she had prophesied, and against which she had incessantly warned the American people, were now taking place, and at the same time the American people, alarmed and distraught over the rapidity of the disasters, were more inclined to listen to Dorothy than ever before.

Public and private lives often move with difficulty together, as every observer knows; and in this period, 1940–1941, I doubt if any kind of private life would have been possible for Dorothy. Even if she and Red had not been already estranged, her intense involvement in public affairs, both national and international, would have made any other arrangement impossible. Red had other interests and other attachments. When this period of high tension was over Dorothy had lost her place in the *Herald Tribune*, America had entered the war and (only three weeks later) her divorce from Red Lewis was granted. These events, coming within a few months of each other, terminate our story.

In the preceding chapter I attempted to differentiate between Dorothy's *historic* mission, as I understand it (and as I think Roosevelt and Churchill understood it), which ended with America's entrance into the war, and her career as a professional journalist, which continued for another fifteen years. The historic mission was, principally, the call to arms, if we may so name it — the awakening of America, in which she had many fellow workers but was in many ways the voice most heeded. Among other things it involved the third presidential term (and finally the fourth) for Franklin Roosevelt, although Dorothy never expected to find herself supporting any such cause until the end of that terrifying summer.

She went to Europe in the spring of 1940. Dinah and I had gone over in March, made a tour of Italy (where I thought I might never again see the treasures which in fact the war so happily spared). We met Dorothy again in Paris and on the night of May 9th we dined at the American embassy and went back to the Meurice Hotel with Dorothy afterwards. With her principal secretary (Madeleine Clark), Air Vice-Marshal Barratt, commanding the R.A.F. in France, and Robert Murphy, then counselor of the American embassy, we sat late in her sitting room, talking of the war which seemed suspended in agonizing uncertainty. On the following morning we all woke up to find that Hitler's armies had invaded the Low Countries in crushing force.

Dorothy's activity in Europe was ending anyhow, and a few days later we saw her off on the train to Genoa, where she sailed on the *Rex*. She was (like everybody else) in a state of alarm and premonition, especially since our own country, averse to war at almost any season, was now about to embark on the paralyzing enterprise of a presidential election (as Hitler perfectly understood).

My wife sailed from England later on, but I stayed through the "blitz" in London until the beginning of October. What I know of Dorothy's activity at the Republican convention that summer and during the election, up to October, I have learned from her and from others, as well as from the newspapers.

She had made up her mind, sometime after leaving Paris, that only Wendell Willkie could keep the Republican party from a neutralist or isolationist policy in the time now at hand. She was therefore more determined on his nomination than ever; she knew him well; she felt sure that he could do what was necessary to (as she undoubtedly said) "save the country." She was among the early Willkie-ites and now she became one of the strongest of them. Mrs Reid has told me of an evening in Philadelphia, during the Republican convention, when Dorothy pounded the table so that the glasses and dishware clattered, declaiming with vehemence: "If the politicians won't nominate Wendell, believe me, Helen, we can elect him ourselves! I'll go into the street and get the people to elect him!"

He was nominated and the campaign began.

During this campaign, as Dorothy told me, she grew more and more unsure that Wendell could take over quickly enough to make a difference in the unfolding of history. She never had liked the idea of a third term — it was always an unsympathetic notion to Americans — but she came more and more to fear the uneasy, faltering footsteps of a totally new administration on what had become, essentially, the battlefield of the world.

Along with this there came, during the summer, a rather unwilling admiration for the President, Mr Roosevelt. She felt a calm assurance in him (everybody who knew him felt it) which was in itself a shield against despondency and suggested, at least for the present ominous circumstances, both courage and wisdom. Dorothy had never greatly admired the President up to this point and she had often criticized and opposed him in print. She was changing rapidly as the campaign went on and the events in Europe became steadily more calamitous. The bombings in London, the sense of England's terrible and solitary ordeal, the regard which she, like everybody else, felt for the indomitable people of that island and for their spokesman, Churchill (it was the summer of his greatest speeches), must have influenced her mind strongly, in the sense that although Wendell's sympathies were as clear as the President's, it was the latter who seemed likely to know how they could be made to count.   .

Thus she reached October, a late stage of the campaign, a month before the elections. I came home just then and found her more downright gloomy (and less talkative!) than I had ever known her. In a few days she presented the *Herald Tribune* with two columns in which she declared that in view of the national emergency she wanted to move her support from Willkie to Roosevelt, and gave her reasons.   .

The *Herald Tribune*, the leading Republican newspaper of the country, was in a most embarrassing quandary and for the moment refused to publish these two columns. Dorothy thereupon invoked her contract, in which her right to untrammeled expression of opinion had been embedded. Rather than make the uproar worse by litigation, the *Herald Tribune* printed these two columns and all the rest that she wrote from then until April 30th, 1941, when her contract expired. It was not renewed.

Republicans in general, especially Dorothy's friends, were aghast at what seemed to them an outright betrayal. Dorothy had been so vehement in support of Wendell Willkie that it seemed incomprehensible now to find her on the other side. Wendell himself, although it must have been a shock to him, met her soon after the elections at a *Herald Tribune* gathering and said to her: "Dorothy, even if you don't want me to be President I still want you to be my friend." That was characteristic of him.

The change in Dorothy's political complexion soon became evident in many ways. She entered upon something like a friendship with the President; in the next few years she saw him more often, he telephoned her frequently, and she was to be a tower of strength to him (in one particular speech above all) in the campaign again four years later. Her attention was constantly on the war from then on until after Roosevelt's death, and opportunities for criticism were therefore less frequent. She supported him to the end, although what her feelings were at successive steps we do not precisely know.

Among the Roosevelt letters in the papers at Syracuse are a number from the President, the most important of which we quoted at the end of the last chapter; there are several from his wife, asking Dorothy to lunch or dinner, or to stay at the White House; and there is even one from his mother, the redoubtable Mrs James Roosevelt, who was not given to such expressions of approval. (My guess is that the President asked her to write it.) It does show, more perhaps than any other, what an effect Dorothy's change from Willkie to Roosevelt had on those concerned. It reads:

HYDE PARK
ON THE HUDSON, N.Y.

My dear Miss Thompson,
    I have always enjoyed reading your letters in the Tribune,

so I allow myself the pleasure of telling you how happy I
have been over the *brave* spirit you have shown in the last
two I have read. I am the Mother of the president so you
will perhaps like to know how happy you have made me.
Believe me

Sincerely yours

Sara Delano Roosevelt

This was written in the large, decisive script of the authori-
tative old lady who had dominated her entire family for so long.

Things had changed, yes — a great deal since that day, only
two years before, when I had my first private talk with Mr
Roosevelt. At that time (March, 1938) he said to me, with
good humor but fully meaning it: "Don't quote Dorothy to me.
She's the oracle of Wall Street."

6

THE JAPANESE ATTACK ON THE AMERICAN FLEET AT PEARL
Harbor brought us into the war in December, 1941, seven
months after Dorothy's departure from the *Herald Tribune*.
Her column was now appearing in the New York *Post* and in
numerous newspapers (not always the same as before) throughout the country. She wrote to the President that she had
"taken no financial loss" in her spectacular switch to him. This
remained true for a while, but gradually her number of newspapers declined. That, however, was for the future.

At this moment, as 1941 met 1942, Dorothy's mind was on
the war and not upon her divorce, which was about to be made
final. In order to show how completely this had become the
fact — how little she thought of the divorce at last, when it
came — I reproduce the first four pages of her diary for 1942.
(It lapses afterwards — there are only five entries, the fifth of

no interest. Each page of the 1942 diary, so quickly abandoned, has the date and other reminders in print at the top: one page is allowed for each day.)

<table>
<tr><td>1ST
DAY</td><td>Thursday 1 January
Happy New Year</td><td>364 Days
to come</td></tr>
</table>

This year I shall attempt to keep a diary, as much for thoughts as for events. Wells is here, and last night in the melancholy that always follows drinking broke into a rather bitter protest against his life in the army — its inactivity, rigidity. "The American army is the oldest democratic army therefore the least democratic, most rigid." He wants officer's training "in the marines, cavalry, or best in the intelligence service." Dr Parker called yesterday to interest me in "vice." How to keep our boys pure. "No one is as interested in this war." Perhaps because the people know more! I asked her whether maybe Hitler didn't have the solution. Fornication for all, and every girl a mother at the cost of the state. Prostitution, I told her, is the price some women pay for the virtue of others.

A terrible etatism will be the result of, not the war, but the way we are prosecuting it.

Max[1] came in this afternoon and we talked at length about the foreign and internal policy about which he is as critical and skeptical as I — the lack of any integration to a clear political line & the Pres's[2] habit of counteracting one agency by another to the end of gen'l chaos and paralysis. We drank tea in the kitchen & Marian[3] came to take him to train & see the house. Mikey at Brooks's for afternoon.

[1] Max Ascoli, anti-Fascist refugee from Italy, economist and philosopher, had become an American citizen.
[2] Roosevelt.
[3] Marian Ascoli, Max's wife.

2ND
DAY
Friday 2 January
363 Days
to come

It was on July 8, 1927, and I had been granted a divorce in Hungary the day before, and I thought I had never seen anyone as unhappy as I except he, with a face like one who has gone through war & "flammenwerfer," and a tongue so cynical & brilliant and he said "I have been looking for you for years. Will you marry me?" And I thought "I have been looking for you, too." Then always those years of intense pleasure & blackest pain. Still the crazy conviction that he loved me & it would all add up to something. But it was so quickly over for him, or maybe never began. On that first day he said "I will buy us a house in Vermont, this shape ⊓ and looking down a valley. And he did. And insofar as we were ever happy we were happy there. Now, to sit in the Woodstock Courthouse, charging desertion . . . . and to feel nothing at all, literally nothing except some faint distaste. To have felt too much is to end in feeling nothing. Four years of loneliness & agony & work, all anodynes. The last terrible remembering in London last spring. But now it is the ratification of something that has been over & done with & not even Michael, any more, reminds me of him. "Far & forgotten like a scene in cameo."[1]

3RD
DAY
Saturday 3 January
362 Days
to come

As my father's diary occasionally wrote, "Hard day." Rather haggard after two nights on the train that backed & filled like the train in Derenko. Wrote a column in the morning. Fodor[2] came in for lunch — unchangingly opti-

[1] This entry is reproduced in Dorothy's handwriting facing page 179.
[2] Marcel Fodor, the old friend from early Budapest days, now a refugee.

mistic. Too optimistic. Liberals are God's children. They blink with pleased anticipation on the edge of the precipice.

Emmy Rado[1] came in the afternoon about Paul[2] and I spent an hour trying to find out where he is.

Ham[3] called me & told me Raoul[4] has T.B. It is stinking. The most civilized mind, the freest spirit, the wisest judgment . . . and he is going to be out when we need him most. There's a jinx on us. Max [Ascoli] came in & we talked about L.Am.[5] & a fête for Madeleine[6]

4TH DAY	Sunday 4 January	361 Days to come

By telephoning all over the place I've found Paul is at Sulphur Springs. Called J.Wheeler Bennet[7], Emmie, and Eleanor [Roosevelt]. He's under the State Dept & from El. I gather will never be freed.[8] I want him in protective custody where we can get at him. Unlike Ham [Armstrong] & John [Gunther] I don't altogether trust him. He's playing some game, but certainly with at least a "blind" opposition.[9] But to send him back to Germany is insane. He

[1] Emmy Rado was the wife of a celebrated psychiatrist from Vienna.

[2] Paul Scheffer, the celebrated correspondent of the old *Berliner Tageblatt*, was now interned with other German-Nazi journalists and diplomats at White Sulphur Springs.

[3] Hamilton Fish Armstrong, editor of *Foreign Affairs*.

[4] Comte Raoul de Roussy de Sales was the most esteemed of French journalists in America at the time, working in Washington and New York and constantly consulted by Dorothy.

[5] *Latin America*, a proposed magazine.

[6] Madeleine Clark, secretary.

[7] Wheeler-Bennett, journalist and historian, was in British intelligence work during the war.

[8] He was to be sent back to Hitler with the other Germans a little later when he suffered a severe accident to his leg and remained in America until his death in 1963 at Woodstock. He had spent most of the twenty years in Vermont on pensions from various sources (Dorothy being one), including the chancellery of the West German Republic. There seems little doubt that his activity at this period had been somewhat obscure and perhaps double in character; an official Nazi correspondent, he afterwards worked for the Americans.

[9] "Blind" opposition, i.e., to Hitler.

knows too much; is too intelligent. I don't think he's a hero. He'd sell out. Then why not to us?

Mikey is darling. I motored him & Den out to school;[1] much slush. I didn't leave the car. Many goodbyes & God bless us — and that darling baby-manly face.

In the eve. I worked on a memo for D.[2]

Thus ends the story of Dorothy and Red. The third and fourth entries of this diary were included to show how little the second entry (that of January 2, the day of the divorce) mattered to her. To Red it quite possibly mattered still less, since he was in Beverly Hills and preparing to write a new play, THE play he called it.

They had traveled far from that birthday in Berlin. As we followed their journey we must all have wondered, sometimes, how much was life and how much literature — how much illusion the habit of word-spinning had cast upon them. We shall never be sure, and indeed it is the property of such lives to leave us bemused by a plurality of meanings. If they had not been thus they might have been otherwise, but they would not have been Dorothy and Red.

[1] In Riverdale.
[2] Probably "Wild Bill" Donovan (Major General, later head of the Office of Strategic Services).

Epilogue

Epilogue

AFTER THE LAST EVENTS DESCRIBED IN THIS BOOK, SINCLAIR Lewis lived for nine more years and Dorothy for nineteen. His death took place in Rome on May 10th, 1951, and hers in Lisbon on January 30th, 1961.

The final years were kinder to her than to him. She attained a tranquil happiness in her marriage to the Czechoslovak painter, Maxim Kopf, of whom she used to say, "He's the man I ought to have married in the first place." His gentle, devoted nature, at variance with his robustious appearance and manner, was accompanied by a genuine plastic talent and a profound sense of form, so that his work both in painting and in sculpture seemed to be edging towards greatness. It did not, in fact, reach that point, but it was at all times his own, the work of a sincere artist. When he died in 1958 Dorothy was inconsolable, gave up journalism and lectures, and went through the series of heart attacks which ended with her death three years later.

The years at Twin Farms after the war were memorable for work and pleasure, for many guests and much good talk as well as the beauty of the seasons and the sheer joy of the Vermont hills. I moved again into the old house (the smaller of the two) in 1946 and remained there, at least from May to October, for eight years, first as a tenant and then as temporary owner. Later on Dorothy sold the Big House, divided the property at the private road between the two houses, and herself resumed living in the old house where her Twin Farms life had begun long before.

Wells Lewis, whom she always loved as a son, was killed in France during the last days of the war. Michael, growing up, studied acting at the Royal Academy of Dramatic Art in London, married and produced two sons, John-Paul and Gregory, who became Dorothy's great delight. It was to see them that she went to Lisbon for Christmas, 1960, and remained to die.

Red in his last decade moved from one place to another, bought big houses and sold them again, in his usual lavish but not wholly extravagant manner. That is, although he did like big houses — such as the one he had for some years at Duluth, Minnesota — he never, so far as I know, sold them at a loss. In 1947 he wrote me a letter asking me to come up to Thorvale Farm, near Williamstown, Massachusetts, for as long as I chose to stay. In this letter (which, like everything else of the kind I ever had, I have lost) he recalled our earliest days at Twin Farms, with all of us working, taking long walks and drinking little or no alcohol. "Let's do it all over again," he said, or words to that effect. I had to reply that I was on my way to Twin Farms for the summer and, of course, he did not renew this invitation. Although I was conscious through those summers that he was not far away, and although we always drove through Williamstown on our way to and from New York, I did not go to see him. The idea of being a liaison officer between Twin Farms and Thorvale never appealed to me in the least, and on the one occasion when I performed that office (1950) it was for a concrete purpose.

Red's work in the last phase was not equal to his best, but he did have two successful novels which would have seemed triumphant to any lesser writer — *Cass Timberlane* (1945) and *Kingsblood Royal* (1947). He had at last, after years of effort, given up the attempt to write for the stage, but he kept enormous scrapbooks of his acting career and the productions of his plays, and sometimes at night he would pore over them.

He also developed an astonishing appetite for recorded music, symphonies, chamber music and everything else, although in my youth he had made endless fun of me for liking such things. An obsession with the Italian language, literature, history and art was another of the uncharacteristic developments of this period.

I saw him, now and then, but always in New York. For some of these years he was drinking no alcohol at all, which was admirable enough, but he had a propensity for asking his friends to share his virtue. This made a dinner at his penthouse on Central Park West rather bleak at times: one could have done quite equably without the alcohol if this abstinence had not been salted down with temperance lectures.

One evening in 1946 Dorothy and Maxim were dining with Dinah and me in New York. We had been asked to go to John Gunther's for an evening party afterwards. It never crossed my mind that Dorothy had not also been invited, but she said she had not been, and that it probably was sheer forgetfulness on John's part. Why didn't I telephone John and inquire? I did so. John replied that he would be delighted to have Dorothy and Maxim, but that Red and Marcella Powers were coming, and he had thought it more tactful, etc., etc. Dorothy said: "Nonsense! I don't mind meeting Red." We went.

So far as I know it was the only meeting they had after their divorce. Dorothy and Red sat rather primly on one sofa and Marcella and Maxim on another some distance away; they made polite conversation. I was so embarrassed that I took refuge in another room.

Michael, too, was to all intents and purposes a stranger to his father. He had paid one rather unsuccessful visit to Duluth when he was a child, and Red had gone to see him act in the theatre school at Peterborough one year. One summer (1949) Dorothy was very worried about Michael's future, his relationship to his father, and Red's refusal to answer letters or make any arrangements for the boy. (The trust fund for Michael now yielded only a small part of his annual expenses.) And Red had just recovered from a really serious bout of pneumonia, as friends told us.

Without consulting Dorothy or Michael, I telephoned Red one morning at Thorvale and asked if I could come down there with Mike to see him. Red was cordial indeed: "Any time," he said, "and I'd be delighted. Why don't you drive down today?" I said the next day would be better and he said he would expect us in the late afternoon.

Michael had to drive my car, since my leg (from a broken kneecap) was in a plaster cast. We got to Thorvale before five o'clock and Red was at first nervous, irritable, and offensive to Mike. (He had been drinking.) He warmed up afterwards; various people came to dinner, including the professor of Italian literature who had been reading Dante with Red; and before we went to bed that night Red had hauled out his theatrical scrapbooks and was showing them to his actor son.

"Remember this, Michael," he said. "Your father may not have been much of a writer but he was one hell of a good actor."

This was the beginning of a reconciliation which, however imperfect, was better than nothing. Red made an allowance for Michael and drew a new will in which the boy came in for half of his estate, the rest going to friends. Michael went from London (where he was still at the Royal Academy of Dramatic Art) to see his father in Italy that next winter and again in the last winter of Red's life.

Dorothy's trip to Lisbon, to see her grandchildren for Christmas of 1960, started from Washington, where she had been sharing the Wallace Irwins' commodious apartment with Tish Irwin, now also a widow. Dinah and I went out to Idlewild to see her off. Michael was there, having driven her out from Pennsylvania Station. She looked harassed, distracted, and the signs of great illness were upon her. At the very last moment, when her flight was called and she dived nervously into the appropriate doorway, I had the sudden feeling that she really did not know one of us from the other, Dinah and Michael and me. There was an irresistible sense of farewell.

In the following May, according to her wishes, her body was taken to Barnard, Vermont, and buried in the village graveyard beside that of Maxim. It was a cold, wet day, not actually raining at the time of the service, but muddy and still. I had gone up to stay the day at Hilda Rothschild's house — Hilda, friend and solace of Dorothy's last years. There were the family, a few other friends and a good many neighbors. There was Sister Peggy, ever faithful. To her, even more than to me, it was like saying goodbye to a lifetime.

Appendix

Appendix

EIGHTEEN YEARS AFTER HER DIVORCE FROM RED, DOROTHY VISITED Sauk Centre for the first time under circumstances which she described for the *Atlantic Monthly* in the following essay. After so much living, it seems to sum up what remained of a lost love and a half-forgotten attachment.

V.S.

The Boy and Man from Sauk Centre

BY DOROTHY THOMPSON

THERE ARE THREE GRAVES IN A ROW MARKED BY SIMPLE, IDENTICAL stones set equidistantly, and flat, in the greensward. Each has the briefest of inscriptions. At the right lies Edwin J. Lewis, 1848–1926; at the left, Emma Kermott Lewis, 1848–1891; and between them one of their three sons, Sinclair Lewis, 1885–1951, "Author of *Main Street*." The world-renowned writer holds the honored place between his parents. But the mother, who died when he was six after a long illness with tuberculosis spent in sanatoriums far from home, he barely knew, and he was not his father's favorite son. Behind them is the Lewis monument marking the family lot, lugubrious, of dark granite, underneath the mournful draperies of the stone.

There is no mention of other books on the marker, nor of the Nobel Prize for Literature, of which he was the first American recipient. For to Sauk Centre, which most of the Western world knew as Gopher Prairie shortly after *Main Street* appeared forty years ago, the book which started Sinclair Lewis' national and international fame is the only one worth memorializing.

Today Sauk Centre, once the "butter capital of America," is all Sinclair Lewis. The Main Street that Lewis, in the introduction to the novel, said would tell the same story "in Ohio or Montana, in Kansas or Kentucky or Illinois" and "not very differently Up York State or in the Carolina hills" is now christened "The Original Main Street." Third Avenue, where the house of his father, Doc Lewis, still stands, is now Sinclair Lewis Avenue. The City Park, lovely with superb oaks and elms and its front on the Sauk Lane, is now Sinclair Lewis Park.

The library, from which the child and youth Harry withdrew so many books that finally "I'll bet he read every one of 'em," now houses in its basement a Sinclair Lewis museum, in which are gradually being collected memorabilia and such manuscripts or copies of them as have not gone, under the terms of his will and along with his library and the Nobel Prize medal, to Yale.

There are plans to purchase the old home and restore it, as far as possible, as it was when he lived there and to open a seminar and establish scholarships for creative writers. It is hoped that money will be found to erect a statue of him as a boy, but the sculptor is put to it to find anything to go on. There seems to be no existing photograph of him after early childhood. I have one taken at the age of three or four, before the characteristic features had developed. There are apparently none taken subsequently until after he left Yale.

Govenor Orville Freeman proclaimed 1960 as Sinclair Lewis Year in Minnesota. The first weekends in July, August, and September were given over to a Lewis festival. Nineteen sixty would have been the year of his seventy-fifth birthday, and is the fortieth anniversary of the publication of *Main Street*, the thirtieth of his winning the Nobel Prize.

I had never before been in Sauk Centre. In the thirteen years that I was married to Sinclair Lewis, he had never urged me to visit the town or proposed taking me. His father and stepmother were dead before we met; only his older brother Fred and Fred's family had never left Sauk Centre, and to them Sinclair Lewis was indifferent; and I do not believe that he visited the town himself during our marriage, except en route to somewhere else.

What drew me there now, to attend this festival in his honor? Some desire to pay tribute to him as an artist? Some appeal to a humorous sense of curiosity about how the satirizer of all boosters might now be celebrated by the same? Specifically so that his two only grandsons, John Paul Sinclair Lewis, aged six, and Gregory Claude, aged three, sons of Michael Lewis, Sinclair's only surviving son, might visit the childhood haunts of the grandfather who died before they were born? Or was there not another reason, wholly unconscious, when I made the decision to take the long and uncomfortable trip from Vermont in what promised to be broiling weather? Was it not a desire to learn, if I could, more about the man who for a few years had been the center of my existence, had fathered my only child, had caused me more grief than joy, but whom, after more than twenty years of total separation, I could never put out of my mind?

My daughter-in-law Bernadette, her three-year-old son Gregory, and I (John Paul had come down with measles in Chicago and had been left in Minneapolis with his nurse) now stood before the three stones.

Why, I wondered, had the writer wished to be buried in Sauk Centre beside his father? His brother, Dr. Claude B. Lewis of nearby St. Cloud, had expressed surprise at the news and concluded, "He must have loved the old town." But was that the reason?

The questions that flashed through my mind at the grave were to be pondered all the while I was in Sauk Centre, and afterward.

Sauk Centre had furnished him with the material for his first great literary success, and the legendary "Zenith," an up-and-coming city of the same Middle West, was the scene of two later superior and successful novels, *Babbitt* and *Dodsworth*. The genesis of his literary insights was here and in this vicinity. It was artistically fitting that his ashes should finally rest here. But why, as he expressly commanded, next to those of his father?

The body of his stepmother, Isabel Warner Lewis, is interred in the family lot, but not next to the husband she loved and served so long, nor next to the famous son, whom she understood and protected more than the father ever did.

There was a certain filial piety in Sinclair Lewis. During his father's lifetime he wrote home regularly. But although he begot two sons, he had no father-son relationship with either of them. Continually separated from both children, he seldom wrote to either, and when living in the same house with one or both of them, wished to see them only briefly, the younger never at meals and only when on his best behavior. He was not affectionate with them. Both children — I had occasion to see much of his older son, Wells, in our home, and eventually in my own, from the time he was eleven until he went away to war never to return again — were afraid of him. If he bantered with them, it was with an irony too far over their young heads to grasp, and it humiliated them.

Wells, sophisticated and humorous, once he got away from his father and was mature, affected and doubtless really felt considerable affection for "the old bastard." When, at twenty-one, Wells published his first and, for his age, distinctly promising novel, *They Still Say No*, his father, who had read the manuscript and picked the title, was excited and proud.

Michael, when he passed babyhood, had toward his father a resentment and fear that he never overcame. At seven he remarked, after a reverie, "When I grow up I think I shall probably kill my father." At thirteen, he said solemnly, "All my life I have felt like a bastard." When he was invited by his father to join him, before and after our final separation and divorce, he looked forward to the event with a combination of hope and anxiety. When a schoolmate asked him about his famous father he replied morosely, "I hardly know the man."

On a very few occasions, his father had invited him to visit, but always arranged some activity for Michael that would remove the boy from his presence and even from his house — a fishing trip with someone else, or a motor tour.

Their last encounter had been catastrophic. Michael was twenty and completing his work at the Royal Academy of Dramatic Art in London, when his father invited him to spend the Christmas holidays with him in Rome. Sinclair Lewis was then very ill. Rumors had reached me from friends and acquaintances who had seen him that his poor head was as emaciated as a skeleton's, and his hands shook with an uncontrollable palsy.

The father had invited the son to lunch with him promptly at one the day after his arrival. Michael had spent the night on the town, getting to bed in the hotel where his father had sent him — was there no room in his large apartment? — at dawn. He overslept and was very late for lunch. His father, in a fury of rage, demanded that he return immediately to London and, in effect, said, "Never darken my door again."

Michael returned to London, took his diploma, and then came home only a day or two before his father died and only some two weeks after he had taken his wretched, humiliating, though not undeserved, dismissal.

Sinclair Lewis had received the news of his older son's death in the fall of 1944 in a manner that seemed utterly feelingless. He was on a lecture tour en route to Chicago when the news came over the radio that Lieutenant Wells Lewis had been shot in Alsace by a sniper and killed instantly while studying a map with General Dahlquist, to whom he was aide-de-camp.

My gentle, sensitive sister, who was devoted to Sinclair Lewis and to Wells and of whom Lewis was fond, felt that the news which he might not have heard should be broken to him lovingly and went to the railroad station but missed him. He had scheduled a party for the evening, to which my sister and her husband had been invited. They phoned the Palmer House, where he was staying, thinking it might have been called off. Lewis had already left for the party, and they went. There they found him in the liveliest possible mood. No one mentioned the death of Wells, but my brother-in-law, finding himself, for a moment, apart with "Red," quietly and simply expressed his sympathy and sorrow.

Sinclair Lewis flew into a biting rage. "People just love to be bearers of bad news." He snarled at Hal (Harrison) Smith, who had telephoned or telegraphed his friendship and sympathy. He attacked me because I had canceled my radio program when I heard of Wells's death a few minutes before I was scheduled to leave for it. "Dorothy's just putting on an act. She wasn't his mother. It's all self-dramatization."

Fanny Butcher, longtime literary critic of the Chicago *Tribune*, was there, and Lloyd Lewis, the newspaperman and historical writer, with his wife. Sinclair Lewis admired Lloyd and had collaborated with him on the play *Jayhawker*, which had not been a success. When I ran into Fanny some months later, she was still shocked at Lewis' conduct that evening. Lewis bragged that he had heard the news just before he went to lecture and had never "been better in my life."

My sister, defending Hal Smith, said, "He is one of your oldest friends. He didn't want to bear bad news, but to offer you sympathy and comfort. And you know that what you say about Dorothy is not true. She loved Wells deeply, and he loved her. She was prostrated."

This reproof Sinclair Lewis took in silence. But my sister was not shocked. She was sorry. She knew only too well that Lewis' reaction to frustrations and griefs was to hit out at those who cared most for him, and often at those for whom he cared most. That was always the trouble: never knowing whether he really cared at all, for anybody or anything except his work.

Neither was I shocked when I heard the story some time later. I commented only that he must have felt perfectly dreadful. He repressed his emotions to a point unbearable for those who wished to share them and had the pride of Lucifer in doing so. But how many writers have ever been good family men? In recalling biographies, one finds that their number is minuscule.

Sinclair Lewis was not a good father. When young he had been a docile, dutiful son of a father who had inspired admiration, often fear, but never, I had gathered, intimacy or warmth of feeling.

So it could hardly be a feeling of family solidarity that led him to wish to be buried here, I pondered. After his father's death he had maintained fairly close ties with only one member of the family, his brother Claude. Theirs was a real friendship that lasted until Sinclair Lewis' death and extended even to Claude's family, with whom he was more at ease than with his own. Claude and his family had visited us several times in New York and in Vermont. The two brothers looked very much alike, except that "Harry" (as Claude continued to call him) was much taller than Claude.

I never heard Sinclair Lewis consistently express as much admiration for any other man as he did for Claude. Nearly six years younger than Claude, Harry had in his boyhood perpetually tagged after his brother and was proud of him as a physician, a surgeon, and a man. Claude had the mind of a scientist, and the author, in keeping with his times, elevated the scientific mind above all others.

Claude was not a country doctor, as his father had been. Like his father he had received his medical training at Rush Medical College in Chicago, a highly reputed school which since 1942 has been incorporated in the University of Chicago, and like his father he chose northern Minnesota for his home and work. But he had lived and practiced in St. Cloud, a town ten times as large as Sauk Centre, comely, prosperous, the seat of the Minnesota State Teachers College and of a splendid Catholic hospital of whose staff he was a member. He had studied internal medicine, was an excellent diagnostician and a skillful surgeon. He had exuberant health. His habits were temperate as to food, drink, and sleep; he loved the outdoors of the northern woods, lakes, and streams, was a first-rate shot and an exceptionally skillful fisherman. And, as laconic in speech as his writer brother was garrulous, he was the very soul of ineffusive kindness.

Sinclair Lewis once remarked to me, "The only people I ever wanted to impress were my father and brother Claude. I never succeeded."

I do not know about the father, who had died before I met his genius son. But impressed or not impressed, Claude had a deep affection and highly protective feeling for his brother. Claude was not, by nature, a reformer (nor, except in his younger days, was his writer brother). He accepted people as they were, when they were beyond the powers of medicine to heal. Sinclair Lewis thought psychiatry a form of quackery. Claude was conscious of its limited power to cure unhappy personalities. But he had respect for modern psychological analysis. "Harry had a huge inferiority complex," he once remarked. "Had it as a kid."

"*Aus meinen grossen Schmerzen mach' ich die kleine Lieder,*" wrote Heine, who made most of his own *Schmerzen* for himself. Claude probably comprehended this generality. But he was a doctor and was outraged by his brother's way of life. When I telephoned him upon receiving the news of Sinclair Lewis' death, he answered in his clipped way: "Doesn't surprise me; doesn't surprise me a bit. Lewises are long-lived. He was basically healthy. Should have lived another

ten years at least. But couldn't, the way he behaved. Drink's
affected his central nervous system. But why didn't that secretary
telephone me? If I'd known of his condition, I'd have taken the next
plane to Rome. Wonder who was taking care of him." (He meant
what doctor, with a strong implication of doubt about Italian
medicine.)

Pitiable as he was, Sinclair Lewis could not endure or give pity.
Nor was Claude a dispenser of it. Perhaps the only person in the
world whom Sinclair Lewis would have welcomed then would have
been Claude — gruff, unsentimental, and competent.

But Claude, who lived to be seventy-eight, is not buried in Sauk
Centre. Sinclair Lewis' ashes are not beside those of his most enduring
friend in the family.

Perhaps he wanted, I thought, to rest here from a sense of tradition,
in the traditional family burying ground. For the iconoclast of
contemporary mores had, like his fellow iconoclast H. L. Mencken,
a deep feeling for tradition. If, like Mencken, he had little use for
the commercial middle classes (the booboisie), and especially their
promoters, boosters, retailers, salesmen, and ad men, it was not
because of a keen social consciousness about the exploited workers
or the oppressed minorities.

He admired the independent entrepreneur industrialist (Dodsworth), and hated the corporation empires; he felt sorry for the dirt
farmers, "Svenska" (Scandinavian) and "Dutch" (German), so many
of whom were his father's patients in his boyhood and whom he saw
being squeezed by land dealers, loan sharks, middlemen, and later by
bureaucratic policies and regulations. He did not think highly of
Jews, in general, because of their predominant economic activities,
though he admired Jewish scientists, doctors, and a few writers.
(Gottlieb, in *Arrowsmith*, is surely one of his most sympathetic crea-
tions.) He thought most lawyers were crooks, adept at circumventing
the purpose of the law, and politicians, almost without exception,
rogues, promising all things to all men, with the single aim of being
elected.

He was basically apolitical, but insofar as his social ideas were
articulate and consistent, he was an old-fashioned populist American
radical.

He attempted over a number of years to write a novel about labor, studied the scene with his usual thoroughness, had long talks with many labor leaders, and finally threw the manuscript away with the dictum that few labor leaders were really concerned with helping the rank and file; rather, they were concerned with feathering their own nests and grabbing power. I went with him to an AFL convention in Canada, and he railed at its leaders all the way back.

Toward American Negroes he had a genuinely warm feeling, and in them a real interest. He left part of his estate to the NAACP and the Urban League. But his interest was more seignorial than egalitarian. He was more against the white South than for the black. "The mountain-whites of the south — purest Anglo-Saxon stock in America — are awful: filthy, inbred, shiftless."

I remembered the remark when *Kingsblood Royal* was published.

His yearnings, if not his tastes as expressed in his way of living, were more aristocratic than democratic. He hankered after the old and long established. He fled to Europe as a cure for all his woes, and always, by preference, to England, France, and Italy, with their long continuity of culture. He disliked urban Germany, even before Hitler, because of its energy, technology, modernism, and Babbittry.

His attraction was to the medieval; he was as versed as an art historian in twelfth, thirteenth, and fourteenth century cathedrals, churches, abbeys, and castles; although, to the end of his life, as far as I know, he was indifferent to pictures and sculpture except as part of architecture. Those that adorned his walls were usually prints, and all conventional.

He discovered music only in his fifties, and then went in for it with the intensity with which he did everything. He left an enormous collection of records, all of them of classical music.

If tradition influenced his desire to be interred beside his father in Sauk Centre, it was not because of the civilized traditions embodied there. When he was born, as I learned there last summer, Sauk Centre had only recently emerged as a settled village. The first white child to be born there had preceded Sinclair Lewis by less than twenty-five years. The Indians, because of the lakes, had been fishermen and loggers, and logging first attracted the small number of white settlers, who lived in stockades. The loggers cut down the

trees, so that the earliest picture of Sauk Centre is of a village bleak
and treeless. Yet it must earlier have been heavily wooded. Oak,
elm, birch, and poplar flourish there, and today its heavily shaded
streets, neat lawns, the Sauk Lake, and the incomparable skies are
its only claim to beauty. Its buildings and homes have none of the
classic grace of the old New England towns and villages that rank
among the loveliest in the Western world.

Many of the Sauk Centre homes of Lewis' boyhood, as well as his
father's, still stand. They are comfortable, reasonably spacious,
gabled, replete with screened porches front and back, but lacking in
any architectural design whatsoever. By the time Sauk Centre came
into being, the great fireplaces of the earlier-settled East had given
way to more practical stoves and hot-air furnaces, burning wood or
coal. There is nothing there one would wish to restore.

The physical description of Gopher Prairie, as seen through the
eyes of Carol Kennicott in *Main Street*, is not very different to this
day. Of course, there are new buildings and new homes, mostly of
the ranch type, some of them of attractive design, but few are in the
village proper.

One recalls Carol's dream of having it all rebuilt in Georgian brick
with shuttered windows and white trim and her efforts to get the only
possible village Maecenas to do it. The dream was grandiose, but
Carol never did anything about even smaller dreams. Except for
refurnishing her husband's home, which is recognizably the old
E. J. Lewis place, Carol was a great improver only in her own mind.

The novelist's stepmother, Isabel Warner Lewis, did do something.
Like Carol, who in the novel had been a librarian in St. Paul, she
was relatively urban. Dr. E. J. Lewis brought her as his second
wife from Wilmette, a suburb of Chicago. She was a leader in the
Gradatim Ladies Club (in the novel, the Thanatopsis) and among
the few movers to create the City Park, which adds greatly to the
town. She was also a mover in providing the first village rest room
for the wives of the German and Swedish farmers from the surrounding countryside, who brought their wives into town along with their
products, the wives to do the week's shopping with nowhere to wash,
relax, and be sheltered from the village heat or cold. She was an
early clubwoman type devoted to improvement. Isabel appears in

the novel as Will Kennicott's widowed mother, who had given over her Gopher Prairie home to the bridal pair and lived elsewhere, but nearby. She has little role in the story, but is sympathetically depicted.

The history of the Lewis family, on both sides, was pioneer. Of British stock, the paternal family was — if the legend is true, and in Sauk Centre I saw it stated with fair evidence in the family Bible — descended from Peregrine White, the first child born to the Mayflower Pilgrims in America. The Lewises were American a hundred and fifty years before there was a United States.

The mother's origins were more obscure. The novelist had told me that the family was "French Canuck," but this, I found from the family annals in the possession of his brother Fred's widow, is not true. The Kermotts came from the Isle of Wight, and the family reached America through a fourteen-year-old boy who apprenticed himself to a ship's captain, trading between Great Britain and Canada. In Canada, the Kermott lad, having had a row with the captain, jumped the ship, and thereafter he and the family he founded remained in British Canada. There is a rumor that the name was not Kermott, but that this name was adopted later, probably by the boy, who jumped the ship and wished to conceal his identity. Emma Kermott's father — none of the family still living in Sauk Centre seems to know when or how — came to the United States and became, or already was, a veterinarian. E. J. Lewis married Emma in 1873. He was then living in and beginning his medical practice in Ironton, Wisconsin, where she was teaching school.

Apparently the ancestral Lewises moved very early from Massachusetts to Connecticut and farmed in the vicinity of Westville. Then, during the Gold Rush of the 1840s, the family sold the farm, pulled up stakes, and went to California. Like many thousands of others, they found no gold and started working their way eastward, getting as far as Pennsylvania, where the author's father was born in Lebanon. From Lebanon, the family moved to Elysian, Minnesota, tracking westward again. E. J. Lewis, after a spell of teaching school in Redwood Falls, Minnesota, went to Rush Medical College in Chicago. He practiced first in Ironton, Wisconsin, where both his oldest son, Fred, and the second son, Claude, were born. The third son, Harry Sinclair Lewis, ten years younger than the oldest, was the first Lewis to be born in Sauk Centre.

The New England tradition persisted in the family's religion. Unlike the Lutheran Scandinavians who, with predominantly Catholic Germans, settled the farms surrounding Sauk Centre, the Lewises were Congregationalists, whose church descends from the Puritans. The well-to-do Protestant Anglo-Saxons in Sauk Centre built and attended the Episcopal Church. The present church existed in Sinclair Lewis' childhood. Designed by Cass Gilbert and built of stone in the Tudor style, covered with ivy and well placed in pleasantly landscaped grounds, it was and is the most distinguished building in town.

The villages and towns of the northwest pioneer territory and their outlying farms were greatly in need of physicians. The Sauk Centre of 1920, when *Main Street* was published, had a population of 3000. It has some 3500 today. In Sinclair Lewis' childhood it was, I heard, under 2000. Yet Dr. E. J. Lewis prospered, and although the family did not rank in the top economic class along with the banker, the commission merchant, and those who had made substantial fortunes in real-estate deals, it was economically not so far from the top. Dr. E. J. Lewis could afford to send both younger sons penuriously to college — Fred, the oldest, never cared about a higher education — and although, among the gilded youth of Yale, a rich man's college, Harry Lewis was too poor, and too eccentric, to belong to the upper crust and too proud to join its outcasts, he never had to tend furnaces or otherwise work his way through. He did do some newspaper work for pittances. When the doctor died in 1926, he left some sixty thousand dollars, mostly in farm mortgages. That was a great deal more than it is now, and considerable for a country doctor to amass.

So, perhaps for social reasons, the Lewis family might have joined the Episcopal Church. Certainly never the Methodist or Baptist, with at that time their hell-fire revivalism which Sinclair Lewis the writer was so bitingly to satirize.

But, except for Sinclair Lewis' adolescent conversion (while preparing for Yale in Oberlin and from which he soon recovered), there is no indication of any particular religious feeling in the Lewis family, father or sons, beyond the purely formal. The father thought the church a good thing for the community, and the family regularly attended morning service together, unless the father were on an emergency call, and the boys also attended Sunday School. The father believed in and practiced the sterner and more puritanical virtues, pre-eminent among them duty, and especially the duties of his healing profession. No storm nor time of night would prevent him from answering a call, and the operation performed on a farmhouse kitchen table by Dr. Will Kennicott in *Main Street*, with Carol, his young wife, giving the ether in the presence of an open flame of light, occurred in Sinclair Lewis' life when he was thirteen, when he, there being no one else, performed the same service for his father at the risk of both their lives. The father fulfilled his duties to his patients, his family, and the community. He did not attempt to collect fees from those who were indigent through no fault of their own, from the widow with children whom she could barely feed or clothe, or from the struggling farmer whose crops and year's work had been destroyed by drought. His ledgers, preserved by Fred's family, which I saw in Sauk Centre in his widow's home, carry laconic comments — "Can't pay."

But he had neither charity nor patience for "ne'er-do-wells," who shifted off onto others responsibilities which, by hard work, they would have been able to bear. The ledgers occasionally carry in red ink in the margins the words "Dead beat," or "No good." One remarks, "Skipped the country with a niece leaving a wife and four children. S.O.B."

How many characteristics of his father the author son displayed! Sinclair Lewis had the same sense of duty toward his work, though it was often interrupted by breakdowns. And how often did I hear him cry, "I'm so tired, so tired!" He never drank while he was actually working, but spent regular uninterrupted hours at his writing table. When he had come to a stalemate in a novel, he would go on a drinking bout, leaving home with a secretary or any companion he might pick up, disappearing for days or weeks; and such a breakdown invariably occurred, during my life with him, at the end of every novel and lasted until another idea for a novel miraculously was born in his fevered mind.

His work was always ordered. He wrote his novels from precise and copious outlines of the characters, their professions or trades, and their haunts, building the structure of the book as an architect designs a house. Characters and incidents developed as he wrote, but they moved within the framework. With the tools of his work he was as scrupulous as his father was with his surgical instruments. Sharpened pencils, notebooks, paper, carbon were always in the same place. His writing table was never littered, and what he had written was neatly stacked each day.

In his home he demanded an orderliness that sometimes drove me to exasperation. He smoked continuously but could not endure a half-filled ash tray. But he also could not endure an ash tray, or anything else, that was not exactly where it should be, nor a meal that was not served punctually to a second. He always hung his clothes on exactly the proper hangers, and his bureau drawers might have been kept by the best-trained valet.

He was scrupulous about paying bills and collecting debts, and, like his father, had no use for dead beats or for the shiftless and lazy, although he might cultivate them briefly out of a writer's curiosity. He was hell on servants, thinking nothing of their hours or recreations — yet they were invariably devoted to him. But he would fire them out of hand for even a slightly unsatisfactory performance of a task, for any familiarity, or for what he might consider an overreaching of a long tacitly granted privilege.

Are such characteristics the result of early environment, even though one rebels against it, or are they congenital?

At any rate, "Like father, like son" was not suspended in the Lewis case. Perhaps the dust did call to dust.

But was it not all much simpler? Where else could he have been buried? Where else had he ever had a home? Where had he spent anything like the seventeen years of his life that he had lived in Sauk Centre before he went away to college?

He had had many homes, but never, until his marriage to me, owned one with the intention of keeping it for the rest of his life. That one was Twin Farms, in Barnard, Vermont. We spent only long summers here (where I am writing this), and although he was often away, it was his home for eight years, and during that time he was certainly happier and more creative here than he was anywhere else.

And this home was also his simplest. In 1933 he bought a large Tudor-style house in Bronxville, New York, as a wedding anniversary present to me. I did not want him to do it. I could not imagine him, or myself, happy in the suburbs. Thereafter, following our separation and eventual divorce, he rented and furnished an enormous New York penthouse, with a living room sixty feet long and views from its windows of every bridge in New York — the specifications he had given to a real-estate agent. Apart from his books, which lined the great room from floor to ceiling, it was as conventionally furnished as if designed by an expensive but not at all imaginative interior decorator.

He kept it for a short time, and then brought a house in Duluth, having decided to return to Minnesota. Again, the house was immense, pretentious, and ugly, a German-style Mid-Victorian castle, looming in the most prominent position in the city — a white elephant, Duluth people said, with a bowling alley and billiard table in the recreation room in the basement. He wrote *Cass Timberlane* and discovered that he was tired of Duluth, traveled again, and bought a large estate near Williamstown, Massachusetts, again in New England. Here the land and view were beautiful, but the large house was nondescript and conventional, such as might have been built for a prosperous executive. That, which held all his household possessions, including his books, and was kept by a caretaker, was in his ownership when he died. Both these houses were sold to Catholic orders, ironic for an owner who had despised all organized religions.

He left Williamstown to lease a huge Neofascist-style villa in Florence, lived there a year or two, did not renew the lease, and after traveling again all over Europe by motor, with his secretary, during which trip he suffered a very serious breakdown in Zurich, drove to Rome and took the furnished apartment there. He had never been rooted anywhere, except in his childhood and youth in Sauk Centre. Nor had he made many real or permanent friends. In England he had had a few friends who were more than admirers of his work. But most of them had predeceased him.

On the European continent he made few, if any, close friends, even among writers, although initially he was much sought after, because his work had been translated into every European language and was a best seller in many countries. So gregarious that he could not bear to be alone except while at work, he sought temporary companions rather than friends.

He was never in the least Europeanized. Although he had spoken German from boyhood, picking up a *"schoenste Langewitch"* version from the German-speaking people of Minnesota, and had studied it in high school, aided by a Catholic priest as tutor, and in Oberlin, and could write it correctly, even literately, his accent was bad, and speaking it torrentially, he forgot grammar. His French was limited and abominable. He had many times started studying Italian systematically, but how well he eventually came to speak and write it, I do not know.

His erudition in English and American literature was phenomenal, but with Continental literature he was only superficially familiar. Of the works of Flaubert he spoke only, during our life together, of *Madame Bovary.* He had certainly read Balzac but never in my remembrance returned to him, as he repeatedly did to Dickens. When, after our marriage, we started together to collect a library, the German and Russian classics were added by me.

On the Continent he drifted toward Americans: journalists, foreign service people, or Europeans with American wives. He was as American as ham and eggs and strawberry shortcake, and always distinguishably so. Although he had written *Babbitt* in England and Rome and most of *Dodsworth* in Naples, there was no fitting resting place for him anywhere in Europe.

In Rome, he died alone, and only his secretary — a strange man of undistinguishable nationality, whom he had engaged in Florence — accompanied his poor body to the crematorium, though his death was front-page news in every American and European newspaper.

No one, as far as I could learn from the secretary, when I saw him in Rome a year or so later, visited him in the hospital to which he had been delivered delirious in a state of total physical and nervous collapse. He emerged only briefly from the coma in which he soon died, and his last words at the hospital are said to have been, "God bless you, Sister," to the attendant nun.

Now, standing before his grave, I saw him, as when I met him for the first time in the foreign office in Berlin, July 8, 1927. "Knick" (H. R. Knickerbocker, the Hearst correspondent in Berlin) had brought him to the regular Friday afternoon tea party at which the then foreign minister, Gustav Stresemann, regularly received the foreign correspondents and answered their questions, for the most part off the record.

He seemed to bring in with him a disturbing atmospheric tension such as that which precedes an electric storm. I saw a narrow, ravaged face, roughened, red, and scarred by repeated radium and electric needle burnings, less of the face below the hawkish nose than above it, where it broadened into a massive frontal skull, crossed by horizontal lines; reddish but almost colorless eyebrows above round, cavernously set, remarkably brilliant eyes, transparent as aquamarines and in them a strange, shy, imploring look; red-blond hair, already retreating, very fine and silky; a small and narrow mouth, almost lipless, drawn away from the long teeth by repeated burnings, and which in the course of a few minutes could smile a dozen ways. The face of a man who had walked through flame throwers. An elegance about the figure, slim, narrow, long boned, very tall, with the tallness all in the legs that seemed to have forgotten where to stop; long and narrow hands and feet. Very well dressed in clothes obviously from Savile Row.

And an immediate aura of greatness, large, torrential, tortured, and palpitatingly sensitive. I felt that if one but touched him with the softest finger tip, he would recoil. My instantaneous reaction was, God, what a lonely, unhappy, helpless man! Somebody *must* love and take care of him! And, of course, I was fascinated.

I did not imagine myself in the role. I did not fall in love with him then, nor really, ever. It was something deeper than that which can happen so many times in anyone's life. I married him a year later in London after a courtship pursued in Berlin, Vienna, Russia, and Italy. What moved me was a compelling sense of his need. Yet neither I nor any other woman who had come into his life before or was to come afterward could fill whatever that need might be. He was autonomous, an elementary force in himself, driving and driven, yearning and resistant. In the end all women left him, driven away perhaps by the impossibility of penetrating the curtain that screened him from any real intimacy; or he left them, forever disappointed.

I remember other things, of course: the incandescence of his conversation, more often than not a monologue; his hilarious gift for mimicry, usually of his own characters or those being created in his mind; and his continuation of a monologue until the listeners were exhausted or bored; his incredible power to ad-lib verse in the manner of any English-writing poet from Shakespeare to Vachel Lindsay or T. S. Eliot, as fast as he could talk, with never a fault of meter or of style; the game we played together and with others, of which of us could most quickly compose a sonnet containing a line usually meaningless — he always won, doing it as fast as he could write. His mind was as swift as light. I remember, too, our playing anagrams, and his fishing words out of never-never land. Challenged, they were always in the dictionary.

His intimates remember his flaring and often cruel temper, at any slight, real or imagined, during which his nostrils would expand like those of a horse, and his unspoken contrition afterward, expressed in introverted sulkiness. They remember the penetrating acidity of his remarks on public figures and on everything that he considered puffed up and overblown. Yet he was himself, as a man and writer, overblown. And one remembers, also, his generous encouragement to other writers, especially young ones, and his ineffable charm.

But he was really happy only in his work. When it was going well, he would often chuckle at his typewriter and tear out a page to read to me. He took special delight, it seemed, in his more monstrous and ridiculous characters. He wrote most of *It Can't Happen Here* in Vermont, and excerpts from the speeches of the preposterous Berzilius Windrip, which head so many chapters, were often composed or recited at table, with gusty relish, with the happy comment, "What a bastard!"

If the child is father to the man, what kind of lad was Harry Lewis in Sauk Centre?

There are still many people there who remember him, a few who went to school with him, and I saw a number of them. Their picture is of a lonely boy, eager to be one of the gang (one of the Club, of which his brother Claude was the mischievous ringleader) but forever repulsed. In a small town, then as now, physical skills are highly admired by other boys and their elders. They fish, hunt, build secret refuges for themselves in the woods, retrieve and patch up discarded wagons and machinery, and earn money by picking berries, mowing lawns, and doing small handyman jobs for the neighbors.

Harry was good at none of these things. He was too nervous and impatient to be a good fisherman, had no pride in killing rabbits and game birds, and, as I knew him, was singularly helpless at anything requiring the concentration and control of his hands or limbs. With his long legs and natural swiftness of movement, he should have been proficient at some games. Theoretically he liked tennis, but although for a time we had the only tennis court in our Vermont township, he rarely appeared on it and was as bad a shot with a ball as with a bullet. His mechanical competence extended to the ability to change a typewriter ribbon, and stopped there.

His exercise was walking, and he walked untiringly until, in his trampings, he had explored an area. Then he was bored with the paths through the woods, ever-changing as they always are. He was not interested in the minutiae of nature. He preferred to walk in Europe, where every village and county is different — in Cornwall from Land's End to Tintagel; clean across Shropshire; along the Main from Mainz to Frankfurt; from Innsbruck through the Alps to Venice. These tours I took with him. He never would make reservations. We stopped overnight at the first inn that appeared when we were tired.

His knapsack was always heavy with books. If, at rest in the evenings, he could not read, he was frantic. He enjoyed conversation only with a group, though he would stop to talk with wayfarers about their lives and occupations, or linger in cemeteries, fascinated by names on tombstones and noting some in a book.

Everyone with whom I talked in Sauk Centre who had known him as a boy remarked that he always had his nose in a book; one recalled him reading on the Lewis lawn with the lawn mower nearby and only a few rows cut. I tried to find out from his contemporaries what he had read and got the impression that it was mostly romantic novels (Scott was repeatedly mentioned) and a great deal of poetry. Later, when a successful writer, he professed to despise poetry — "People write poetry who can't write prose" — and his insistence on this was once the cause of a heated quarrel between us, but he may not have meant it. He had started his literary career with writing poetry — better described as verse — and his knowledge and memory of the English and American poets were prodigious. He had a photographic memory of any printed page. A Harvard don, English teacher, and poet who was once visiting us started to quote from a poem by John Donne. We were sitting before the fire in the big room at Twin Farms, and Lewis had rudely retired behind a newspaper. Our guest halted in his recitation, groping for the next lines. Sinclair Lewis put down his paper — he had been listening all the time — and finished the whole passage.

Probably the boy who was forever reading found in books an escape from an environment which was not uncongenial but whose demands he could not meet.

He met its demands as a student in the Sauk Centre grade and high school. The education, then, was less inclusive, but in the subjects taught, more rigorous and demanding. For some reason or other, he kept many of his report cards and school essays. Even in mathematics he was very good, and some of the essays were quite astonishing for his age. He told me that he had graduated at sixteen, fifth in a class of seventeen.

Mrs. Kells, who as Laura Thomason had been through high school with him, though a class ahead, denied this. "There were nine in his class, and he should have been graduated at the top. He was easily the brightest scholar in all subjects, though he was best, of course, in English and literature. Early in high school he had something published in *Scribner's*, and I remember how excited everybody was in school. But some of the teachers didn't like him; he was too odd and had ideas of his own." In defense of his prejudiced teachers, it must be noted that his marks in deportment were bad. His awkward, show-off antics perpetually disturbed the classroom.

She recalled also that his power of observation of human behavior showed itself very early. "When he was thirteen, the first cream separator was demonstrated in town, and many of us youngsters went to see it. Harry watched with a superior air and said on the way home, 'The machine's all right, and the principal words of the operator are *me, myself,* and *I.*'"

Mrs. Ben DuBois, formerly Cecelia Gallagher, and younger than Harry, lived next door to the Lewis place and remembers only that he had remarked to her, "I don't like cotton tops." Her husband remembers when Harry ate grass. "I eat grass," he had remarked ostentatiously, and promptly illustrated it by cropping the lawn on knees and elbows. This desire to call attention to himself as a compensation for normal inabilities persisted all his life. He would drag the Nobel Prize into the conversation in a most embarrassing way. He was conscious and self-critical of his showing off, but he seemed unable to help it.

Sauk Centre remembers that he walked ten miles to Melrose to get a train to Minneapolis to enlist in the Spanish-American War as a drummer boy. He was then thirteen. The stationmaster, after establishing his identity, telephoned his father, who came in a two-horse rig to drive him back home. The story has it that Harry bragged to the stationmaster that he would undoubtedly be the youngest drummer boy in the army and intended to become another Richard Harding Davis. But the self-confident pose was quickly abandoned with the arrival of his irate father (who had to pay two dollars for the buggy), and as he drove through Sauk Centre he was good-naturedly greeted by the jeers of his contemporaries, yelling "Doodle" and whistling *Yankee Doodle*. No one in Sauk Centre recalled his ever getting into a fist fight, yet there is no record that he ever had but one close boyhood friend.

The committee that thought up and managed the festival, the museum, the restoration of the old home, and a scholarship fund for creative writers is not the Chamber of Commerce primarily bent on boosting the town. The driving spirit has been the editor of the Sauk Centre *Herald*, Gary Sukow, twenty-four years old and an atomic phenomenon of energy. He wants to be a creative writer, "though none of us today could write like Sinclair Lewis or any of those writers of the twenties and thirties. They might pan the hell out of America, but they hadn't any doubt about it. At base they were all optimists. We aren't sure whether anything will survive our own lifetimes."

Another member of the committee is Don Hipschman, author of the pageant *A Man from Main Street*. He is assistant editor of the *Independent Banker*, published in Long Prairie, twenty miles from Sauk Centre. Others are an attorney and his wife, an investment counselor, a restaurant owner, a chain-store manager, the Episcopalian rector, and housewives with a literary interest.

Mr. Hipschman's pageant of Sinclair Lewis' life is faithful and written with talent. It was acted on the fairgrounds after dark on a lighted stage, in a series of scenes. With a nice attention to unity, it begins and ends in the graveyard with the burial of the author's ashes, and throughout his ghost carries on a commentary on himself, his times, and his contemporaries, most of which is taken from what he himself had written or said.

It revives the incident to which eyewitnesses at the interment testify. The January day was the coldest in the year, 22° below zero and blustery. Dr. Claude Lewis, in pouring the ashes into his brother's grave, spilled some over its side, and a snowy gust blew them away. "He couldn't be quiet even in his grave. He's scattered all over Stearns County."

But what does it matter where a handful of ashes lies? What was once Sinclair Lewis is buried in no ground. Even in life he was fully alive only in his writing. He lives in public libraries from Maine to California, in worn copies in the bookshelves of women from small towns who, in their girlhood, imagined themselves as Carol Kennicotts, and of medical men who, as youths, were inspired by Martin Arrowsmith and his associates. He survives in every college and university library. He does not live as do those few stupendous novelists revealing the human condition for all places and all times. He never really penetrated the soul. He was not a poet of either verse or prose.

But he is an ineradicable part of American cultural history in the twenties and thirties, and no one seeking to recapture and record the habits, frames of mind, social movements, speech, aspirations, admirations, radicalisms, reactions, crusades, and Gargantuan absurdities of the American *demos* during those twenty years will be able to do without him.

I did not go back to the grave.

Index

Index